DOUGLAS F4D-1 SK

DESIGN HISTORY

When the graceful, compact features of the Skyray were first unveiled to the public, early in February, 1951, many observers were at a loss to describe the airplane. Although the F4D-1 seemed to have some of the characteristics of a "delta" and a "flying wing," it was neither.

Others wondered aloud why a company like Douglas El Segundo, long famous for producing straightforward attack and light bomber aircraft, ever designed such a radical looking interceptor. The answer lies partly in the influence of two early "flying wing" proponents: America's Jack Northrop and Germany's Alexander Lippisch.

The El Segundo Division of Douglas Aircraft Co. had been investigating tailless aircraft since the late 1930's, as a result of studies begun by Jack Northrop when the plant had been known as the Northrop Division of Douglas Aircraft. After Northrop's departure in 1938, these studies had continued under Edward H. Heinemann as Chief Engineer, but did not produce any significant results as the division was busily producing a successful series of more conventional designs.

Then, in May, 1945, the German defeat in Europe enabled two Douglas aerodynamicists, Gene Root and his assistant A.M.O. Smith, to travel to Paris as part of the U.S. Naval Technical MIssion there. Their assignment was simple: to bring back any aeronautical information from captured German documents or personnel. Arriving in Paris within a week of VE-Day, Root and Smith soon found an amazing cache of German wind tunnel data and reports. These documents had been retrieved from the bottom of a well, dried in the attic of the Technical Mission Headquarters, and microfilmed for future inspection. Among the papers were the studies of Alexander Lippisch,

R.G. Smith, Configuration Engineer on the F4D-1 project, depicted this intermediate stage of its development, the D-571-4. (Via Harry Gann)

designer of the tailles Me-163 rocket fighter and early proponent of delta wing designs. Root and Smith also had listened to Lippisch, during a seminar at Paris-St. Germaine, where he was incarcerated, and his descriptions of future jet-powered flying wing interceptors he had designed fascinated the Americans.

After their return to the U.S., the Douglas engineers studied Lippisch's work and began applying the captured German data to Douglas' own studies on tailless aircraft. Initially, these studies involved only small-scale wing sections tested at the California Institute of Technology's Cooperative Wind Tunnel, in Pasadena. The progress the El Segundo Division was making on these early designs was followed closely by the Navy's Bureau of Aeronautics, as their interest in the practical applications of the "Lippisch Principle," as it was known, coincided with that of the Douglas group's.

That these Douglas studies were of a general nature is indicated by a Sept., 1946 memorandum from A.M.O. Smith to Leo Devlin, Chief Designer at El Segundo. In this memo, Smith proposed a remedy to the problem of poor range for jet aircraft: "The solution appears to be a delta wing jet airplane; a flying wing, of very low aspect ratio, using boundary layer control to reduce the drag. Its appearance will be much like that of the low aspect ratio wing model just tested, although the aspect ratio may go as low as 1. As a type, such an airplane will show about equal superiority over present configurations whether used as a fighter, bomber, or cargo plane".

In Oct., 1946, construction of four scale wing models was started; three small semi-span half models with various NACA airfoils, and a six-foot span complete model with control surfaces. These models featured a 50-degree leading edge sweepback, as previous tests with a wing model of 45-degree sweep, three-to-one taper, and straight trailing edges indicated that no arrangement of its internal components would balance correctly.

Initial wind tunnel tests provided surprising results, as few had previously considered any design with an aspect ratio as low as two-to-one. Once tests had begun, the large model exceeded the maximum design capacity of the tunnel's balances, while the smaller models gave results below the tunnel's minimums!

Smith also launched a series of wind tunnel investigations into boundary layer control using the delta wing planform. Originally, tests had been planned for mid-1947 with a flow generator model. However, a Swiss report dealing with similar studies that had already been completed furnished Smith with the data he was seeking. Douglas applied the Swiss findings to their own, and resumed their investigations into boundary layer control. These tests continued for several months, but various problems developed with the system, and the program was dropped. In general, it was decided that any boundary layer control system required too much perfection for a practical service airplane.

In the meantime, design parameters were being proposed for a delta-winged interceptor. In one study, a jet interceptor with a 2:1 aspect ratio wing of 703 sq. ft. and two-24C (Westinghouse J34) afterburning engines was projected to take 3.35 min. to accelerate and climb to 40,000 feet to intercept a bomber cruising at 550 mph. This senario assumed that the carrier's radar had detected the bomber's approach 100 miles from the ship. In similar studies, various combinations of wing area and engines were investigated at this time (Dec., 1946). Preliminary design studies centered around a "low aspect ratio swept wing" operating with and without afterburner as a general purpose fighter and as an interceptor at gross weights ranging from 14,7000 lbs. to 25,400 lbs.

Finally, in Jan., 1947, Navy specifications were written for an interceptor, and the studies were given an offical company specification design number, D-571. With the investigations narrowed to an interceptor design, wind tunnel work continued more rapidly. Throughout 1947 and 1948 many models were constructed and tested to determine control surface designs, low and high speed flight characteristics, duct inlet designs, and spin characteristics.

The initial model D-571, as designed by R.G. Smith, Heinemann's Configuration Engineer, was a true "flying wing" of 50 degree sweep and an area of 700 sq. ft. Power was provided by two-24C engines with afterburners. Normal gross weight was projected at 15,000 lb. The pilot sat near the leading edge of the wing under a small bubble canopy, surrounded by four-20 mm cannons in the nose. A tricycle landing gear was featured, with the nose wheel swinging aft and the main wheels folding inward.

Results from extensive wind tunnel tests gradually thinned the wing and enlarged the fuselage to the point where the interceptor appeared more conventional in its final form than the Douglas engineers would ever have expected when the studies were begun. Though no simple progressions were made in this design evolution of the interceptor, the D-571 generally went from a thick-winged true delta to a thin-winged modified delta airplane. Again, many combinations of several engine types and placement were studied during this process. Due to the excessive weight of these early turbojets, a conventional rear tail wheel landing gear arrangement was even studied, but was dropped after a short time.

At this stage of the design's history, the Navy voiced their concern about the "flying wing's" reported habit of tumbling uncontrollably, end-over-end. A.M.O. Smith recalls a meeting with Navy officials in Washington, D.C.

The design evolution of the Skyray progressed from the initial D-571, a true "flying wing" of 700 sq. ft., to the D-571-4, an intermediate stage with a 676 sq. ft. delta wing, ending with the final F4D-1 planform, a highly modified delta wing of 557 sq. ft. (Drawings by Don Williams, Douglas Aircraft Co.)

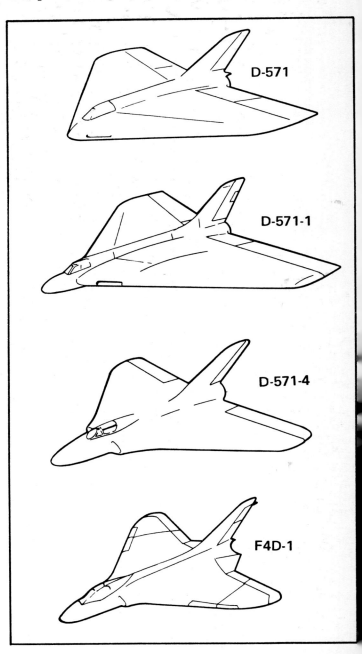

AT RIGHT: TOP - Skyray mock-up. MIDDLE - XF4D-1, 124586 after preliminary shop completion on 10-9-50. Note bureau number is painted incorrectly. Also note prototype tailhook. BOTTOM - The two X-Rays 124586 and 124587 at Edwards AFB in the early 1950s. Note the added fin on the tailcone of 124587. (Douglas)

4

Front view of the two XF4D-1 Skyrays at Muroc Dry Lake in the early 1950s. Note the test booms and the yarn tufts on the tail of 124586 in the foreground. (Douglas photo)

in which the subject came up. Armed with some crude cardboard cutouts he had made for the occasion, Smith gave the Navy officers a quick course in delta wing aerodynamics, as the men playfully tossed the models about the office. Apparently, this impromptu demonstration convinced the officers of the design's inherent stability.

Later, a more serious study of tumbling was made in a curtained-off section of the Douglas plant in El Segundo. Several dynamically similar and balanced balsa scale models were constructed; one of early D571 design, and a couple of the high aspect ratio flying wing designs Douglas had studied previously. To test these, Heinemann, Smith, and several others on the staff waited patiently for several hours after the building had been cleared for the day. This was done to provide security for the project, and to allow the large building's air currents to stablize. The models were carried to the rafters and dropped to a net far below while their free-fall behavior was observed and filmed for future study. The results were heartening as the low aspect ratio delta design refused to tumble from any position.

By March, 1948, design work had progressed to the D571-4, an interceptor based on the new Westinghouse XJ40 turbojet. With a gross weight of only 15,700 lb. and a wing area of 676 sq. ft., this variant featured a short fuselage projecting ahead of the wing, continuing back to house the engine and fuel cells.

Continued testing refined this design until the final planform was chosen in Aug., 1949 as the best compromise between the original "flying wing" concept and a conventional swept wing delta. The first contract for two prototypes, now designated XF4D-1, was awarded in Dec., 1949 by the Fighter Branch of the Navy's Bureau of Aeronautics.

As detail design progressed through 1949 and 1950, the Douglas XF4D-1 emerged as one of the most unique aircraft of its time. The initial design's square-tipped wings were rounded off considerably to shorten the main landing gear and save weight (and to acknowledge the fact that the final few feet of wing didn't add much lift or control).

An amazing 557 sq. ft. of wing area was packed into the XF4D's 44-foot length and 36 ft. 6 in. span. The tricycle landing gear arrangement was supplemented by a small, retractable tail wheel that absorbed shocks resulting from the design's inherent high angle of attack when landing. Directional control was conventional, provided by a single tail fin and rudder. Longitudinal and lateral control was maintained by trailing edge "elevons" that functioned as both elevators, when used together, and as ailerons, when used opposite one another.

To solve the problem of longitudinal trim, Ed Heinemann devised a set of wing root trimming surfaces. These "trimmers" enabled the elevons to operate through neutral much more effectively than if the entire trailing edge of the wing were used for both longitudinal trim and lateral control. A complicated hydraulic power assisted control system was designed, featuring an artifical force feel, with manual reversion in the event of power failure. This system, one of the first of its type, was to prove one of the most troublesome aspects of the airplane's design. Another innovative design feature that resulted in maintenance headaches was the XF4D's very thin guage aluminum skin with pilled reinforcements (stamped indentations). This provided a light airframe structure, but was difficult to maintain and repair.

Fuel for the XF4D-1s was carried in two 320 gal. tanks buried in the enlarged wing fillets surrounding the engine. These provided the airplane with an endurance of only about 45 minutes, short by fighter standards, but adequate for the Skyray's intended interceptor role.

Finally, the Navy specified the airplane's four wing-mounted 20-mm cannons, Aero 1-A fire control system, ejection seat , and various items of equipment. The Navy also had specified the J40 engine for the XF4D-1s and later production models. However, since Westinghouse was beginning to encounter difficulties in perfecting this engine, Heinemann insisted that the fuselage cavity be made large enough for the J57 in the event of a decision to use this engine at some future date.

The Douglas design staff had no difficulty in naming this a new interceptor. The aircraft had a striking resemblance too the giant manta rays that effortlessly cruised the oceans. By combining this with the traditional Douglas "Sky-" prefix, the Skyray" name was born.

Construction of the two prototype Skyrays was begun in an isolated corner of El Segundo's Building 1, under a veil of security that was much heavier than usual. Due partly to the nature of the Skyray's mission and partly to the outbreak of the Korean War, this security was to surround the airplane and its activities for several years. All publicity it received was heavily censored. Most early descriptions of the interceptor were vague, and sometimes ridiculously incorrect as writers of the day were given photographs in which all control surfaces panel lines, and markings had been airbrushed out.

In Oct., 1950, the first prototype, BuNo. 124586, was towed into the Southern California sunlight to begin an extensive program of testing. Upon its preliminary shop completion, 586, and and later its sister ship, BuNo.124587, was painted a glossy midnight blue featuring a stubby, rounded nose contour. By December, however, a long, tapered pitot boom was fitted to both aircraft in preparation for flight testing. The noses of both aircraft were also decorated with a red stripe outlined in white with the name "Skyray" above it, also outlined in white.

As the Westinghouse XJ40 was unavailable at this time, both prototypes were fitted with the Allison J35-A-17 engine, producing barely 5000 lb. of thrust and exiting through a miniscule exhaust cone.

FIRST FLIGHT

In preparation for the Skyray's first flight, Douglas began accepting bids from its large staff of test pilots. Presumably, the lowest bid from a qualified pilot would be chosen for this initial trip. But a minor controversy arose in the Douglas organization when it was announced that Larry Peyton would make the maiden flight. Peyton was an experienced test pilot with the Santa Monica Division, but mainly on transport aircraft. He had been flying the F3D Skyknight to build up his jet time, but his experience was rather limited compared to other Douglas test pilots then in the division. Naturally, the question arose as to why Peyton had been chosen over others who were not only senior to him in the company, but who were vastly more qualified to handle the Skyray on its uncertain voyage.

In any event, on the morning of Jan 21, 1951 Peyton sat in the cockpit of the glossy blue fighter at Edwards AFB and prepared himself for what was to become one of the most terrifying flights of his life!

The purpose of this first flight was twofold: to evaluate the control forces and effectiveness in the "manual" control configuration, and to make a preliminary evaluation of the Skyray's stability. As a safety factor, Peyton was to leave the wheels down during the entire flight. Fortunately, this decision was one of only a few good ones to be made in preparation for the flight and possibly saved the airplane.

Though the unique nature of the Skyray's design doubtless caused some apprehension among the Douglas engineers and pilots, their only real concern before the first flight was in determining the best takeoff trim setting. During the ground evaluations there had been no way to find the correct amount of "up" trim to get the Skyray's nose wheel off the ground before flying speed was reached. As a result, it was decided to attempt the first flight with full up deflection of the pitch trimmers. Also, to avoid the possibility of over-controlling the airplane during the flight, the inboard portions of the split elevons were locked in the neutral position by inserting bolts in place of centering pins.

Unfortunately, flying the airplane in the manual mode involved lengthening the stick as well as cutting the surface deflections in half. This would make it more difficult for Peyton to counteract the nose up forces caused by the pitch trimmers. This combination of reduced control surface and deflection, and the large "up" pitch trimmer setting, not to mention the greatly reduced thrust of the J35, caused Peyton some thrilling moments.

At 10:20 that morning, Peyton revved the engine up to 95% rpm and slowly rolled down the Edwards lake bed. At 78 kt he eased back on the stick as the nose wheel began to lift, and the Skyray's pitch gradually increased. At approximately 121 kt the XF4D-1 gently lifted from the ground and Peyton prepared for a slow climb to 10,000 feet.

As the Skyray's speed increased, however, Peyton found to his dismay that the pitch angle of the airplane also increased. When this rise continued even after he had pushed the stick fully forward against the panel, Peyton gave the trimmers one short burst down. This caused the nose to rapidly pitch downward. To counteract this, Peyton again pulled the stick fully back, but with no effect, so he brought the trimmers once more to the full up position. This action caused the airplane to flare suddenly, and it settled back to the ground. To those watching Peyton fight the bucking Skyray, it appeared that the airplane was about to be lost!

Undaunted, Peyton continued the take-off, and after the second lift off he reduced the power slightly to limit the Skyray's tendency to pitch up. As the XF4D-1 settled into a climb at 140 kt, Peyton discovered that flying the Skyray in this configuration was a little awkward, to say the least. The stick was against the instrument panel and he could only control the climb angle by use of the throttle. By lowering the trimmers in short blips, Peyton brought the stick neutral point to a comfortable position inside the cockpit, and the power was increase until a stabilized climb was achieved at 140 kt and 100% rpm. At 10,00 ft. Peyton leveled off and began checking the Skyray's handling qualities.

He found the Skyray to be surprisingly solid laterally, until disturbed by a gust of wind or the application of rudder. Longitudinally, the airplane was very sensitive to a change in power or the control stick. The rudder was also very sensitive, and effective in counteracting a slight right wing heaviness. Peyton noted an excessive amount of stick slop during this phase of the flight: approximately six inches fore and aft and four-and-one-half inches to each side! This made it very difficult for him to determine the stick neutral position and to control the airplane.

Peyton next made some mild turns with the rudder fixed, to check elevon effectiveness. He found that it took about 25-pounds of stick force to obtain half elevon throw, and 30-degree rolls to each side were made. A strange phenomenon was discovered as the roll stopped momentarily at the wings level position and then continued without any noticable change in stick force or position.

Peyton next checked the rudder for yaw and roll effect and found that the rudder was twice as effective as the elevons in rolling the airplane. The nose of the Skyray followed the roll into a smooth turn immediately after the roll had developed.

During longitudinal checks Peyton decreased the Skyray's speed in steps from 148 kt down to 113 kt and found that a 5% change in the power output required an immediate change in the trimmer setting. The pitch increase that was required to maintain altitude during these slow speeds was quite startling, Peyton noted.

Flight testing of the J-35 powered XF4D-1 124586 in May 1951. (National Archives)

Finally, the Skyray's gliding characteristics were investigated before landing. In his report of the flight, Peyton wrote, "This airplane seems to have some very unusual gliding angle characteristics and rather erratic trim requirements. The trim requirements vary considerably from the power on to the power off condition."

Satisfied that he had accomplished all that he could, Peyton line up the XF4D-1 for a straight in, power on approach from 2000 feet. Once over the end of the runway, he carefully flared the airplane and reduced power. The stick neutral point again went out of the cockpit and the airplane began settling rapidly with the stick fully aft. Peyton applied full up trimmers immediately, and the Skyray once again ballooned, and Peyton once more found himself pushing the stick against the instrument panel in desperation. The skyray touched down on the main and tail wheels, however, just as the stick was beginning to come back off the panel.

Once safely on the ground, Peyton rather disgustedly came to two conclusions: stick slop in the airplane's control system was entirely unsatisfactory for any flight conditions, and the trimmer action was too fast for control during take-off and landings.

Due to contractural problems with Douglas, Peyton never flew the Skyray again, and Douglas test pilot Russ Thaw continued the Skyray's preliminary evaluation program at Edwards..

Douglas engineers had realized their mistakes on the first flight, and taxi tests were made by Thaw to determine the pitch trim setting that would enable the pilot to lift the nose wheel off at 90 percent of the stall speed. In other words, letting the pilot unstick the nose wheel when he wanted to get it off.

While Thaw continued his preliminary elvaluation in the Spring of 1951, Douglas test pilot Bob Rahn was assigned to the program. As Rahn later recalled in his memoirs, "My first flight in the aircraft was in Oct. 1951, after Thaw had made 25 flights. After observing Thaw's flights, especially his landing approaches, I wasn't so sure that I wanted to check out in the airplane, as this type of aircraft, with its modified delta wing planform, has a very high angle of attack which looks as if the airplane is about to stall at any moment. After my checkout, however, this high angle of attack during landing approach did not bother me due to the excellent visibility over the nose. I soon realized that this aircraft was just what I had been looking for in a fighter since my flying days in the Spitfire. The F4D was a fighter pilot's dream as it combined 1) maneuverability at altitude, 2) extremely high rate of climb, 3) short takeoff and landing distances, 4) excellent low speed handling characteristics, 5) extremely high service ceiling, and 6) high level flight speed."

Because of the Skyray's lack of power with the J35, its test program proceeded rather slowly in the beginning. To reach supersonic speeds, for instance, the Skyray had to be put into a mild dive. And due to persistent problems with rudder buzz and tail buffet, supersonic flight in the XF4D-1 was not made for a year-and-a half, until the summer of 1952. "When this first supersonic dive occurred," relates Rahn, "I was not aware of the fact. The Douglas ground observers at Edwards called me on the radio asked if I had made the dive in their direction. My answer was 'affirmative' and they informed me that they had heard a supersonic boom. Since there was no other aircraft in the area, it was assumed that the F4D had made it first supersonic flight. On the very next dive, however, I increased the dive angle slightly which in turn increased the speed and caused the characteristic Machmeter, altimeter, and airspeed jump to occur."

"This was not the last of our problems with supersonic flight testing," Rahn continues, "as the aircraft was designed to fly supersonic 'on the deck,' which had not been accomplished by any aircraft, including the research types. During the following months approximately 150 dives with as many as 14 changes to the area around the tail cone and rudder were made in an effort to eliminate the tail buffet and rudder buzz. It was necessary to install telemetering in the aircraft so as to enable the flight test engineers to observe the air loads that were occuring on the rudder and fin during these low altitude, high Mach number dives. So, in essence, these flight test engineers on the ground were my co-pilots, and very important ones at that because they could tell when the aircraft was approaching its structural limit whereas the pilot could not."

"On one particular flight with Major Chuck Yeager as chase pilot, I was attempting to go supersonic in a dive at low altitude, and I was determined to let the dive continue until the flight engineers, who were observing the air loads on telemetering, told me to pull out. The aircraft was buffeting fiercely and the rudder was at a high frequency 'buzz' when I 'chickened out' and terminated my dive just as the flight test engineers advised me to pull out. This advice from the ground rather startled Yeager as he did not know that the flight was being monitored by telemetry. He commented that he saw that the rudder buzz was of a rather high amplitude, but he didn't realize it was high enough for the ground observers to see with the naked eye!"

Spin recovery in the Skyray was of special concern to the Navy, and Douglas conducted an extensive spin program throughout 1952 and 1953. Again, Bob Rahn, the most qualified person to speak on the subject, relates, "The spin program on the F4D was approached with much timidity and caution on my part—yes, even fear—due to the fact that a delta wing had never been spun before. It was decided early in the flight test program to conduct one 5-turn spin at a forward center of gravity to determine at the outset whether or not any major aerodynamic redesign was necessary. So the aircraft was spun in March, 1952 at a forward cg. Al Carder, who was the project coordinator on the aircraft and is of a cautious nature, was possibly even more concerned over the outcome of the flight than I.

"The procedure established for working up to a 5-turn spin was to work up in intervals of a quarter of a turn at a time up to one turn, then half turn intervals up two turns, then in one turn intervals up to the required 5-turn spin. During the flight I commented that my yaw damper was causing heavy rudder pedal forces, and Al Carder suggested that I bring the airplane back. After several preliminary workup spins, Carder suggested over the radio that I again bring the aircraft back because he thought that I was getting tired, but actually he just wanted to get the aircraft back on the ground in one piece. A third excuse Carder used to try to get me to land was that he felt that the duration of the flight was of such length that my fuel guage must be inaccurate. However, a successful 5-turn spin was accomplished with excellent recovery and we felt that our problems were over.

"Several months later we again resumed the spin tests, but at a more aft cg. which caused the spin characteristics of the aircraft to become more oscillatory in pitch and the turns required for recovery were increased. During the first few spins on the renewed program, I was attempting a two-turn spin to the left. The aircraft spun one turn and, while holding full pro-spin controls (left rudder and full aft stick), the aircraft stopped its rotation and then started slowly spinning in a flat attitude to the right. Recovery was attempted from the reversed flat spin; however, the aircraft quickly rolled to the inverted position and started spinning inverted. The nature of this inverted spin was highly oscillatory in pitch, at times giving me the impression that I was in an upright spin which thoroughly confused me. I wasn't sure whether I was upright or inverted. In fact, I wasn't even sure in which direction I was spinning. To add to complications, the seat broke loose from its mountings due to the high negative load factor during the pitching oscillations, causing me to fall against the top of the canopy. I was not having any success in recovery from the spin so I decided it was time to pull the spin chute, which again save me and the airplane, and recovery to level flight was accomplished 4000-feet above the terrain. The entry altitude was at 36,000 feet. Luckily for me the spin chute functioned properly because while taxiing back in after landing, I found that the canopy could not be opened and this would have prevented me from bailing out!

"As a result of this incident, exhaustive wind tunnel tests were again conducted and NACA forwarded the movies of the model tests in the spin wind tunnel. Careful study of these tests left me highly apprehensive of any further spin tests on the XF4D as the movies showed that the spin characteristics and recovery characteristics were extremely hairy. Therefore, much effort was required on my part to force myself into the proper frame of mind to continue with the spin tests. What finally convinced me to go ahead with the test was the fact that I felt that I had to master the airplane instead of it mastering me.

"I requested of Al Carder that we make every effort to accomplish at least two flights per day so that I could maintain this frame of mind. We cautiously re-entered the spin program by providing a still stronger chute, which would withstand higher opening shock loads, and by going back to the maximum aft cg. of the aircraft in small increments. The prototype XF4D-1 was satisfactorily spun in all the different types of spin entries required by the Navy. Completion of the program was a great relief to me and created the occasion for a big drunk that night."

At some time during this period (mid-1952), the two XF4D-1's were repainted. Presumably, it was found that their midnight blue color was very difficult to spot in the clear blue skies over Edwards AFB. Hence, the airplanes were repainted in glossy white overall, except for the area around their tail cones, which were left in varying amounts of bare metal as modifications were made to reduce the troublesome tail buffet at near-supersonic speeds. Each airplane retained its red nose stripe, however, as well as the name "Skyray," also in red.

PRELIMINARY EVALUATION

While 587 was being flown by Rahn in the spin program in mid-1952, the Navy was conducting a preliminary evaluation of the first prototype Skyray, which had just received the XJ40 engine. From July 16 to July 26 three Navy pilots from the Naval Air Test Center at Patuxent River made ten flights in 586 at Edwards AFB for a total of 7½ hours of flight time.

Two flights were made on the 16th, after which the

XJ40-WE-6 was removed for a routine 50-hour check. However, several discrepancies were discovered during the check and flying was delayed until July 24.

All evaluation flights were conducted with a full internal fuel load of 640 gallons, which gave the Skyray a gross weight of 18,030 lb. at take-off. During ground measurements Douglas engineers found that the XJ40 produced only 6,000 lb. of thrust, due in part to the 2,300 ft. field elevation at Edwards. Whatever the cause, the evaluation pilots were obviously disappointed at the prospect of flying the interceptor with limited thrust.

In addition, the Naval evaluation team noted that the Douglas pilots had at that time yet fly the Skyray past Mach 0.96 due to the persistent rudder oscillations. Con-

Walk-around photos of prototype XF4D-1 124586 on 12-20-50 at El Segundo. Aircraft is in the initial flight test configuration with the Allision J35-A-17 engine installed. Skyray and nose flash are red with white outline. (Douglas)

The empennage area of the XF4D-1s underwent more than two dozen modifications in an attempt to reduce tail flutter and excess drag above Mach 0.95. (Douglas)

AT RIGHT - XF4D-1 124586 in flight on 6-9-52. All blue scheme was changed to white to improve visibility in the skies of the Mojave Desert. (National Archives)

BASIC J35 ENGINE   1st REVISED J35 ENGINE   2nd REVISED J35 ENGINE

3rd REVISED J35 ENGINE   1st REVISED J40 ENGINE   4th REVISED J40 ENGINE

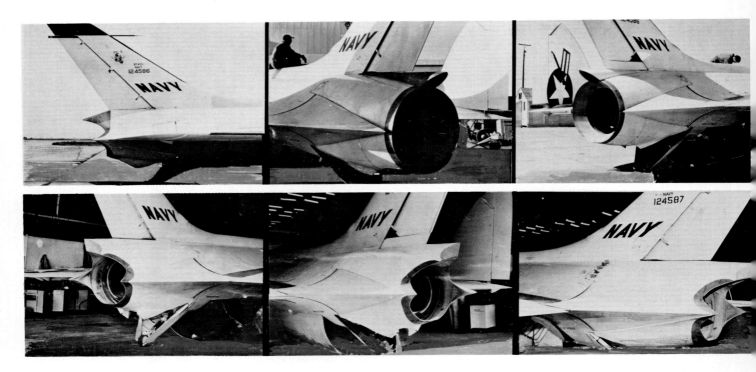

5th REVISED J40 ENGINE   6th REVISED J40 ENGINE   7th REVISED J40 ENGINE

8th REVISED J40 ENGINE   9th REVISED J40 ENGINE   10th REVISED J40 ENGINE

sequently, they locked the rudder mechanically above Mach 0.92 and restricted their speed to a maximum of Mach 0.95.

In their final report of the evaluation, the team acknowledged that there were many Douglas-proposed changes for the production models of the F4D that the prototypes did not have. Among these was a standby hydraulic system independent of the main hydraulic power control system. In the XF4D-1's a failure of the power control system meant unlocking the outboard elevons from the inboard sections and controlling these manually, while the inboard elevons floated freely. As demonstrated during Peyton's first flight, this procedure left the pilot with a greatly reduced control surface area as well as the removal of a power backup.

Douglas also proposed replacing the XF4D's magnetic clutch artificial force feel system for the elevons with a more conventional set-up using springs an a bob weight. The Skyray's one piece rudder also was found to be unsatisfactory as the action of the yaw damper could be felt by the pilot through the rudder pedals. Consequently, Douglas proposed a two-piece rudder for the production aircraft, with the upper surface serving as a yaw damper and the lower half acting as a rudder. Finally, Douglas planned enlarging pitch trimmers and the speed brakes on the production Skyrays as flight tests clearly showed these to be largely ineffective, at least in the case of the speed brakes.

During this evaluation, the team found that high "g" buffet boundary of the XF4D-1 was one of its most outstanding feature. They reported, "At 40,000 ft, in wind up turns to the left steady accelerations without airframe buffet about 3.4g at M-0.90, 3.2g at M-0.80, and 3.0g at M-0.70 were obtained. The F-86E chase plane was lost immediatley on the such maneuvers." However, it also was noted that these maneuvers caused a considerable loss of altitude due to the low thrust of the J40.

As was expected, Skyray's performance with the J40 was rather unacceptable. Time-to-climb from a standing start to 40,000 ft. took 18 to 20 minutes! By comparison, the F-86E chase plane normally used 97% rpm to maintain position with the XF4D-1 in a climb. A maximum speed run at 40,000 ft. gave a true Mach number of 0.896 and a true airspeed of 520 kt. Another maximum run at 30,700 ft. gave a true Mach number of 0.926 and 559 kt. The F-86E could not maintain position on either run, as was the case any time the XF4D-1 approached an indicated Mach number of 0.90, particularly in a dive.

To give the team an indication of the Skyray's suitability for a carrier use, each pilot made several carrier-type approaches to a strip marked off on the lake bed which represented a Essex-class carrier deck. Vision of the deck and LSO was found to be extremely good, even at the minimum approach speed of 115 mph. However, vision in light rain was found to be rather poor as water tended to accumulate on the side panels and the forward windshield.

Again, during the carrier simulation phase of the tests the J40 was given several unsatisfactory marks due to its long engine staring cycle and due to its poor acceleration form idle rpm to full military thrust.

Overall, the evaluation team found the Skyray satisfactory enough, although there were many discrepancies. Among the most troublesome were the fin and rudder buffet, insufficient thrust and excessive acceleration time with the J40, excessive longitudinal maneuvering forces and sensitivity, an unreliable artifical force feel system, an unacceptable emergency manual flight control system, an excessive minimum trim speed, marginal speed brake effectiveness, and several cockpit control discrepancies.

However, in their summary the Navy pilots stated, "The evaluation team was particularly impressed by the capabilities and potentialities of this airplane as being superior to anything flown to date. It is recommended that every effort be made to hold the aircraft at its present weight and provide it with sufficient power to realize the performance of which it its capable."

CONTRACTOR DEMONSTRATIONS

Douglas spent the next year reworking the prototypes to incorporate the changes suggested in the preliminary evaluation, and included several developmental changes intended for carrier use by production Skyrays. Although neither prototype was fitted with the split rudder that later characterized the production F4D-1's, both underwent a noticable change in their elevons. This involved replacing the unbalanced elevons with ones that were balanced both statically and dynamically by the addition of weighted tips that projected ahead of the hinge line.

To comply with the Bureau of Aeronautics' recent change in their policy of conducting carrier suitability testing of new aircraft, Douglas was requested to conduct

The repainted XF4D-1 124586 prior to carrier trails. It was equipped with four 16-mm cameras, carried under left wing, on its tail, and two under its belly. The belly mounted cameras were protected by a small cage. These cameras were used to photograph catapult bridle and tailhook actions. Note chalked on number 27 on intake. Aircraft had fifth revised J-40 engine tail configuration. Aircraft colors are white with black fin tip, leading edges, wing-walks and anti-glare panel. Nose strip, "Skyray" and intake lips are red Note thin black line around red nose flash. Drop tanks and landing gear are blue. (National Archives)

Testing the XJ40-WE-8 engine at night while in afterburner and producing 11,800 lbs of thrust. (Douglas via R.G. Smith)

their own demonstrations prior to the Navy's tests. Consequently, Douglas staged six simulated carrier landings at Edwards to check for structural integrity during high touchdown rates of descent. Then, in July, 1953, 586 was flown to the Naval Air Test Center, Patuxent River, Maryland, where company pilot J.O. Seay flew a series on contractor demonstration flights. Between July 23 and July 31 Seay made 13 field catapult launches and 12 field arrested landings in the prototype while NATC Carrier Suitability Engineers observed.

Various components and accessories required for carrier use were used during these tests, including two catapult bridles, two arresting hooks, and the holdback and tension bar needed for launches. In addition to the normal bridle, a special instrumented bridle, manufactured by the Naval Aircraft Factory, was used to determine catapult towing loads. Due to its electrical fittings to an on-board oscilloscope, the bridle was retained on the airplane after each launch. Bolts were installed on the toes of the Skyray's catapult hooks which prevented the bridle from slipping off. The center section of the bridle was supported with bungee cord, which was attached to the Skyray's structure in the nose wheel well. In the event of an inflight emergency the gear could be retracted, but normal procedure was to leave the gear extended after each launch. The XF4D's V-shaped arresting hook also was instrumented with vertical and side bending gauges and axial load gauges attached along its length.

The testing facilities at Patuxent River consisted of a fixed catapult and arresting gear set up on two of the station's runways. The catapult, an H4B with a 96 ft. power stroke, was arranged on the runway so that approximately 3000 feet of ground run was available for the remainder of the take-off. This was especially comforting as the Skyray, at its design catapult gross weight of 20,630 lb., reached only 80 kt at the end of the power stroke, and a considerable ground run was required to get the airplane airborne.

The arresting gear used was the Morest type with two one-inch diameter arresting wire spaced 40 feet apart on the concrete runway. The wire was capable of 293 feet of runout, and 5000 feet of runway was available beyond the arresting gear.

Instrumentation used during the catapult launches consisted of a Douglas oscilloscope to record the various strain gauge readings, and wingtip-mounted motion picture cameras to record the nosewheel and bridle action. A fixed high speed motion picture camera also photographed the entire airplane at the end of the power stroke to check the shuttle end speed and the Skyray's attitude, an electronic timer clocked the shuttle end speed, and several meteorological instruments were used to record the wind and atmospheric conditions. A 16 mm camera also took panoramic shoots of each launch. During the arrested landing phase, instrumentation to record the XF4D-1's touchdown rate of descent and its "cut" speed also was used.

The catapult tests began on July 23 with 10 launches. Then, 12 arrested landings were made on the 24th, 27th, and 29th, and a final series of maximum gross weight launches were made on the 30th and 31st.

During the catapult tests the Skyray was launched at gross weights ranging from 16,000 lbs. to 20,500 lbs. To determine the F4D's particular tracking characteristics during the launches, the nose gear was spotted in varying degrees up to 10 inches off center, with the main gear spotted six inches off center. Also, a few launches were made with the nose wheel yawed angles up to 70 degrees with the catapult track.

Each launch was controlled by a Catapult Officer to simulate Navy carrier procedure. The airplane was spotted on the catapult according to the engineers' test schedule and launched. Due to the limited ground run available and the light headwinds at Patuxent, the catapult could not accelerate the Skyray to full flying speeds, and Seay had to continue each takeoff run an additional 1500 feet to 2500 feet down the runway before becoming airborne.

After takeoff, Seay would make a short flight around the field, land, and taxi to position for the next launch. Several launches were made successively with each fuel load before shutting down the engine for refueling. Approximately 500 lbs. of fuel was burned during each cycle of launch, circuit of the field, landing, and taxi to position. Additionally, each time after Skyray's return the airplane was inspected for any structural damage that might have occurred during the previous launch.

The first seven launches were made "clean," without any external stores. The remaining six launches were made with full external stores and varying quantities of water ballast in the two 150 gallon Aero 1A fuel tanks. These external stores included four Aero 3A rocket launchers with seven dummy rockets in each pod.

Before attempting the actual arrested landings, Seay flew three period of field carrier landing practice at Patuxent River. These flights were used to familiarize Seay and the LSO with each other's technique, determine the best approach speed, and to investigate the XF4D-1's wave-off characteristics.

Again, the LSO controlled each landing according to the test program that had been established. After each arrestment, the airplane was quickly inspected for damage. Seay then made a takeoff, circled the field, and entered the approach pattern for another landing. Several landings were made on each load of fuel before stopping the engine for refueling. Each cycle required 300-500 lbs. of fuel, and a minimum of 700 lbs. was reserved for emergency situations.

Although Douglas engineers were confident in their planning, Seay's first arrested landing undoubtedly was a little more eventful than they had expected. The Skyray had been loaded with 2200 lbs. of internal fuel, and empty drop tanks and pylons were installed on the wings. Unfortunately, Seay came in rather "hot" at 140 kt, engaged the wire, and lumbered down the runway pulling out all of the available cable and "two-blocking" the arresting gear! The Skyray jerked to an abrupt stop and was pulled backward by the wire.

Beyond a few pulled screws and rivets, inspection of the XF4D-1 revealed that no major structural damage had occurred, although approximately 135% of the arresting hook load limit had been reached. Actually, the peak load factor obtained on the landing was unknown, as the accelerometer trace left the oscillograph paper at -5.57 g's!

As a result of this incident the internal fuel load was reduced by 500 to 1000 lbs. on the remaining flights, and all wing stores were removed until the seventh arrested landing.

During the 12 test landings Seay attempted to duplicate nearly every type of poor carrier landing possible, exceeding the design limits of the airplane on several occasions. Three free-flight engagements were made, and a high sink rate (16.8 ft./sec.) was induced on one occasion. Seay also landed the XF4D-1 up to 28 ft. to the side of the deck center line, and once intentionally rolled and yawed the airplane upon engaging the wire.

Overall, the Skyray passed these tests remarkably well. One interesting exception was a complaint by Seay regarding the jolt he received during the catapult launches. He regarded this as especially severe in the Skyray, and probably an inherent trait of the airplane due to its catapult geometry and cockpit location.

NAVY CARRIER SUITABILITY TESTS

The final carrier suitability tests of the F4D-1 were conducted late in October, 1953 at NATC Patuxent River.

The project pilots for these demonstrations where LtCdr. Verdin and Cdr. Marshall V. Beebe, an experienced Navy test pilot Beebe had been flying 586 since it was first received at Pax River in late July, 1953. He had recently taken over an administrative post at the station as Director of Flight Test, but was anxious to put the Skyray through its Carrier Suitability Trials.

These tests were conducted in five phases: a preliminary evaluation, and tests for catapult launching, arrested landings, barrier engagement, and deck handling.

During the preliminary evaluation phase, the Skyray, especially the cockpit, was carefully inspected and judged from the pilot's viewpoint. Several discrepancies were noted in the headrest, ejection seat face curtain handle, and several control switches and indicators that were not properly located.

As Verdin had previous experience with 587, a special mention was made about the relative merits of 586's clamshell canopy versus sliding canopy on 587. Verdin noted that the clamshell was slow and difficult to pen and close, did not have adequate "canopy locked" indications, and that the canopy could not be opened during high speed taxiing. The sliding canopy on 587, however, was power operated, required no special pilot checking for the locked position, and could be opened to any interemediate position during high speed taxing and high wind conditions. In retrospect, these comments are noteworthy, as the Navy chose the clamshell canopy for all production models of the Skyray.

The catapult launching phase began with a series of 35 field catapult launches at Patuxent River. Various configurations of internal fuel, external drop tanks, and rocket launcher packages were used during these demonstrations. As with the previous contractor demonstrations, the Skyray was positioned off center and the nose wheel was angled to the side before launching to determine the airplane's tracking characteristics.

Following the satisfactory completion of these field launchings, Beebe flew the XF4D-1 to Chambers Field, NAS Norkfolk on Oct. 23, and the Skyray was hoisted aboard the USS Coral Sea (CVA-43) for shipboard catapult and arrested landing test. During 14 catapult launchings aboard the ship, the Skyray was again subjected to various load configurations in an attempt to reach its design load limits.

During these launches, Verdin and Beebe experienced the same jolting starts that Seay had reported earlier. After careful observation, it was discovered that as the holdback mechanism released, the Skyray rotated nose down, compressing the nose gear, before any appreciable forward motion had occurred. Once the airplane began accelerating, the nose would rise again smartly. This peculiarity of the Skyray first forced the pilot's head backward, and then forward off the headrest, then backward again, hard against the headrest as the airplane accelerated, all within a fraction of a second! Both Verdin and Beebe reported that they had been jolted more in the XF4D-1 launches than in any other launching either had experienced. To lessen the discomfort, they recommended that the fleet Skyray pilot brace his feet on the rudder pedals, keep his knees away from the sides of the cockpit, (standard carrier techniques), and hold his head as hard against the headrest as possible.

Today, Marshall Beebe recalls that carrier qualifications or the Skyray required more of the pilot than just flying the airplane. "There was some telemetry on the XF4D-1, but the procedure in those days was to sit down with the Project Officer and decide what we needed to do. All of the testing had to be integrated with the catapult crew, because they had to take measurements and pressures, angles of attack, and nose depressions on the the catapult shots. So you would write out all these things you were doing to do on a knee pad. After the flight you'd sit down and make out a report that might take three hours to write for a one hour flight. You made out a report on every flight you went on, even if it were an unsatisfactory flight for one reason or another."

The arrested landing phase consisted of 56 field landings at Patuxent River and 13 shipboard arrested landings aboard the Coral Sea. This part of the carrier qualifications went smoothly, although some brief rain squalls in the area caused some delay in the trails. Beebe did have his moments of excitement, fortunately though not during his carrier landings. One occurred during a routine landing at Patuxent. As he was about to roll wings level before setting the Skyray down, the pistol stick grip suddenly came out in his hand! With no elevon control and only seconds to react, Beebe fought the airplane with the rudder. The XF4D-1 hit the runway at an angle and careened off the strip towards the right, chewing up grass along the way. Beebe shut everything down and managed to stop the Skyray before hitting anything. "Recurrent trim problems required frequent maintenance," recalls Beebe, "and the trim control switch was in the 'pistol grip' extension of the control stick." For some reason the pistol grip lock screw had backed off. The Skyray was not damaged, and after the grip had been reinstalled the test schedule continued.

The Skyray completed its carrier qualifications aboard the Coral Sea without further incident. Overall, the airplane was judged suitable for carrier operations, although over 20 recommendations were made to improve the production models.

Following the carrier qualification trials, both XF4D-1's returned to Edwards AFB and continued contractor developmental testing throughout 1954. A new set of airflow problems arose with the afterburning XJ40 which required another extensive "cut-and-try" flight program.

Though the two XF4D-1's had been flying for over three years, several incidents indicate that much work still had to be done with the design. One flight in particular stands out in Bob Rahn's mind as illustrative of the problems that plagued the Skyray.

During a high Mach number dive, Rahn discovered a total loss of hydraulic pressure to the elevons. He activated the emergency electric-hydraulic elevon system, which limited the control power needed for recovery.

However, during the dive recovery, the XF4D-1 went into a sudden uncontrollable wing roll. After fighting the

XFD-1 124586 being towed during deck handling phase of carrier suitability trials aboard the USS Coral Sea (CVA-43) in Oct. 1953 PHOTO BELOW - LCDR James Verdin taxis 586 on CVA-43. Note main wheel spats that disappeared shortly after the production models appeared. (National Archives)

TOP & MIDDLE - LCDR Verdin launches from CVA-43. BOTTOM - Touch down on a touch-and-go pass. (National Archives)

Blue once again, XF4D-1 124586 as it ended its days at Naval Weapons Center China Lake in 1961. It was destroyed as a fire fighting exercise. Note original one piece rudder and retrofitted clamshell canopy. (Via Clay Jansson)

Skyray into level flight, an abrupt nose down pitch occurred, convincing Rahn that his control system was malfunctioning. Regaining level flight once more, he found that the J40 had no oil pressure, and began a dive to land the airplane before engine seizure occured. Rahn reconsidered this action, though, and pulled out of the dive to test the controls before attempting any landing.

By this time Rahn's chase pilot had joined up with the Skyray and reported that the airplane's tail wheel was extended. This explained the Skyray's nose down pitch and eased Rahn's mind enough to attempt a landing. During his descent, however, Rahn found that the afterburning J40's variable exhaust nozzle was stuck near the full open position, which reduced engine thrust considerably during the landing. After a safe landing had been made it was discovered that a hydraulic fire also had occurred! Such was the harried life of a Skyray test pilot.

RECORD FLIGHTS

As Douglas prepared 586 for the official Navy carrier suitability trials, test flights continued at Edwards with 587 through the summer of 1953. However, in September and October 587's regular tests schedule was interrupted for a special task: an attempt at the world's air speed record.

Previously, upon receipt of the prototype examples of Westinghouse's J40-WE-6, the Skyray began achieving the speeds it had been designed for. Finally, when the afterburning XJ40-WE-8 at last became available in mid-September, Douglas began thinking seriously about taking the speed record for the 3 km straight course.

After several false starts, On Oct. 3, 1953, LtCdr. James Verdin set a new world's absolute speed record of 753.4 mph in XF4D-1 587 over a course laid out beside Southern California's Salton Sea. Two weeks later, Robert Rahn flew 587 to a new 100 km closed course record of 728.1 mph at Edwards AFB.

To achieve these record speeds, 587 was extensively reworked to streamline the aircraft and lighten it. Outwardly, the only noticable difference in the airplane was the absence of the small tail wheel, which had been removed and the area faired over. After setting these records, 587 was put back into its flight test configuration, and the test schedule was resumed.

Partly as a result of these records, the Skyray was bestowed a special honor when Edward H. Heinemann shared the 1953 Collier Trophy with North American's James H. Kindleberger. Awarded each year for the greatest aviation achievement in America, these two men accepted the trophy for designing the first supersonic airplanes to enter service: the Air Force's F-100 Super Sabre, and the Navy's F4D-1 Skyray.

3 KM RECORD

In the early 1950's a flurry of speed records were being set across the country and in Europe. On Nov. 19, 1952, an F86D piloted by Capt.J. Slade Nash set a new 3 km record by averaging 698.505 mph over a course set up by North American Aviation Co. over the shores of the Salton Sea in Southern California. Jacqueline Cochran next made the headlines on May 18, 1953 by flying a Canadian-built F-86 to a new 100 km closed course speed record of 652.337 mph at a course she had personally set up at Edwards AFB. Just two months later the 3 km record was broken again by the Air Force as Lt. Col. William F. Barnes flew his F-86D over the Salton Sea course, averaging 715.7 mph. To further re-emphasize their air superiority, the Air Force broke the 100 km record again on Sept. 2, 1953, When Brig. Gen. J. Stanley Holtoner piloted his F-86D over the closed course at Vandalia, Ohio. The American record-setting was cut short, however, as England entered the headlines two and a half weeks after the flight at Vandalia. On Sept. 19, Sqdn. Leader Neville F. Duke set a new 100 km record at Dunsfold, England by piloting a Hawker Hunter to a 709 mph average.

Thus, in little less than a year, five new records had been set at the 3 km and 100 km distances alone. As reports of other aircraft and countries' preparations for record attempts became known, the aviation world became charged with the excitement of competition. The stage was set for the Navy and Douglas to step in with the Skyray.

It's uncertain as to how long the Navy or Douglas had been thinking about breaking the world air speed record with the Skyray. Robert B. Smith, a Douglas engineer, had the continuing job of determining what world records any El Segundo-designed aircraft could set. As today, whenever someone wished to try for a speed record and have the results offically recognized, they had to notify the world governing body for all air speed records, the Paris-based Federation Aeronautique Internationale (F.A.I.), pay a sanction fee, and submit the aircraft to an official inspection team to insure that it conformed to the rules that separated the various classes of aircraft. The course also had to be certified as being accurately laid out. In the United States the F.A.I.'s representative, the National Aeronautic Association (N.A.A.), and its officials timed

XF4D-1 124587 over the Mojave desert where it broke the 3 km and 100 km speed records. Douglas photo taken on 9-28-54. Colors are white with black leading edges, wing-walks and anti-glare panel. Nose flash, Skyray and intake lips red.

recorded the speed attempts made in this country. If successful, the speeds or times were forwarded to the F.A.I. for official registration.

In any event, sometime in the late Summer of 1953 Ed Heinemann decided to try for the 3 km record. This relatively short (1.86 mile) straightaway course had long been recognized as the "classic" event by which aircraft were compared. The highest average in four passes was considered the world's "absolute" speed record, as opposed to other records for class of aircraft used or distance around a circular course.

Heinemann wired the Navy's Bureau of Aeronautics for their approval, which was soon granted. The record attempt would be a joint effort of the Navy Douglas. Cdr. Vic Rowney was assigned as the Navy Project Officer for the attempt.

Actual preparations for the attempt were started in mid-August at the Douglas testing facilities at Edwards Air Force Base, located in the Mojave Desert 70 miles north of El Segundo. Since the course at Edwards was Air Force property, it was necessary for Douglas to request permission for its use. This, too, was soon granted by Edwards officials.

On Sept. 14, 1953 Douglas submitted its formal application for the speed attempt to both the National Aeronautic Association and the F.A.I., requesting that official observers, timers, and their equipment be furnished at the course at Edwards. Shortly after this, however, North American Aviation Co. also submitted an application for the 3 km record try. Upon learning of the Douglas intent, North American officials naturally felt that their new F-100 should have been given the first chance at the record. The Skyray, so their reasoning went, had not been fitted with the afterburing J40, and had yet to exceed 650 mph. The YF-100, on the other hand, had been equipped with the afterburning J-57 for some time, regularly flying in the 750-mph range. However, the Natioanl Aeronatuc Assocation insisted that Douglas and the Skyray had the right to make the first attempt by virtue of their earlier application date, and that they could keep this priority until Oct. 15, 1953.

The Skyray's record attempt was to be flown by Lt. Cdr. James B. Verdin, age 35. Verdin had been a Navy combat pilot in World War II and Korea with over 100 missions to his credit before becoming a Navy test pilot. Hollywood could not have come up with a more photogenic choice. Boyishly handsome, Verdin looked the part of a test pilot, and the Navy took full advantage of this in publicity photographs and films of the event.

But the more immediate chore of getting the F4D ready for the speed runs fell to veteran Douglas test pilot Robert O. Rahn, 32. Bob Rahn, born in Harvey, Ill., but raised in Dayton, Ohio, had joined the Douglas Testing Division in 1945 after serving as an Air Force fighter pilot flying Spitfires in North Africa. After 204 missions, Rahn was assigned to Wright Field's Special Weapons Branch. There he flew B-17's, B-24's, and B-25's before being transferred to Fighter Flight Test, where he piloted the long-range P-47N and P-38L. In all, Rahn had over 3,500 hours to his credit in 60 different types of aircraft, including the original developmental stability and control flights with the Skyray. Tall and handsome in how right, Rahn was to play an invaluable part in the development of many Douglas aircraft.

By mid-September, the afterburning J40-WE-8 was finally installed in the F4D, and the record attempt was scheduled for Saturday, Sept. 26. Rahn made the first unrestricted afterburner flight on Sept. 20. To everyone's surprise, this engine worked flawlessly. After only a few test hops with the afterburning engine, Rahn flew the Skyray through the Edwards 3 km course at low altitude. Bringing the F4D down on the deck at military power, he lined up the aircraft with a long strip of black asphalt that recently had been applied to the desert course to aid visibility. As a further aid, old tires had been piled at either end of the course and ignited, and tall plumes of coal-black smoke rose for hundreds of feet. As he approached the entrance, Rahn fired the afterburner and quickly accelerated to over 700 mph. The desert floor just 100 feet below sped past in a blur as the F4D started buffeting as it approached the speed of sound.

To Rahn at that moment, the experience was terrifying! "I said to myself, 'What the hell am I doing here?'" An instant later the Skyray suddenly yawed uncontrollably and skidded violently off the course. Rahn quickly cut the afterburner and climbed for altitude, testing the controls for response. After a safe landing has been made the cause of this yaw was soon discovered. The metal shroud covering the Skyray's small tail wheel had peeled back into the airstream during the high speed run.

While Rahn was conducting these preliminary flights over Muroc, the Douglas Flight Test crew were preparing what was hoped an ideal flight plan for the record try.

Prior to each flight the aerodynamicists worked out the flight pattern and time, depending upon the current temperature and weather conditions. At the conclusion of each afternoon's practice flights, Douglas technicians often worked until midnight developing motion picture film of the Skyray's instrument readings taken during the runs. These pictures were used in preparing flight plans for the following day's flight.

Over the next couple of days Rahn flew five more high speed flights through the course at Muroc, determining the proper handling technique and the number of seconds of allowable afterburner time. During these speed runs it was necessary to fly the airplane with a fixed longitudinal trim settings. This was due to the rapid acceleration and deceleration of the aircraft with the afterburner on or off. The pilot couldn't take time to worry about trim while flying at these speeds. This resulted in a "tuck under," or nose down trim while flying at maximum speed in afterburner, and a nose up trim condition while using military power in the turns. The odd result was that the pilot had to exert a pull force on the stick while in level flight and a push force during the steeply banked turns.

Handling the airplane in these turnaround was also tricky. Stringent F.A.I. rules prevented the aircraft from exceeding 500 meters (1,640 feet) in the turns. At the speeds being flown by the F4D, the afterburner had to be cut off the instant is passed out of the course, and the aircraft banked around in a wide, low turn. This rule was originally intended to stop aircraft from diving into the course to gain speed. For the Skyray, however, this maneuver would have been futile. The airplane was flying at its maximum speed near the "sound barrier," and the effects of compressibility quickly brought the Skyray back to the "Vmax" as drag rise took effect. As it was, the 750 mph speed took the F4D-1 many miles beyond the course, in a five mile diameter turn!

The number of seconds needed for afterburner operation was a critical aspect to the success of the record try. Every pound of fuel carried by the Skyray was crucial to its speed. If the afterburner were turned on too soon before entering the time portion of the course, the aircraft would reach it maximum speed before entering and waste fuel. If it were applied too late, the F4D-1 would still be accelerating after it had entered the "traps," and the average speed would be correspondingly lower.

To get as much fuel as possible into the Skyray's tanks, the Douglas crew piped the JP-4 through coils immersed in alcohol packed with dry ice. This reduced the fuel temperature to about 35 degrees., which also reduced its volume.

During this period in which Bob Rahn was testing the Skyray with its new engine, Cdr. Verdin was assigned an F9F Cougar from NAAS El Centro. He flew this airplane over the course several times to locate and familiarize himself with the various landmarks.

After only one hour and 55 minutes of flight time in the afterburner-equipped Skyray, Rahn turned the airplane over to Cdr. Verdin on Friday, Sept. 25. Up to this date, Rahn's best unofficial speed over the 3 km course was 737 mph average, bettering Duke's recently set 100 km record by some 18 mph. Unknown to them at the time, however, was the fact that on the same day in 103 degree heat in the Libyan Desert, Britain's Mike Lithgow had officially flown the same speed over a 3 km course. Piloting a production Vickers Supermarine Swift with a cockpit packed with dry ice. Lithgow had broken his countryman's record with a 737.3 mph average.

Back in the Mojave Desert, however, Cdr. Verdin used this Friday to make several high speed familiarization flights in the F4D-1. He felt ready for the attempt Friday afternoon, so the go-ahead was on for the scheduled try the following day.

Unfortunately, a 35 mph wind developed on Saturday, kicking up clouds of sand so thick that the visibility was questionable and the turbulence dangerous. To assess the situation, Verdin and Rahn flew over the course in a company Navion and decided to cancel the flight.

A conference was called that afternoon, and it was decided to take advantage of predicted higher temperatures in the Salton Sea area, some 140 miles south of Edwards. North American Aviation Co. graciously gave Douglas permission to use its privately owned course, along with timing equipment and technicians.

Douglas Testing Division personnel and their tools, along with the National Aeronautic Timers and their equipment, were flown overnight to the El Centro Naval Auxiliary Air Station, 40 miles south of North American's course, and were set up and ready for the runs by noon Sunday. This was no easy feat. In addition to the Douglas mechanics, technicians, engineers, and administrative personnel that had to be moved, there were the N.A.A. officials and timers, and a battery of "impartial observers" that were required to witness the attempt. Stationed at various points along the course, these observers were required to sign notarized statements as to the height of the Skyray during the run. Also helping the Douglas crew with the preparations for the flights were personnel from both the Air Force Flight Test Center at Edwards AFB, and the 6511th Parachute Development Test Group at El Centro.

Verdin, meanwhile, left for El Centro in his F9F, while Rahn had the job of ferrying the F4D to the station. Before landing at El Centro, Rahn flew the Skyray through the course at maximum speed. As the Salton Sea course was actually below seal level, some 2,600 feet lower than the one set up at Edwards, there would be an expected rise in the indicated airspeed of about 25 mph. It would be interesting, he thought, to find out the effects, if any, this would have on the handling of the F4D.

The results were better (or worse) than he had expected. Rahn located the course, and as he was accelerating across the east end of the sea, a pronounced yaw developed at about 5 mph below the maximum speed. While trying to determine what was causing the yaw and whether or not it could be trimmed out, the F4D skidded across the sea to the west side! Although a couple of additional flights were made the next day to try to find out what was causing the problem, it remained a bothersome but acceptable mystery and Verdin decided to take the aircraft as is for the record attempt, now re-scheduled for Monday, Sept. 28.

It was at this time that the Douglas crew learned of Lithgow's attempt at the 3 km record. This was rather disheartening news as Rahn's best unofficial run at Edwards was no faster, but it was decided to try again regardless since it was thought the Swift's record was still unofficial.

On Sunday afternoon, Cdr. Verdin made two practice passes over the course, but the F4D developed a fuel gauge malfunction and the Skyray was grounded while repairs were made that night. Monday's attempt was also canceled, however, due to a pitot tube that had to be sent to the El Segundo factory for repairs.

On Tuesday, Verdin managed to complete four officially timed passes, but not without further mishap. Flying the course late that afternoon, when the temperature was below 90 degrees, the first three passes were satisfactory enough: 748.4 and 746.9 mph on the downwind passes and 740.8 mph on the first upwind run. On the final upwind pass, however, Verdin made a sudden climb for altitude near the end of the course as the engine fluctuated due to fuel starvation to the afterburner. "The gauges did a little dance," Verdin later remarked to reporters, "and I thought I'd better head for someplace to land. But it settled down and flew just great." The slow last pass of 734.6 mph brought Verdin's average for the run down to 742.7 mph. He had needed to make 744.6 mph to beat the British mark by the required 1%. However, as it was still not known that the Swift's record of 737 mph was officially recognized and the speed to beat, there was some agonizing decision-making by Navy and Douglas officials on whether or not to submit the 742 mph run as an official attempt.

There were several factors to be considered. The Navy and Douglas were both eager to submit the record attempt because it would be the first time in Naval air history that a carrier aircraft had held a world speed record. However, several other factors went against a decision to submit the attempt. It was all too apparent that North American was waiting with its F-100, and would probably beat the F4D mark on the first try. The Supermarine Swift was also preparing for another try at the distance, and Hawker was reportedly taking its Hunter down to the Libyan Desert to make another official attempt at the 3 km record. Despite these considerations, the fact that it was known that the Skyray could do better than the 742 mph average was the main reason why it was decided not to submit the speed as an official attempt.

The Americans were not about to give their British competitors any indications of their progress, either. Stated Rahn, "To add to the tension that was already prevalent at this time, trans-Atlantic telephone calls were being placed from London to El Centro and also from Paris, headquarters of the F.A.I., to Thermal, California, where the N.A.A. timers had set up their headquarters. Therefore, we knew that the British were closely following our progress. So, to add to the tension on the other side of the Atlantic, we refrained from giving them information as to what speeds we were obtaining or when we would make an official try."

After the record attempt on Tuesday, Rahn flew the F4D back to El Segundo for minor repairs to the afterburner and to patch some tears in the wing skin and tail cone. The next attempt was rescheduled for Friday, when higher temperatures were predicted for the Salton Sea area. Douglas mechanics took advantage of this delay by completely reworking the aircraft. Every hole in the Skyray was sealed over, the wing slats sealed up, the arresting hook removed, and every protuberance smoothed out or removed. As Bob Rahn observed, "The plane was waxed and really looked like a 'racer'."

Also during this brief intermission, Douglas and Naval personnel from El Centro combined forces to improve the course markings. As the course was laid out over hilly sand dunes and small arroyos draining into the nearby sea, it was impossible to mark it with a strip of asphalt as was done at Muroc. Because of this, Cdr. Verdin had some difficulty determining when to turn the afterburner on and off despite the use of smoke pots.

After discounting several schemes, Douglas, Navy, and National Aeronautic Association officials finally settled on a method that worked quite well. At either end of the course posts were sunk eighty feet apart diagonally to the flight path, and a red nylon material was stretched back and forth between them. Then, with a Navy helicopter and pilot borrowed from El Centro, 5,000 pounds of lime were dropped in a straight line at each end of the course. This helped Verdin eliminate the necessity of making any last-second directional changes.

When rework on the Skyray had been completed at El Segundo, the pressure was on to fly the aircraft back to El Centro as soon as possible for the expected high temperatures on Friday. Again, the weather conspired to delay the record attempt. A thick fog had settled over Los Angeles Airport, precluding any takeoff by the F4D. It was then a test aircraft in the Douglas Testing Division, and long-established procedure was that no test airplane would be flown in instrument weather. However, the tight schedule of the record attempt enabled Rahn to make his instrument climb through the fog, leaving behind many turned backs at the El Segundo plant. On the cross-country flight to El Centro, Rahn made another maximum run over the Salton Sea course in the cleaned-up Skyray, and the true airspeed he achieved was most encouraging!

In any event, the expected high temperatures on Friday never materialized. Although it reached into the low 90's, it was still too "cool" for an all-out attempt at the record. A temperature of around 98 degrees would put the speed of sound at approximately 792 mph. The F4D was going to need all the help it could get to set a respectable record, too, for the Douglas crew now learned that the Swift's record was official, and had to be bettered by the required one per cent. This meat that a speed of 745 mph would have to be averaged, and that temperatures around the 100 degree mark would be vital for a successful flight. The attempt was re-scheduled for the next day, Saturday, October 3rd.

Saturday morning arrived with dismal hopes for a record try. A wind began blowing and meterological forecasts indicated that the winds would not diminish. Reluctantly, it was decided to cancel the attempt until the following Monday. Everyone had been working seven days a week for the past month, and morale was getting low in the desert heat. As the Douglas personnel were waiting for the company DC-3 to arrive at El Centro, however, the winds began to slacken, causing a slight but definite increase in the temperature. At the Salton Sea a plot was made of winds and air temperature every half-hour. Not surprisingly, this clearly showed a increase in air temperature with the decrease in wind velocity. Encouraged by this turn of events, Verdin made a test run over the course in his F9F and reported that the turbulence was not excessive. Suddenly, thoughts of a weekend at home were shoved aside as an attempt at the world speed record was on!

While the temperature climbed toward 100 degrees, the F4D was hurriedly prepared for the flight. Rahn spent the last hour with Verdin in "solitary" in any empty room containing a couple of bunks, and sat and talked about things unrelated to flying.

When the temperature peaked at 98.5 degrees at 3 p.m., Verdin made his way out to the Skyray while Rahn and Douglas Test Pilot Quentin Burden each climbed into one of the red, white, and blue company Navions. The Navions were used to carry an official observer at each end of the course, circling to make sure that Verdin did not exceed

**AMERICAN AVIATION HISTORICAL SOCIETY
P. O. BOX 99,
GARDEN GROVE,
CA 92642**

Tailhook Association
Box 40
Bonita, CA 92002

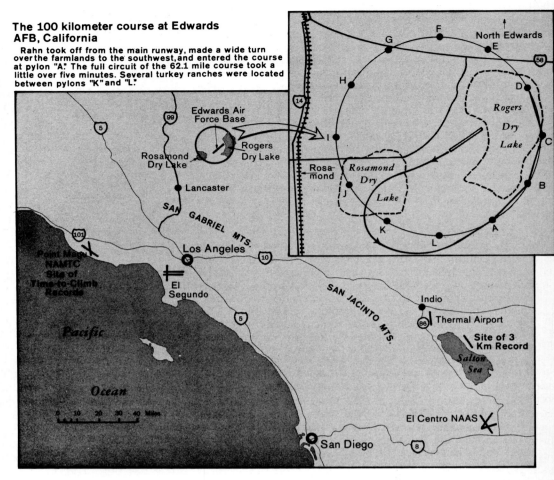

The 100 kilometer course at Edwards AFB, California

Rahn took off from the main runway, made a wide turn over the farmlands to the southwest, and entered the course at pylon "A". The full circuit of the 62.1 mile course took a little over five minutes. Several turkey ranches were located between pylons "K" and "L".

Map by Peter Mersky.

500 meters in the turns. Rahn's Navion also carried a Douglas engineer aboard, who kept track of Verdin's afterburner time during his passes over the course, and made a plot of his remaining fuel.

At El Centro, meanwhile, Verdin was strapping himself into the Skyray, which had been loaded with some 700 gallons of pre-cooled fuel. Several mechanics spent the last moments polishing the Skyray's wings and fuselage to ensure the least air friction possible. Finally, the Skyray, with Verdin riding in the cockpit, was towed quickly to the end of the runway. Two white-overalled mechanics sat at the F4D's wingtips as it made its way past the El Centro flight line.

A portable starter was hooked up to the aircraft once it was stationed on the runway, and as the engine came to life the Douglas and Navy mechanics quickly backed away. Verdin checked the Skyray's instruments for a few moments and then eased the throttle forward. The Skyray slowly gained momentum and, after a long takeoff roll to save valued fuel, was airborne at 3:22 p.m. Verdin headed north toward the course, and in only a few moments, brought the F4D up to full military power as the smoke from the burning tires came into view. While still several miles from the course entrance, he lit the afterburner and the F4D accelerated to its maximum speed just as he entered the traps.

To observers standing near the course entrance it was an eerie sight. The only sound as the hot desert breeze rustling the sage-brush, and the commotion of various observers as the call came over the radio: "Verdin is airborne!" Moments later the Skyray appeared silently on the horizon; a small white speck against the clear blue desert sky, trailing a faint wisp of smoke behind. The speck quickly grew as it approached at near the speed of sound. Suddenly Verdin and the Skyray had passed and entered the course, accompanied by a deafening roar as the afterburner rumbled and glowed and faded into the distance.

By unofficial watches, Verdin's first pass against the wind was a relatively slow 745 mph. Not fast enough in itself to capture the world record, but the downwind runs would more than make up for this.

As soon as Verdin passed the end of the traps, he cut the afterburner, rolled the Skyray into a steep 70 degree bank, and made a wide, level 180 degree turn that took him several miles beyond the course. Each time the F4D shot through the course and started its turnaround, Verdin radioed his remaining fuel to the engineers so that an accurate plot of his fuel situation could be made. There was a real concern that he might not have enough fuel left to make it back to El Centro.

Verdin's next three runs through the course went as smoothly as the first. The Skyray seemed to be performing well, but only the official's photos and measurements would tell if a new speed record had been set.

Exactly 20 minutes and 25 seconds after taking off, Verdin set the Skyray down at El Centro 3,450 pounds lighter, as it had burned approximately 575 gallons of fuel during the brief flight.

After exchanging congratulations, Verdin, Rahn, and some of the Douglas crew flew from El Centro aboard a

TOP LEFT - Bob Rahn, 32-year-old Douglas experimental test pilot, in record-breaking XF4D-1 124587. This was the only Skyray to retain the sliding canopy. 124586 was retrofitted with a clamshell canopy. (Via Rahn) TOP RIGHT - LCDR Jim Verdin in 587 several weeks after his record flight. (Via Lee Saegesser) AT LEFT - Verdin and Rahn in USAF pressure suits used for record altitude attempts at Edwards in Dec. 1953 with 124587. BELOW - 124587 after breaking 3 km world's absolute speed record in Oct. 1953. (National Archives)

company DC-3 to the Thermal Airport, 30 miles north of the speed course. Here, National Aeronautic Association officials were beginning the tedious process of developing the films taken of the flight. They had to measure the pictures and compute the Skyray's speed using slide rules, magnifying glasses, and a comptometer. This was done in a dingy back room of the airport office building. As darkness was approaching, a single naked 50-watt bulb burned over a small table where the timer had their equipment spread out. Broken glass lay by the window and paint was peeling from the walls.

Observing this scene of tired and unkempt men huddled around the now-darkened room, Rahn later observed, "We appeared more like bandits dividing their loot rather than

A black and white tent which protected N.A.A. timers and equipment during Verdin's 3 km record attempt. Cameraman at right filming scene for Douglas produced 16mm documentary, "New Wings for the Navy." Douglas Aircraft Co. via Los Angeles Intl. Airport Public Relations

officials from the National Aeronautic Association figuring out a new world speed record."

The computational process took nearly six hours, but the wait was well worth it. The photos showed that the Skyray had indeed broken the record. With passes of 745.075, 761.414, 746.053, and 759.499 miles per hour, Verdin had averaged a remarkable 753.4 mph to give the United States the absolute world speed record over 3 km!

By a curious twist of circumstances, the Skyray's absolute speed record lasted but a month, although its 3 km record remained unbroken for nearly eight years. As expected, within weeks of Verdin's flight, Lt. Col. Frank Everest, Jr., piloted the YF-100 over the same Salton Sea course, breaking the F4D's record. Due to lower temperatures, however, Everest averaged only 757 mph. This was faster than the Skyray, but not by the required on percent. Undaunted, North American officials took advantage of a little known technicality in the FAI rules. It was discovered that the FAI recognized the absolute speed record as the fastest average over either the 3 km or 15 km straight courses. A 15 km course was hurriedly prepared at the Salton Sea and Lt. Col. Everest set a new 15 km record 755 mph. As this was faster than the Skyray's average it was recognized as a new absolute speed record.

Remarkably, Verdin's 3 km record stood until August 28, 1961, when Navy McDonnell F4H Phamton II flew 902.7 mph over a course set up at Holloman AFB, N.M.

100 KM RECORD

After Verdin's successful 3 km flight, everyone connected with the attempt took a much-needed rest over the weekend. The next Monday's activities would be back to business as usual: that of resuming the Skyray's busy flight test schedule at Edwards. Bob Rahn had a better plan in mind, though. As the F4D was in a "racer" configuration, it seemed to Rahn a waste not to try for the 100 km closed course record, too.

That following Monday, Rahn approached Donald Douglas, Jr., with the idea. Douglas saw no objections, and suggested that Rahn look into the possibility of using the 100 km course at Edwards AFB that had recently been set up by Jacqueline Cochran. Rahn flew north to Edwards in a company Navion, obtained the location of the course, and spent most of one morning spotting the pylons from the air.

Located at the north end of the Antelope Valley, the circular 100 km course was made up of 12 tall poles used as pylons. These were set equidistantly around Edwards AFB at 8.3 km intervals (approximately 5.2 miles), for a total distance of 100 km, or 62.1 miles. The east side of the course broadened the eastern end of Rodgers Dry Lake, and proceeded north of the highway between the towns of Mojave and Boron, west to the west side of Rosamond Dry Lake and continued south to the southern edges of both Rosamond and Rodgers Dry Lakes. The whole area was made up of flat, dry lake beds with shallow arroyos draining into them. It was largely unpopulated, except at the southern end of the course where there were a few large turkey and chicken ranches. These ranches, just northeast of the town of Lancaster, caused Rahn a bit of apprehension, but more on this later.

After satisfying himself that the course was indeed usable, Rahn telephoned Ms. Cochran at her ranch in Indio, Calif., to request permission to use it. She was in Japan at the time; however, her husband, Floyd Odlum, told Rahn that the course was available to anyone who wanted to use it.

Once again, Douglas requested permission from the Navy for an attempt on the 100 km record. The Navy was agreeable to the idea if it could be done with a minimum of delay to the testing program with the Skyray.

As this was to be another Navy record attempt it was assumed that a Navy flier would be chosen to pilot the F4D. Much to Rahn's surprise, however, a teletype was received from Bob Canaday, the Douglas-Navy liaison representative in Washington, D.C., stating that BuAer had approved Rahn as pilot. The last line of his message read, "Tell Rahn he owes me a beer." Said Rahn later, "Needless to say, I sent Canaday a case of beer posthaste to show my appreciation for what he and the Naval officers at BuAer had done to obtain the approval for me as pilot." As far as is known, this was to be the first time that a "civilian" was allowed to set a world record in a military airplane.

Another application was submitted to National Aeronautic Association and FAI officials for the record try, now nicknamed "Operation Merry-Go-Round." The official timers and their equipment were once more on their way to Edwards. Whereas this was an attempt on a world class record, rather than the "absolute" one, the NAA/FAI required a sanction fee of only $150 from Douglas. If the at

TOP - Bob Rahn taxis out in 124587 to set 100 km closed course record. Note no nose flash. (Via Rahn). AT LEFT - Robert Rahn streaks past the finish pylon on his second, and official 100 km flight with an average speed of 728 mph. Smoke of burning tires marks pylon A. (Via Rahn). BOTTOM - 587 prior to the 100 km record and low over the Mojave. (Douglas)

tempt was successful, an additonal registration fee of $150 was required. Rahn was also told by the officials that he had to buy a "Sporting License" for the flight! "To this day," says Rahn, "I still don't know why I had to buy a Sporting License. I should think that my Commercial Pilot's License would have been sufficient but I have had $3 (the cost of the license) worth of fun just telling the story about it."

During the next week Rahn made many practice runs around the course in an F3D Skyknight, saving valuable engineering flight test time on the Skyray. During these flights, Rahn built up a mental log of landmarks surrounding each pylon as they were very difficult to spot at the high speeds and low altitudes at which the course had to be flown.

At least one account of the record attempt stated that Rahn flew a circular path around the course in a constant

35-degree bank, but this was not so. In order to minimize the distance traveled between pylons, Rahn elected to fly directly from one pylon to the next, rounding each turn in a tight 70-degree bank. After banking around each pylon, Rahn would roll the Skyray back into level flight for the 15 seconds or so it took to reach the next pylon. He would then roll the airplane into another 70-degree bank and change course 30 degrees toward the next pylon, continuing in a counterclockwise direction around the course.

By FAI rules. Rahn was restricted to a maximum altitude of 100 meters. But, as in the 3 km flight, diving into the start of the course would have been futile as the drag rise would have quickly brought the aircraft back to its maximum level speed.

Finally satisfied with his flights in the F3D, Rahn made one final practice flight over the course in the Skyray. During these runs it was necessary for Rahn to secure his lap and shoulder belts as tighlty as possible. Moving through the course at over 700 mph, the F4D was constantly shaken by rapid sharp jolts as it passed through the severe desert turbulence. After negotiating only half of the course at high speed, Rahn cut the afterburner and completed the remainder of the flight in military power. This was done because of the turkey rances at the southern end of the course. It was discovered that the noise of the afterburner and the Skyray's loud shock wave literally scared the fowl to death!

Rahn encountered no major problems on these practice flights, and so it was decided to make an offical try for the record on Thursday, Oct. 15. To help him spot the pylons a pile of old tires was stacked near each one and burned so that the dense, black smoke would mark the turns. In addition, two obvservers were stationed at each pylon; one to make sure that Rahn stayed outside of the pole, the other to flash a small mirror at the approaching plane.

The day of the record attempt turned out to be a relatively cool one, as the temperature slowly peaked at only 76 degrees. As the many officials, timers, and observers took their stations, the XF4D-1 was loaded with 640 gallons of fuel. Douglas test pilot Bill Davis took off in an F3D and circled the course as a "lamplighter," a signal to the observers at the pylons that the official flight was minutes away, and that the tires should be set afire.

As Davis rounded the course, Rahn sat in the Skyray's cockpit listening on the radio as Davis called out each pylon. When he reached the tenth one, Rahn started the Skyray's engine and was off the ground within a minute and 20 seconds. Rahn quickly brought the F4D to 600 mph using military power, making a wide turn to the southwest of the course. Then, while still several miles away from the first pylon, he lit the afterburner and rapidly jumped to maximum speed just as the first pylon was reached.

Rahn had no difficulty in negotiating the course. The day was beautifully clear and he easily spotted the mirrors, the smoke, and the pylons. Continuing through the course, Rahn's only real concern was in maintaining his speed through each turn. If he slowed too much while pulling the high-G turns, there was a possibility of "backing through" the Mach trim change. Had this happened, it would have caused increased control sensitivity, which would have induced a severe longitudinal control problem by inadvertent overcontrolling. It would have been more of a concern with higher temperatures, but the day was cool and the entire flight was made at speeds above this point.

As it was, the flight was uneventful. Overcoming his first reactions to the situation, Rahn later reflected, "Flying at this speed so close to the ground especially where longitudinal control is at its worst is quite frightening at first, but after two-thirds of the flight was over, I was fairly relaxed and wished that I could get more speed. I actually found myself trying to move my upper torso fore and aft trying to get more speed."

The full circuit of the course took little more than five minutes. As he passed through the traps, Rahn pulled the Skyray up into a vertical climb and did victory rolls up to 10,000 feet before landing.

Upon landing, Rahn was congratulated by the crew and ground observers. They had timed the flight with stop watches, and after some quick calculations had determined that a new closed course speed record had easily been set. The flight had lasted a little over 10 minutes from takeoff to landing, consuming 600 gallons of fuel.

The Douglas team's rejoicing was cut short, however, as the N.A.A. timers reluctantly notified the group that the official timing mechanism had malfunctioned, and that the attempt would not count. However, the flight was repeated the following day, Friday, Oct. 16, with complete success. According to the unofficial observers stopwatches, the second run was only .2 mph slower than the previous day's. The new official record established by Robert Rahn and the Skyray stood at 728.11 mph. This beat the previous record of 709 mph by a substantial margin, and gave the 100 km record back to the United States.

As fate would have it, this record flight would come with an unexpected, but certainly predictable, cost. The Douglas Aircraft Co. soon received a bill for $1,800...for 450 turkeys that had been frightened to death by the Skyray's two full-afterburner circuits of the course!

Bob Rahn's 100 km record stood for over five years, but not because of any lack of aircraft capable of besting his speed. Rather, it seems to have been a combination of several factors. There was growing dissatisfaction in the aviation community over the outdated F.A.I rules that required the courses to be flown at dangerously low altitudes at speeds never imagined decades earlier. Performance-wise, these records had little bearing on a fighter's true capabilities, as the turbojet was never intended to excel at low altitudes. Also, their measurement in ground speed rather than Mach number didn't give a true picture of a modern fighter's performance.

In any event, as far as is known, Rahn's 100 km record was the last one set at low altitude. With sophisticated radar tracking and timing devices, all record attempts could be flown at high altitudes where speed, as well as safety, could be achieved. Rahn's record was eventually broken on Feb. 25, 1959, when Gerald Muselli piloted a Dassault Mirage III to a 1,095 mph average, set at an altitude of 22,970 feet.

WORLD'S ALTITUDE ATTEMPT

Not all of the Skyray's attempts at world records were successful. In Dec., 1953, the Navy was apparently basking in the spotlight of the F4D's record-breaking flights two months earlier. So much so, in fact, that it was decided to try for the world's heavier-than-air altitude record of 63,668 feet, set the previous May by a British Canberra Bomber.

It appears that the Navy wanted to score a publicity coup by making the official announcement of still another Skyray record at the Wright Brothers Memorial Dinner, to be held on Friday, Dec. 18, in Washington, D.C. Cdr. Verdin was assigned to fly the attempt, even though he had never flown the F4D at altitude before. Thusly, a great deal of pressure was placed on the Douglas crew to produce results.

When the trial flights were begun at Edwards AFB by Bob Rahn, however, balky afterburner controls developed on the J40 and continued to cause problems. Fuel starvation and erratic running were to plague the Skyray for some time due to this. Although many high-altitude flights were attempted, Dec. 18 arrived with Rahn still unable to make the Skyray perform at altitude due to the afterburner fuel control problems. After an unsuccessful official altitude attempt on the morning of the 18th, it was decided to make one more small adjustment to the fuel control and have Verdin make a final attempt that afternoon.

TOP - 124587 prior to unsuccessful altitude attempt on Dec. 18, 1953. (NASM) BELOW - 124587, at NAF Inyokern (China Lake) in Nov. 1954. Note starter cart and unique tailhook bumper wheel used on XF4D-1s. A different configuration was used on the production aircraft. (Fahey)

It took several hours to locate the official observers in Los Angeles, and it was late in the afternoon before they arrived. Still more time was used for the necessary inspections of the aircraft by the officials. By the time everything was ready for the flight it was 15 minutes before sunset. To make matters worse, the sky had become overcast, a definite hazard to a high-altitude flight.

What happened next is best left for Robert Rahn to tell: "As Jimmy was being strapped in the cockpit, and I was giving him final instructions and advice. I felt that it was foolhardy to make an official attempt at this time and risk losing the aircraft. So I called Al Carder (Manager of Douglas Flight Test at Edwards) up on the ladder and the three of us held a 'secret' conference. We decided just to make a familiarization flight for Verdin. The reason for this secrecy was that considerable effort and time had been expended on the part of the official observers, and we didn't want to cancel without making some attempt. Also, the crew had made an all-out effort in order to prepare the airplane for its second flight this day, and we felt their disappointment would be keen."

Good as their intentions were, this agreement between Rahn, Verdin, and Carder turned out to be unnecessary. Verdin could climb no further than 25,000 feet as the fuel control problems persisted and he was unable to light the afterburner.

The GE crew prepares 587 for a ground run prior to its first flight with the J79 on Dec. 8, 1955. Aircraft is polished aluminum with red da-glo canopy and pitot boom. Tail band is dark blue with yellow borders; engine is yellow with red shock diamonds on white background. (General Electric via Virgil Weaver)

GENERAL ELECTRIC USE

By 1955, the prototypes were completing their testing assignments as Douglas began using the early production airplanes to continue the F4D-1 flight test program. Evidently, the XF4D-1's were beginning to show their age, as "Old Fireball" had been stencilled in small black letters above 587's nose stripe.

Though these aircraft seemed destined for the scrap heap, to one observer, Virgil Weaver, Manager of General Electric's Flight Center at Edwards, the Skyrays were just the type of aircraft he had been looking for.

General Electric was preparing to test its new J79 engine, designated for the F-104. But as the engine was ready for flight test prior to production of the Starfighter, a flying test bed was needed to determine operating procedures and limitations before installing the J79 in the airplane.

To Weaver, the Skyrays represented a ready solution to GE's problem. The XF4D-1's large engine bay would easily accept the J79, and the airplane's performance potential would enable GE to test the engine at high altitudes where the F-104 would be operating.

After some involved discussions with all concerned, Weaver got the Navy to agree to a rather roundabout arrangement. Both fighters were relieved of their test commitments and bailed to the Air Force who, in turn, arranged their bailment to General Electric for their test purposes.

After checking out the condition of the two prototypes, Weaver decided to use 587 as the actual test aircraft and 586 as a spare aircraft, to be cannibalized for parts as they were needed. At this time, for some unknown reason, 586 was back into a dark blue paint scheme, with orange da-glo panels and stripes on its tail and wings. It never flew again. Its J40 was removed and through the following years was reportedly moved about the GE flight test area at Edwards, sometimes being chained to a large jet engine shipping container to keep it from blowing away.

In any event, both aircraft were received by GE on July 6, 1955, and the company shop began the process of reworking 587, which was to be GE's first attempt at major modifications to one of their growing stable of test aircraft. A new instrument panel was installed that retained only the basic flight instruments. Engine instruments were given priority in a bewildering array that monitored the J79's temperatures, pressures, fuel flow, and other vital functions.

Since the J79 was actually shorter and smaller than the original J40, a new set of engine mounts had to be con-

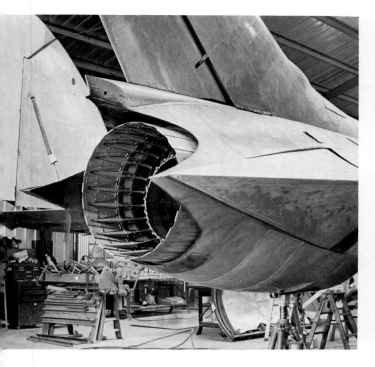 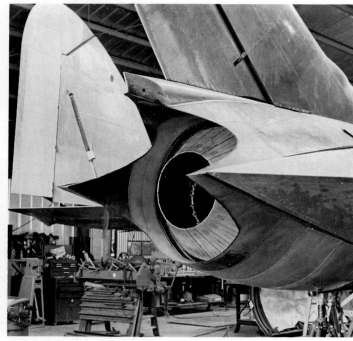

TOP - Open and closed nozzle configurations of the General Electric J-79 as installed in the XF4D-1. BOTTOM - 124587 with the J-79 in Feb. 1957. (G.E. via Virgil Weaver)

tructed and a new inlet duct extension designed. Fabricating this duct by hand soon proved to be more than the GE shop could handle, and Weaver was forced to hire a Los Angeles auto body craftsman who hand formed the Y-shaped duct by hammering sheet aluminum on sandbags. This new duct turned out to be a work of art that worked flawlessly throughout the test program.

The Skyray's tail wheel was again removed and the area reskinned by GE. Additional engine instruments were mounted in the Skyray's nose, photographed by a 16-mm camera in a photopanel turned out to be the limiting factor for many flights, as the Skyray would usually run out of film before it ran of of fuel. Finally, the Skyray's glossy white paint was completely stripped away and its aluminum skin was given a high polish.

During this rework period, several GE test pilots studied the Skyray's manuals and talked to the Douglas test pilots at Edwards about is flying qualities. Bill Todd, one of these GE pilots, recalls spending hours in the XF4D-1's cockpit when the technicians weren't working on it, and going over his cockpit procedures during the ground calibration runs before the first flight.

This maiden flight of the J79-equipped Skyray was made on Dec. 8, 1955, by GE test pilot Roy Pryor. Todd remembers his first flight in the Skyray, made shortly after Pryor's with some humor. He had previously been an Air Force F-86 pilot with the 4th FG in Korea, and had flown the afterburning F-86D and F-94. But the Skyray's thrust-to-weight ratio, delta wings, and rather poor control response combined to give Todd a wild first ride.

"On the first flight I remember releasing the brakes as the J79 went into afterburner," Todd said recently, "and the airplane just shot down the runway. The next thing I knew the airplane had built up more airspeed than I wanted, so I pulled it off the runway. By the time I got the gear

XF4D-1 587 on its maiden flight with the CJ805 on April 12, 1958. Aircraft is polished aluminum with red da-glo nose, dorsal spine, and fin, with broad stripes on wing. (General Electric, courtesy of Tom Emmert)

up and was in control of the airplane, it was going through 20,000 feet! The control system just wasn't very sophisticated. It was probably the worst control system I have ever flown. It was oversensitive, and there weren't proper null points. It wasn't relative, from how far you moved the stick to where you got a reaction...it hit you all of a sudden. But once you got used to it, it didn't detract from the aircraft." Todd continued his first flight in the Skyray by making some high speed turns and rolls to get the feel of the airplane. "The F4D had a higher rate of roll than just about any airplane ever built. There was no restriction on the Skyray on roll as there is on most airplanes. If you could physically do it, you could slam the stick over and do about 360 degrees per second, but you just couldn't hold it."

Over the next two years GE conducted flight tests with the J79 powered Skyray. Flying without drop tanks, the Skyray's endurance ranged from an hour to an hour-and-a-half. This was much better than with the J40, due to the J79's better specific fuel consumption. Initially, the YJ79 engine produced up to 13,500 lbs. of thrust with afterburner. Later, the XF4D-1 was re-engined with the -3 variant which produced 14,700 lbs of afterburning thrust. Tests run on these engines included compressor blade stress measurements, trans-sonic operation, and fuel schedules for both engine and afterburner altitude relights. Testing of the J79 in 587 was terminated on Dec. 31, 1957, after 297 flights and 202 flight hours had been accumulated.

Early in 1958, the J79 was removed and replaced by the CJ805-3, General Electric's first commercial engine, destined for the Convair 880. As the CJ805 was the commercial version of the J79, and basically similar to it, the only noticeable external difference on the Skyray was an extended concial tail pipe.

As one might expect, flight testing the commercial engine was considerably different from that of testing the military J79. Airline use demanded careful determinations of engine reliability and fuel consumption at various altitudes and power settings. To simulate airline use, normal procedure was to take off at a certain power setting and hold this for several minutes, throttle back into a climb power setting until cruise altitude was reached (say 35,000 ft.), then simply "bore holes in the sky" to duplicate an intercontinental flight.

To Todd, the final 1000-hour accelerated service test phase was especially boring. The Skyray was now equipped with 300-gallon drop tanks that raised its endurance to 2½ hours. The GE pilots flew in shifts: two or three flights during the day and two or three each night. In theses 2½ hours, the Skyray was usually flown from Edwards south to San Diego, east to Yuma, Arizona, up the Colorado River to Las Vegas, across Nevada to Reno, west to Monterey, down the coast and back to Edwards for a total distance of roughly 1500 miles

And rough it was. Several factors made this type of flying especially agonizing to the GE pilots. The Skyray had no autopilot and was not a particularly stable airplane. And since the engine tests required precise attention to airspeed and altitude in order not to change the test parameters, each pilot found himself constantly having to fly the airplane, especially in pitch and roll. Todd soon devised a partial solution to the problem Takeoffs and maneuvers would be made in the normal "automatic," or power-assisted control mode. But for the long cruises he switched the controls to "manual" and extended the stick, which made the Skyray much easier to fly for extended periods.

Another problem that got progressively worse as the program continued was the cockpit pressurization. Though GE had visited the Douglas factory warehouse to rummage for spare parts for the XF4D-1, none could be found for the Skyray's pressurization system. Toward the end of its career with General Electric, the Skyray's cockpit pressurization was nil. On one flight to 35,000 feet, Todd recalls that the Skyray's cabin pressure was at 31,000 feet! During the flight a slight twinge in his shoulder gradually developed into a case of air embolism, or the "bends." Realizing what was happening to him, Todd descended to below 10,000 ft. and finally had to cut the flight short.

One final agony of these flights resulted from the Skyray's cramped cockpit, which had certainly not been designed for long trips, and two pressure points on the seat. This latter feature caused a condition that can be appreciated by anyone who has flown or driven long distances with little room for periodically adjusting one's weight. The completion of these accelerated service test flights in the Skyray must have been especially welcomed by the pilots!

There were a few moments of excitement, however, and sometimes the job could even be fun. An example of the former occurred during one takeoff with Todd at the controls. While barreling down the Edwards runway with full

Skyray 587 with CJ805-23 "aft fan" engine model mounted on lengthened right wing pylon. Over 20 flights were made with this model in place of wind tunnel test. (Via Jim Sullivan)

AT RIGHT - Model is all-wood mock-up to simulate installation on a Caravelle which was purchased by G.E. for flight test and demonstration to prospective customers. (G.E. via Virgil Weaver)

drop tanks, one the Skyray's main tires blew approximately 20-kt short of takeoff speed. Realizing that the flight would have to be aborted, Todd fought to keep the airplane on the runway. But without nosewheel steering or a drag chute, and with only one brake, it proved to be exciting indeed. Todd used nearly all of the 15,000-foot runway to stop the airplane, and came within inches of going off side.

But the sheer boredom of these Accelerated Service Test flights occasionally surfaced the instincts of a fighter pilot. Despite its age, the Skyray was an extremely maneuverable airplane, and within its own flight regime other aircraft had a great deal of difficulty with it in mock combat. Flying throughout the southern half of California, as they did, the GE test pilots had several opportunities to demonstrate the Skyray's qualities. The Navy had some old Cutlasses and F9F's at El Toro and Miramar and F-8's in San Francisco Bay area. The Air Force had F-100's out of George AFB and had just received F-104's at Hamilton AFB.

The net result was that, through this period of Accelerated Service Test flying, many of these military pilots landed their pride and joy unwilling to discuss with friends their losing encounter just experienced at the hands of an antiquated, non-afterburning, something-or-other. The only aircraft, it seemed, that could give a good account of itself against the XF4D-1 was a clean F-100. Other than this, nothing could stay with the Skyray in a turn.

As the XF4D-1 finished its testing duties with the CJ805, one final modification was made in March, 1960, when a wooden scale model of General Electric's CJ805-23 "aft fan" engine was mounted on a lengthened pylon under the right wing. Hand-built by GE cabinetmaker Jerry Blackburn, the model and pylon replaced the Skyray's 300-gal. drop tank. This model was instrumented with

pressure probes, and over 20 flights were made in lieu of wind tunnel tests.

From its first flight on April 12, 1958, to its last in May, 1960, the CJ805-engined Skyray accumulated an amazing 1492 hours in 723 flights. Along with Roy Pryor and Bill Todd, General Electric pilots Dick Scoles, Swede Davis, and future Astronaut Elliot See flew the XF4D-1 while monitoring the various tests: plotting the engine's fuel regulator schedule, specific fuel consumption, stall margins, and checking its altitude restarts.

At the termination of their testing program with the Skyray in May, 1960, GE removed the CJ805 and all test instrumentation, and the aircraft was returned to the Air Force, who returned it to the Navy. Both prototypes were taken to the Naval Weapons Center, China Lake, where XF4D-1 124586 was eventually destroyed while serving as a firefighter's practice dummy.

The second XF4D-1, BuNo. 124587, was used for

several years for static environmental testing of many locally developed weapons. In 1968, the aircraft was refurbished and used for static display at the year's Armed Forces Day celebration.

Today, 587 rests at the entrance to the Naval Air Facility at China Lake, occupying a place of honor alongside another former GE-engined record holder, Grumman F11F-1F, BuNo. 138647

TOP - G.E. CJ805 engine being installed in 124587 on 1 April 1958. (G.E. via Weaver) BOTTOM - The record-setting XF4D-1, BuNu.124587, as it rests today at the entrance to China Lake's flight test area. (Roy Lock)

UNOFFICIAL TIME-TO-CLIMB RECORD TO 10,000 FEET

As previously mentioned, the key point in the Skyray's design was it climbing ability. This was first officially demonstrated during carrier qualification trials in 1953 aboard the Coral Sea. Then, Cdr. Verdin flew the XF4D-1 to 40,000 feet in under five minutes to meet the Navy's contract requirements.

But although the Skyray was designed to be a fast-climbing interceptor, its ability at this was never really demonstrated until 1955, more than four years after its first flight.

In the early months of 1955 a series of highly publicized, unofficial time-to-climb records was being established by various Navy aircraft. These flights were timed from brake release to 10,000 feet and presumably served to emphasize the Navy's increasing air might. McDonnell's F3H Demon posted the best time at 71 seconds, being set in St. Louis on Feb 13.

At the time, Douglas was conducting routine stability and control flights with early production models of the F4D-1 at Edwards AFB. Late one Friday afternoon, a week after the Demon flight, Bob Rahn and Al Carder were sitting in Carder's office at Edwards discussing the next day's test schedule when the subject of the various time-to-climb flights came up. Somewhat puzzled, both men wondered what the other companies were trying to prove, since the Skyray, whatever its other failures, could surely take any climbing contest. After some discussion they decided to see what the Skyray could do in the event the next day "just for the hell of it," and without any special preparation to the aircraft they were then using for testing.

At dawn the next morning, Saturday, Feb. 19, Rahn streaked down the runway and pulled the F4D into a near-vertical climb, reaching 10,000 feet in just 56 seconds! Said Rahn later, "I had though that my Thunderbird, in accelerating up to 60 mph in 10 seconds, was terrific, but acceleration of the Skyray was astounding as 160 mph was acquired in the same 10 seconds. I was so busy during the remaining 46 seconds after takeoff trying to fly a prescribed course on instruments that little reaction was felt on my part until the climb was terminated, and I looked back over my shoulder and saw the runway almost directly underneath 10,000 feet away. The climb performance of the aircraft at 10,000 feet was astounding as the aircraft was in a 70-degree climb and was going at a rate of 28,000 fmp."

TIME-TO-CLIMB RECORDS

Though it was widely publicized Rahn's flight was unofficial. And though it was obvious in 1955 that the Skyray could have easily broken the existing world time-to-climb records, an official attempt was not made for three more years. Then, in Feb., 1958, Douglas submitted a proposal to the Bureau of Aeronautics, Fighter Branch, requesting that an F4D-1 make an attempt on the four French-held records of 3,000, 6,000, 9,000, and 12,000 meters. These records had been set by Michel Chalard in a Nord 1405 Gerfaut 88 at Istre, France, on Feb. 16, 1957. Douglas engineering data indicated that the Skyray could take the records by a substantial margin. The Douglas engineers also hoped to set an entirely new record of 15,000 meters, nearly 50,000 feet.

Although BuAer had also received a "feeler" from Vought and their F8U-1 Crusader, it was evidently decided that the Skyray stood a better chance to break the French marks, as Douglas received permission to proceed with the attempt.

The Chief of BuAer, Rear Adm. Robert Dixon, authorized funds for the planned record attempt, now dubbed "Operation Intercept." Though Intercept was termed a development project, the only intended development was publicity for the Navy, Douglas, and the Skyray.

Adm. Dixon also authorized Maj. Edward N. LeFaivre, 37, to pilot the F4D-1 in the attempts. LeFaivre, the F4D Project Officer at the time, was born and raised in Baltimore, Md. After leaving the Martin Company in 1942, LeFaivre entered Aviation Cadet training and was commissioned a Second Lieutenant, USMC, in 1943. As a night fighter pilot in the Pacific, LeFaivre participated in the Marshall Islands and Okinawan Campaigns. On one sortie he destroyed two enemy aircraft while flying an F6F-5N equipped with an APX-6 radar. In Korea, LeFaivre flew F7F-3N, F4U-5N, and AD-4 aircraft on night interdiction missions, destroying approximately 150 enemy vehicles. Before becoming the F4D Project Officer, LeFaivre had been on exchange duty with the Air Force as an all-weather interceptor pilot with the 354th FIS, based at Oxnard AFB, Calif. LeFaivre was a logical choice for these time-to-climb flights. His skill at flying on instruments would serve him well during these attempts.

The National Aeronautic Association was notified of the record attempt and was requested to furnish verifying officials would certify the times established and, if successful, would forward the results to the F.A.I. in Paris for final certification and recognition.

On Monday, May 12, LeFaivre met with Douglas personnel in Los Angeles to discuss the techniques to be used during the trial flights. A specific program was established during the two-day planning conference. There were many problems in logistics and in plotting the correct flight profile for each altitude attempt. What climb angle would be used? What was the maximum allowable engine temperature? How much "G" force should be applied during rotation? What measuring and recording instruments would be required? These were but a few of the problems to be worked out prior to the record attempts.

The particular aircraft to be used was the sixth production airframe, Bu.No. 130745. "745" was government-owned but on permanent bailment to Douglas because of the continuing need for Douglas to retain a test aircraft, plus the high cost that would be required to rework it to operational configuration. Contrary to publicity releases, "745" was far from being strictly a "standard production model." Various articles had been removed to lighten the aircraft, including the four 20mm cannon, wing and belly stores and pylons, various electronics, and the tail hook and wheel assembly. Special test instrumentation was carried, including a long, tapered pitot boom on the nose that projected ahead of the Skyray's shock wave to give more accurate readings.

The funds authorized for the project also included rapid installation of new Wasp-alloy turbine blades in two J-57-P8 engines. These blades allowed higher engine operating temperatures which substantially increased the afterburning thrust of the normal -P8's 14,500 pounds. Only one modified engine was to be used. The other served as a standby in the event the installed engine failed.

As a further aid to the success of the flight, it was decided to conduct the actual record attempts at the Naval

The photos on this page are of F4D-1 130745. Over-all color was standard light gull gray with white under surfaces. The wings, fin and tail cone carried broad red bands, and all landing gear doors and speed brakes were painted with narrow red bands running lengthwise, except for the right main door which was natural metal. A narrow red band was carried behind each side of the cockpit. The radome and pitot tube were painted dark gray with a white design. (Douglas)

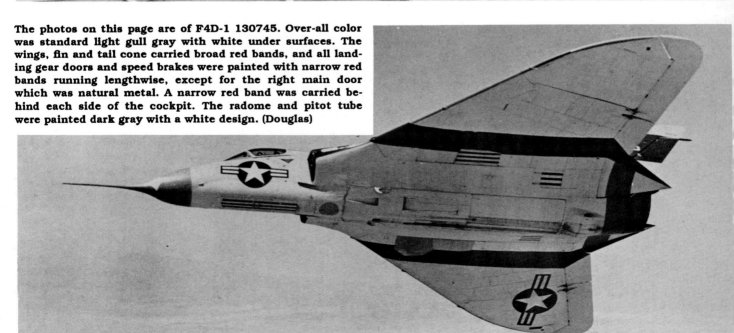

Major Edward N. LeFaivre, USMC, 37. Despite reaching altitudes in excess of 50,000 feet, LeFaivre did not wear pressure suit. (Via Col. E.N. LeFaivre)

Air Missile Test Center, Point Mugu, Calif., 50 miles northwest of Los Angeles. Here, the cold, dense sea air would enable the engine to operate at its maximum efficiency to provide the maximum rate of climb. The prevailing onshore winds would also help reduce the Skyray's takeoff roll.

On Wednesday, May 14, the project team met at Edwards AFB to conduct some practice flights. On the 14th through the 19th, LeFaivre flew nine separate trial flights to test the aircraft's performance with the modified engine and to practice some spin recoveries and the many tasks required during the rapid full instrument climbs.

Each separate altitude try required a slightly different flight profile. The technique for the 3,000-meter mark was simple enough: lift off at 150 kts pulling 1.4 G's and zoom to 3,000 meters holding a 70-degree climb attitude. But for each succeeding height the flight profile became more complicated as the Skyray's climbing ability varied with altitude.

The 15,000-meter profile, for example, was especially troublesome. After lifting off at 170 kts, it was necessary to accelerate to about 540 kts up to 10,000 feet. LeFaivre then had to maintain a specified Mach number (about M-.79) in a climb to 40,000 feet. At this altitude the aircraft was zoomed, pulling up at about 1.5 G's until 50,000 feet (a little over 15,000 meters) was reached. What made the flight especially uncomfortable for LeFaivre was the fact that a 10 to 15 degree engine overtemp occurred on each flight above 35,000 feet. Furthermore, at around 43,000 feet the afterburner flamed out, followed shortly by a basic engine flameout at around 46,000 feet. After this happened, LeFaivre held his zoom attitude of 60 degrees until he reached 50,000 feet. At this altitude his airspeed was around 70 kts, and he let the airplane fall forward in a dive to 25,000 feet, where he restarted the engine.

During all of these climbs the Skyray naturally put high load factors on the pilot. But on the 9,000 and 12,000 meter runs LeFaivre was subjected to a constant 2.5 g acceleration during the latter part of the zoom climb. This made it difficult for him to think and observe clearly. As all of these flights were made entirely on instruments, LeFaivre spent much of his time memorizing each individual flight profile.

During these practice flights the combination of desert heat and altitude at Edwards caused the initial thrust and acceleration of the Skyray to suffer somewhat. Because of this the times recorded for the various flights were greater than those needed to break the records, but this caused no real concern to LeFaivre or the Douglas crew.

On Monday, May 19, LeFaivre flew the Skyray to Point Mugu, and preparations were made for the official flights. That afternoon and during the next two days LeFaivre practiced each climb once more, except for the troublesome 15,000 meter climb, which he tried three more times. The effect the denser sea air had on thrust and acceleration was fantastic, and during the initial practice flights at Point Mugu a major problem developed because of this. Due to the rapid acceleration of the aircraft, the hydraulically actuated landing gear doors would not close! LeFaivre tried three times to start the retraction cycle the instant the aircraft left the ground, but in each case the doors were torn by the on-rushing airstream. Fortunately, the problem was solved by simply increasing the hydraulic system operating pressure. This closed the doors several seconds earlier, and no further problems were encountered.

By late Wednesday, May 21, LeFaivre and the project crew felt ready to begin the measured record attempts, and preparations were made to start the following morning. Bert Rhine and Dr. W.S. Dixon, official representatives of the National Aeronautic Association, had jurisdiction over the flights and the special clocking instrumentation. Radar tracking devices would verify the altitudes achieved and the timing clocks would be started as Maj. LeFaivre made a countdown over the radio.

To take advantage of the cold morning air, the first attempt, to 3,000 meters, was started at dawn. With a minimum of fuel in his tanks, LeFaivre taxied to a starting line marked on the runway and ran the engine to full speed while checking the instruments for proper readings. Ten seconds away from brake release he started a countdown over his radio. At zero he released the brakes, engaged the afterburner, and thundered down the runway, gaining momentum rapidly. At the same instant, cameras began recording the flight and the tracking radar was triggered.

As the full afterburning thrust took effect, LeFaivre was subjected to the tremendous acceleration of the lightened Skyray. In only a few seconds the F4D-1 reached 150 kts and LeFaivre pulled the Skyray into a near-vertical climb. The airplane literally stood on a tail of flame as it streaked to 3,000 meters in 44.39 seconds, bettering the French mark by nearly seven seconds!

LeFaivre landed a few minutes later, after having used only 400 pounds of fuel during the brief flight. After congratulations were exchanged, the F4D-1 was fueled again for the 6,000 meter attempt.

The same procedure was used for the remaining flights,

TIME-TO-CLIMB RECORD SUMMARY

Altitude Meters	Feet	Lift-Off Speed	Acceleration To V;Kts	Alt.	Initial Altitude of Zoom (Ft)	Zoom Load Factor (g's)	Final Speed (V;Kts)	Final Attitude (Degrees)	Expected Times (min:sec)	Actual Times (min:sec)	Nord Gerfaut (2-16-57
3,000	9,843	150 kts	150	S.L.	S.L.	1.4	215	70°	:42	:44.39	:51.15
6,000	19,685	170 kts	350	S.L.	S.L.	2.0	200	70°	1:03	1:06.13	1:17.05
9,000	29,527	170 kts	540	5000ft	10,000ft	2.5	200	70°	1:25	1:29.81	1:33.75
12,000	39,370	170 kts	540	5000ft	30,000ft	2.5	190	60°	1:49	1:51.23	2:17.7
15,000	49,213	170 kts	540	5000ft	40,000ft	1.4	158	40°	2:29	2:36.05	(none)

Summary of the five time-to-climb record flights flown by Col. Edward N. LeFaivre at Point Mugu NAMTC, Calif., on May 22-23, 1958. Expected times are those projected by Douglas Engineers when the record attempt was first proposed. The 15,000 meter climb was an entirely new record set by the Skyray.

with LeFaivre taxiing to the starting line, counting down, and kicking in the afterburner as he released the brakes.

The 6,000 and 9,000 meter time-to-climb records were also broken that day. The Skyray climbed to the first mark in 1:06.13 minutes and the second was broken in 1:29.81 minutes, both substantially bettering the French times.

The final two altitude tries were saved for the next morning, May 23, 1958. The 12,000 meter record was set by the Skyray as LeFaivre flew the run in 1:51.23 minutes. The final 15,000 meter flight was also successful, establishing an entirely new time-to-climb record for the altitude at 2:36.05 minutes.

Thusly, upon recognition of these time-to-climb marks by the F.A.I., the Skyray held a total of seven world records, although briefly. By 1958, time and progress were to rapidly catch up to the F4D-1, not to mention the disgust of Air Force pilots who naturally felt that all speed records should have been exclusive property of Air Force fighters.

THE MAYDAY SKYRAYS DOUGLAS TESTING DIVISION F4D-1s, 1954-1959

"When we got the J-57 in the Skyray we began going through all of the inlet problems...making the afterburner work at high altitudes with the early production aircraft. We had about five airplanes in that high altitude inlet duct test program with different things in the inlets. During this period, when Bill Bridgeman and Bob Drew were flying the airplane, it was an awful lot of work. The airplane would take off and head for altitude and the afterburner would blow out, sometimes blowing the engine out. Nobody knew at that point in time whether they'd get a relight or dead stick it in, so it was not all uncommon that daily we'd picking up the phone saying, 'Hey, we got a flameout on an F4D and the guy may land on the lake bed if he doesn't get a relight.' At that point we were going through the bit of whether the guy should stay on the company test frequency and let dispatch work with the tower as to where he was and all that. Obviously, the military said, 'No, you've got to got to emergency frequency.' Well, whenever anyone goes to emergency frequency you assume it's a Mayday call. It became a damned joke in the bar: There's another one of those Mayday Skyray!"

The speaker is veteran Douglas Aircraft Company test pilot George Jansen, commenting on the nickname applied to the early production F4D-1 Skyrays flown at Edwards AFB by the Douglas Testing Division. The term reflected the often frustrating, if not hazardous, task of molding the production aircraft into reliable weapons platforms. From June 1954 to November 1959 over two dozen production "Mayday Skyrays" bore the brunt of developmental testing of the F4D-1. The aircraft were flown during numerous programs designed to investigate the airplane's characteristics with its new J-57-P2 (later -P8A and -P8B) engine, yaw stabilizer rudder, transonic trim change compensator, Aero 13F fire control system, and other improvements over the prototype aircraft. Dozens of detail design changes made throughout the Skyray's production run complicated this task, tying up a relatively large fleet of test aircraft in "cut and try" programs of modifications made primarily to the air intakes and engine bay, fuel and flight control systems, armament, and empennage. Admittedly, the original "Mayday Skyrays" included only a small number of aircraft flown during a specific test program. But, as is typical with test aircraft in general, most Testing Division Skyrays certainly experienced more than their normal share of hair-raising, "Mayday" situations.

Douglas Flight Test had been formed in 1943 at Mines Field, now Los Angeles International Airport, becoming know as "Location E". In 1947 the organization was renamed the Testing Division after joining with the A-1 Facility at Santa Monica. With the mission of providing aircraft product development, evaluation and certification testing, the Testing Division later expanded to include facilities at Edwards AFB (A-8 Muroc), El Segundo (B-3),

The first production F4D-1, 130740 on rollout at El Segundo. This aircraft was bailed to the Douglas Testing Division. Plane is white with black leading edges, wing-walks and anti-glare panel. Black fin tip, red nose markings and intake lips. Landing gear is blue. (Douglas)

Long Beach (C-1), White Sands, New Mexico, Point Mugu's missile center, and the Edwards Rocket Base. For the El Segundo Facility alone, the Testing Division of the mid-1950s was a busy place, being involved in flight programs with later models of the AD Skyraider, the A2D Skyshark, A4D Skyhawk, and A3D Skywarrior as well as the F4D-1.

The Testing Division aircraft were Navy-owned, but on bailment to Douglas Aircraft for company test program. Each aircraft history card carried the notation, "BAR R&D ES," or Bureau of Aeronautics Representative, Research and Development El Segundo.

By 1948 Douglas artists had developed a comical insignia for the Testing Division, a takeoff on the Douglas Company's longstanding "First Around the World" emblem: two young birds peering down from a nest built on a globe of the Earth, with a third fledgling racing around the world while wearing a flight helmet and stopwatch. This insignia was displayed on the tails of Douglas Testing Division aircraft as was well as on company tool boxes, autos, etc., although not necessarily every Testing Division airplane carried one.

The prototype XF4D-1s, 124586 and 124587, were the first Skyrays to display the Testing Division insignia. Beginning with the initial flight of 586 in January 1951, these aircraft remained with the Testing Division until mid-1955 when they were bailed to General Electric for developmental testing of the J-79 engine.

The first production F4D-1, 130740, joined the Testing Division upon its rollout in June 1954. It and the next two aircraft (an possibly 130744) in the initial production series of twelve (130740-1307541) were painted gloss white overall, as were the prototypes, presumably for improved visibility by chase pilots and ground personnel. The remaining production aircraft of this first batch were painted glossy blue overall. Later, with the exception of these white aircraft, most were repainted in what then became standard for Navy fighters: gull gray upper and gloss white lower surfaces. The Testing Division Skyrays might have remained only in these colors had it not been for the fatal crash of Douglas test pilot James Verdin (who had set a World Absolute Speed Record in XF4D-1 124587 in 1953) on January 13, 1955, while flying A4D-1 Skyhawk 137815. Apparently, air search teams had considerable difficulty in spotting the wreckage of the natural aluminum airplane, and very soon afterward flamboyant markings were adopted for the Skyrays as well as other Douglas flight test aircraft.

While there was wide variation, early on the standard scheme seems to have consisted of broad insignia red bands on the tail and inboard on each wing, longitudinal two-inch-wide red stripes painted on the landing gear doors and speed brakes, with similar stripes applied to the top and each side of the rear portion of the canopy and forward dorsal spine. The last three digits of the airplane's serial number were repeated in large white numerals on the red tail ban, while the Testing Division insignia was carried at various places on the tail.

Toward the late 1950s the Testing Division appears to have adopted a different scheme for its Skyrays: while retaining the two-inch-wide insignia red stripes on the gear doors, speed brakes, and rear canopy, da-glow was painted on the outer wing panels (excluding elevons), slats, tail fin (excluding the rudder and fin tip), the intake area rearward for two feet, and in a wide band on the nose.

However, while standard Testing Division markings schemes seem to have been adopted on paper, in practice they were only partially followed. Each Skyray was given its own identity with various sized da-glo or insignia red panels, bands, stripes, and other eye-catching designs. The F4Ds flew with both blue or white drop tanks, irregardless of the airplane's basic color. Flashy designs often were painted on these tanks, apparently for no other reason than apperance's sake. One Skyray's NavPac, a small bomb-shaped pod carried on the centerline pylon which provided marker beacon and omni-range receivers, was even the recipient to a Testing Division insignia along with three red "racing" stripes painted along its length.

Of the initial production run of twelve aircraft, only two did not fly with the Testing Division. F4D-1 130746 was sent directly to the Naval Air Test Center, Patuxent River, Maryland, for the Navy's own carrier evaluation program. In six short months the airplane was stricken at Pax River after having accumulated a total of only 105 flight hours. Skyray 130751 was used as a static test airframe at the El Segundo plant, being gradually reduced to scrap during fatigue testing of the airplane's subassemblies. Of the remaining ten Skyrays, 130740, 130742, and 130744 were earmarked by the Testing Division as aerodynamics demonstration ships; 130741 initially was used for static structural testing, flying later for intake duct and autopilot tests; 130743 was flown briefly by the Testing Division during the carrier suitability program; 130745 was employed on autopilot and fire control system evaluations, later being modified for a successful assault on the world time-to-climb records; 130747 replaced 130743 on the carrier suitability test at Pax River; 130748 was used during structural demonstration tests, determining maximum load factors, maximum roll rates, rolling pullouts, and stall and spin characteristics, being flown later during missile launch tests; and 130749 replaced 130740 as an aerodynamics test ship when Douglas test pilot Robert O. Rahn, holder of the 100 km closed course record in the second prototype Skyray, bent 740 beyond repair on February 25, 1955. Rahn had been testing the airplane's controls at maximum speed and low altitude when, after cutting the afterburner, the Skyray suddenly made a 9g pitch-up while decelerating through the transonic trim change region at over 700 mph. Recalled Bob Rahn: "An incident occurred after one test was completed which consisted of determining if enough pitch trimmer was available to compensate for the tuck under at Vmax at sea level. The aircraft was accelerated to approximately a true Mach of .98 and the tuck under required full trimmer deflection which was limited structurally to 8 degrees TEU. Thinking that the test was successfully completed, the afterburner was non-chalantly cut and within 1.5 seconds, the vehicles decelerated subsonically, which increased trimmer effectiveness, eliminated the tuck under, and a pitchup to 9.1g occurred.

"Needless to say, a blackout occurred because I was not wearing a g suit - after all, it was only a Vmax level flight test hop. Fortunately, vision reoccurred just in time to prevent a vertical dive into the water. The next few moments were spent nervously surveying the bent wings - not knowing the extent of internal failures at the time.

This tense period was relieved somewhat when (Chuck) Yeager, the chase pilot, who was unaware of what happened, radioed, 'I lost you - couldn't follow you in that maneuver.'"

Rahn was able to land the Skyray safely, but the airplane's spars suffered a permanent set, its wing skin

Photos are of the third production F4D-1, 130742, used as an aerodynamic demonstration ship by the Douglas Testing Division. TOP - White with red nose trim on 5-19-55 at Edwards AFB. (Swisher) MIDDLE - On 1-10-56 with red tail stripe and white 742. Also note thin red stripes above red wing stripe and blue drop tanks and seven shot rocket pod. (Douglas) BOTTOM - 742 minus engine in a hangar at Edwards in 1957. Note flight recorder in the nose. (Robert Cooper)

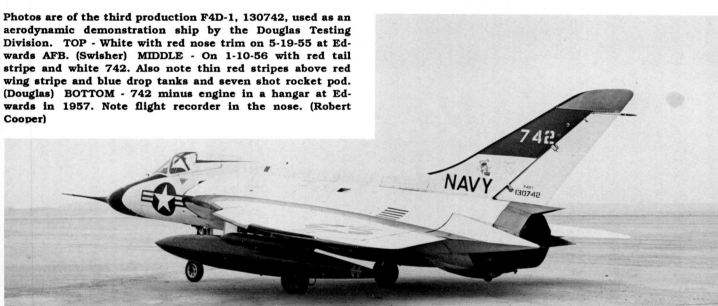

ABOVE - Fourth production F4D-1, 130743, in overall blue as flown by the Testing Division during carrier suitability trials. MIDDLE - Fifth production F4D-1, 130744, on 12-15-54 in all blue scheme. Note main wheel spats used on first F4Ds. BOTTOM - Same Skyray on 3-14-56. White with black leading edges, fin-tip and anti-glare panel. Natural radome with red test probe. All other trim red. Landing gear is blue. 744 was an aerodynamic demonstrator. (Douglas)

looking as wrinkled as a prune.

Perhaps the most troublesome program, commented on by George Jansen previously, involved the Skyray's high altitude compressor stalls and flameouts with its new J-57 engine, which had not been evident on the first flight of 130740 with the J-57-P2, a supersonic hop flown by Bob Rahn on June 5, 1954. A series of duct revisions was initiated on October 25, with the first flight of a J-57-P2 engined Skyray with modified intake duct lines occurring on February 2, 1955. Perhaps illustrating the capriciousness of the problem, 130744 made an initial flight on March 18, 1955, powered by a "J-57-P2 Special" engine and revised ducts, attaining 52,500 feet, but two days later 130742, equipped with the old ducts and the basic J-57-P2, achieved a remarkable 57,300 feet. The problem became so acute that, on April 15, 1955, Douglas embarked on an Accelerated Engine Stall Test Program. Many possible solutions were evaluated. On June 1, 130741 made a first flight with 18 inch extended ducts, while on July 28 a Testing Division Skyray first flew with "bellmouth" ducts. While the Skyray's high altitude engine stall problems never were completely solved, a decision was made on August 5, 1955 to incorporate in all production F4D-1s the best compromise design: a "zero extended duct" with a boundary layer blade and bleed ramp to vent the turbulent air near the intakes.

On another front, in 1956 a Flying Quality Improvement Program was begun by Douglas which at least partially solved some of the Skyray's handling shortcomings. Douglas test pilot George Bright, an ex-Navy Patuxent River graduate, did most of the developmental test flying on this improvement program. The core of the problem was a result of the rush to have the Skyray service accepted at the earliest possible date so that the Navy would have a truly supersonic airplane. Unfortunately, these early aircraft exhibited some amazingly poor flight characteristics, including the transonic trim change which caused the scrapping of 130740. A solution was devised in the form of a transonic trim change compensator (TTCC), which was developed to automatically provide the proper control inputs during transonic operation.

Jim Stegman flew the Skyray extensively while with the Douglas Testing Division. A former World War II Marine Corps enlisted pilot who joined Douglas in June 1955, Stegman recalls this program designed to tame the Skyray's transonic pitchups, which required that he make countless excursions through Mach 1 by putting the airplane into a shallow dive:

"After we got the trim change compensator in the airplane we had to go out and adjust these in flight. We had a little wrench, the trim change compensator wrench, to adjust this. It would throw the pitch trim up at the right Mach number to compensate for the pitch down, or pitch up when decelerating, while in the transonic region. It was an automatic system, but it had to be adjusted and set, so we would always have to go supersonic."

While on another program, Stegman most likely established a speed record for Skyrays, an airplane designed to be only marginally supersonic: "I've gotten pretty close to March 1.5 in the F4D-1. During autopilot testing I got special permission to go to 50,000 feet in a clean airplane (no wing tanks). The dive was a little steeper than normal!"

Another problem area, the Skyray's rudder buffet at near sonic speeds, was caused by flow separation over the aft fuselage. A new tail cone fairing was designed to smooth this airflow, and in November 1956 a decision was made to install this "half dog house" tail cone on all production aircraft. In addition to improving the rudder buffet problems, this new tail cone reduced rudder forces, improved stability, and actually increased the Skyray's top speed. Finally, the Skyray's improvement program made revisions in the lateral and longitudinal control force systems, the rudder hydraulic and dampening systems, and changes in the maximum angle of the servo (upper) rudder operation.

A key figure in the production Skyray's development programs was Robert "Tiger" Drew, who makes some interesting observations about the airplane and its test program: "I came into the F4D test program in the mid-1950s as the 5th Project Pilot. There had been considerable problems with the test program and the test aircraft, such that all of the prior Project Pilots had quit for one reason or another. Most felt the aircraft was too hairy to test.

"Bill Bridgeman and I as his backup pilot did the SR-38 Part 1 Test Program. Later I did the Part 2 Test Program including the full Aerodynamic and Structural Demonstration Tests at NATC Patuxent River, Maryland. These tests were not conducted without incident - wherein I gained the name of 'Tiger'. I can't remember the number of emergency landings, dead sticks, structural failures, etc., and in looking back I can see it was one of the most difficult aircraft to test I have flow. But I nevertheless like the aircraft and had a high respect for its performance capabilities at the time. Like the article says ('Like a Bat Out of Hell'), when you engaged that afterburner she took off and you hung on. The main problem with the aircraft was a bad trim change (aerodynamically) as you were approaching the speed of sound, consisting of a significant nose tuck which presented rather severe controllability problems at times. At lower speeds, however, the maneuverability was superior to most. I remember the Air Force chase pilots like Iven Kincheloe, Bob White and others trying in vain to find an Air Force fighter that could out-turn the Skyray. It used to drive them crazy."

Drew's last comment refers to the little-known fact that the Skyray evoked more than a passing interest from the Air Force. An Air Force Evaluation Team made up of Gen. Stanley Holtoner and Colonels Al Boyd, Frank Everest, and James S. Nash flew XF4D-1 124587 on December 3, 1953, two months to the day after the airplane had set a new Absolute World Speed Record. A second Air Force team evaluation of a production Skyray was conducted on July 1, 1955. While the results of these evaluations are not know, it is safe to say that the Air Force was clearly concerned that the Nay fighter had bested, however briefly, anything the Air Force had at the time.

It should be emphasized that while these Testing Division Skyrays were production models, they still flew as full-fledged test aircraft. Instrumentation carried by the Testing Division F4D-1s was extensive, and varied with each test program. The aerodynamics demonstration aircraft (130740/742/744) all had an identical 35mm photo recorder mounted in their noses, replacing the airplane's radar, and an ocillograph installed in the electronics bay behind the nose wheel. The flight recorder camera could be operated continuously or in a pulsed mode, depending upon the length of the flight or the type of maneuver to be performed. Data reduction was off the exposed film, while the ocillograh readings were taken from ocillograph paper and fed into a computer.

The high speed recorder (HSR), a separate recording

The ninth production Skyray, 130748. TOP - Paint scheme used during structural demonstration tests. Blue with black leading edges, radome and anti-glare panel. Da-glo nose, tail, wing stripes and rear canopy. Red intake lips with white outline. Note blue and white NavPac. BELOW - In-flight and head-on views of 748 while being used for missile tests. Drop tanks and rocket pods are white. Radome is natural and canopy and wing stripe is da-glo. Fin and spine are white and red checkerboard and intake chevron is red. (Douglas)

device used on many flight tests Skyray's was a Douglas developed system which allowed data to be telemetered to the ground and monitored while the aircraft was airborne. It consisted of a signal conditioning and mechanical switching device which took the various inputs, sampling each signal, resulting in a output of pulses which could be recorded on a tape recorder in the aircraft and/or telemetered to a ground station. Typically, the HSR occupied the Skyray's nose, replacing the radar set, with the tape recorder in one gun bay, the transmitting equipment in the other gun bay, and the transmitting antenna mounted in a wingtip. On the ground, data was received by a Douglas Testing Division telemetry trailer and monitored on a large TV-type scope as well as recorded on tape, which later would be fed into a computer for data reduction.

These early high speed recorders used mechanical switches rather than the later solid state electronic switch-

TOP - 748 at Naval Ordnance Test Station China Lake in May of 1957. Note camera fairings on wingtips and on fuselage behind nose wheel. Note red stripes on speed breaks. (Doug Olson) **MIDDLE** - 748 at the Pima County museum in 1976. (Ginter) **BELOW** - Tenth Skyray 130749 at Edwards AFB. (Via Clay Jansson)

Top photo shows production line with fifth production F4D-1, 130744 in front. Photo below shows 134801 and the revised intakes and added splitter plate. (Douglas)

Static fatigue test airframe thought to be 130751. (Douglas)

PHOTO ABOVE - F4D-1 134760 from the second production batch which was utilized by the Douglas Testing Division in May 1956 at Edwards AFB. Colors are grey and white with red tail and wing stripe and intake chevron. Note white test probe and dark grey anti-glare panel. (Swisher)

ing, and were subject to considerable contact surface wearing. This caused occasional odd readings and resulted in a shortened service life. The HSRs also tended to eat up vacuum tubes - more than "Hogan's Goat", it was said. Consequently, one of the later Testing Division Skyrays which used the HSR as its primary recording device had a painting of a goat chewing on a vacuum tube applied to its nose along with the words, "Hogan's Goat".

For missile tests, a few Skyray's were equipped with 35mm wingtip cameras housed in streamlined pods. Additional forward looking 35mm camera was mounted on the airplane's belly, just behind the nosewheel.

As attrition took its toll of the original complement of ten flight test Skyrays, and development problems cropped up with later modifications made to the design, aircraft of the second production series soon were assigned to the Testing Division. Known flight test aircraft from this series include 134746/748/752/754/760/762/763/765/771/774 830/853/and 876. Of this batch, 134752 is known to have participated in the testing of the Skyray's splitter plate modified intake and the NavPac.

The most fascinating program in which Testing Division Skyrays participated began early in 1956 when five F4D-1s were modified for development of the F5D-1 Skylancer all-weather Aero 24A Armament Control System and its Douglas developed Sparrow II missile (XAAM-N-3). Similar in size to the Sparrow I, whose airframe was also built by Douglas, the Sparrow II was an active homing, air-to-air missile utilizing a tiny radar dish hidden behind a blunt nose. The Sparrow II's guidance system was described as "advanced and very accurate," and "compatible with any aircraft fire control system."

The Aero X24A flight test program was designed to test all phases of the system concurrently by assigning separate portions to each of the five airplanes. F4D-1 134748 made radar evaluation flights; 134754 and 134762 flew gun and rocket runs in both lead-collision and lead-pursuit modes; 134763 concentrated on the Sparrow II missile phase; and 134765 was earmarked for autotracking tests, whereby "the autocontrol system controlled the airplane on a firing course as directed by the Aero X24A System."

F4D-1s 134754/762/763/and 765 entered rework and modification at El Segundo between Mid-May and mid-December 1955, being completed between mid-January and late April 1956. 134748 was modified between late April and early September 1956.

For the armament tests, 134754 was equipped with two rocket pods mounted on the outer pylons, each pod con-

TOP - 760 again, but without test probe and with red stripes en-circling drop tank nose cones. Note red stripe on canopy. (Douglas) BELOW - Two photos of F4D-1 134763 which was used as a test aircraft for the Douglas Sparrow II weapon system that was being developed for the F5D Skylancer program. Nose cartoon shows an eagle riding a sparrow missile. Note wing-tip cameras and camera fairing behind nose gear. (Douglas)

TOP - Grey and white F4D-1 134830 leaves the USS Intrepid (CVA-11) in Dec. 1957. Aircraft is in Douglas Testing Division colors. (National Archives) MIDDLE - F4D-1 134853 assigned to the Douglas Testing Division at Edwards AFB in May 1957. Note red stripes on Navpac and late model intakes. (Robert Cooper) BELOW- Production Ford with Navpac and starter cart in grey and white scheme.(Via Clay Jansson)

An F4D-1 being towed out of the Torrance plant for trucking to El Segundo. Note "Ballast."

Partially complete "Ford" being loaded aboard special trailer for movement to El Segundo for final assembly.

Trailers carry assembled F4D's to El Segundo.

taining six 2.75" FFARs, while 134762 had four similar pods, two on the outer pylons and two replacing the airplane's 300 gallon drop tanks, F4D-1 134763 was equipped with two special Sparrow II missile racks mounted outboard of the drop tanks, each carrying one missile.

All five aircraft were modified to carry three Flight Research Corp. 35mm scoring cameras, one in each wingtip in a streamlined pod, and one mounted on the centerline of the lower fuselage just behind the nosewheel door. An additional N-9 16mm camera was mounted in the cockpit to photograph the cockpit counter and radar scope presentation. The modified Skyrays began their individual test programs between April and September 1956.

Jim Stegman flew the missile test aircraft, 134763, at NOTS China Lake, eventually making the first supersonic missile launch with the control system tie-in: "That first time gave me quite a ride! The airplane would automatically guide in on the target that appeared on the scope and bring it to zero. I kept complaining about jitter on the scope...the little thing was bouncing up and down and side to side. Every time that thing would bounce, the autopilot, and the airplane, would follow it!"

By early 1957 the overall program had reached "an assessable point in its progress," and the Bureau of Aeronautics was invited to make its own review of the project. A Navy Preliminary Evaluation (NPE) of the Aero X24A System was conducted at China Lake from March 4-16, 1957. Navy test pilots Tony Nollet and Jerry O'Rourke made 27 flights consisting of firing and non-firing passes at a Dart target and an F2H-2 and A3D. Also, nine flights were made to assess the radar's capabilities, while two classified runs were made to study the effects of chaff and electronic countermeasures (ECM) equipment on the radar portion of the system.

Overall, the NPE uncovered a few areas of deficiencies in the Aero X24A Fire Control System, but it was felt that these were offset by several desirable capabilities. Unfortunately, while the system proved successful it never was refined as the F5D-1 failed to receive a production contract, and both the Aero 24A and the Douglas Sparrow II missile died a sudden and quiet death. Between June and August 1957 all five Skyrays were transferred from the Testing Division, continuing with new test programs at the Naval Air Development Unit, South Weymouth (134748), and Naval Aviation Ordnance Test Station, Chincoteague (134754), Massachusetts, the Naval Air Development Center, Johnsville, Pennsylvania (134763), and NAF China Lake, California (134762 and 134765).

A gradually diminishing number of Testing Division Skyrays were flown in 1958 as the last production batch of 178 aircraft was completed following the earlier cancellation of 230 F4D-1s. Douglas delivered the final F4D-1 in December 1958, with the Testing Division ending its various programs on the Skyray by November 1959. In its annual report, the company would make the somewhat puzzling boast that over the previous nine years the Testing Division had accumulated 1,573 flight hours on "20 different versions" of the Douglas fighter.

In retrospect, it would be an exaggeration to suggest that the "Mayday Skyray" nickname applied to any more than a few of these aircraft. But Douglas test pilot Bill Bridgeman, a man noted for his sense of humor as well as his skill in a cockpit, might have argued the points as indicated by the following incident which, in its retelling, still brings chuckles from sympathetic ex-Testing Division Skyray pilots: "Douglas would have its pilots go around to talk to civic groups, and Bill was assigned to visit a bunch of Boy Scouts. He had been talking about flying the Skyhawk, and started to discuss flying at high altitude in the Skyray: the physiological effects of high altitude, that your blood would actually boil because the nitrogen in your blood would form bubbles. When he got down to the question and answer part one kid asked, "Mr. Bridgeman, just when does your blood start to boil?' Bridgeman looked at the kid and scowled, "Every time I crawl into an F4D!"

TOP - Factory fresh F4D-1 134749 in early configuration with small pylons and starter cart on wing. Note early rear fuselage and absence of small intake lip scoop. MIDDLE LEFT - Good view of early aft design. MIDDLE RIGHT - Late rear fuselage configuration on VMF(AW)-513 Ford. BOTTOM - Rear view of early production Ford. (Douglas)

TOP - Factory fresh F4D-1 134765 from above. Note dark grey anti-glare panel and grey radome that would turn creme color after prolonged exposure. The late Fords had black radomes.

PRODUCTION CHANGES

Hal Andrews via Tommy Thomason provided some comments on the configuration changes which occurred during production: In an effort to improve transonic flight characteristics (drag, trim change, and buffet), Douglas continued to work on the back end of the airplane while production was well under way. The Final results applied to production airplanes were an extensively revised upper rear fuselage and more gradually faired forward lines for the tail wheel fairing.

The revised upper fuselage did not fair inward as did the early one, but maintained essentially a constant section to the aft end. This resulted in the upper line of the flat portion where the trimmer butts against the fuselage being almost a horizontal line (parallel to the fuselage upper surface under the rudder). This change was incorporated in production from 134857 on and retrofitted to earlier airplanes in the late 1957/early 1958 period.

Incorporated somewhat later was the redesigned tail wheel fairing. The leading edge intersection was extended farther forward, giving a shallower slope back to the maximum depth point which did not change.

Mr. Thomason goes on the say that the upper rear fuselage change was not retrofitted on all aircraft: BuNo. 134748 at the Pima Museum still has the early rear fuselage. It is, however, one of the first twelve production aircraft (BuNos 130740 - 130751) which did not receive other retrofits like the Martin-Baker ejection seat and armament changes. The redesigned tailwheel fairing was not in aircraft as late as BuNo 134936 (photographed at the Pueblo, Colorado aviation museum) and may not have been a retrofitted change; I would guess that this configuration was on 139xxx aircraft only.

The F4D had aerodynamically actuated leading edge slats. They were therefore always extended on the ground except when the aircraft was posed for Douglas publicity shots. (When the wings folded, the slats on the folded portion of the wing closed due to gravity.) The elevons operated as both ailerons and elevators. The inboard and outboard sections on each wing moved together and almost all pictures show them streamlined. The large triangular surfaces inboard of the elevons were really giant pitch trimmers; these were positioned trailing edge up for takeoff and landing and are often seen in this position. The trim capability was 28.5 degrees above faired but only 1.5 degrees below. The rudder was in two sections. The lower was a true rudder. The upper was used for trim and yaw damping as well and was often in a different position than the lower rudder.

The F4D is almost never seen without external fuel tanks for a good reason — they almost doubled the amount of available fuel. Later on, the left drop tanks was modified in some squadrons with a refueling probe because there are always times when carrier aircraft have to have more fuel. The only thing carried on the centerline pylon was the navigational pod or "navpac". This contained VHF navigation and instrument approach marker radios and antennas, an interesting commentary on the space available in the F4D and the size of radios at that time. This pod was not normally installed for carrier operations.

The original armament for the aircraft was to be four 20mm cannon and unguided rockets carried in pods on as many as six wing store stations. According to Hal Andrews, the cannon were seldom carried and the gun ports were usually faired over although the shell chute holes remained. On early production aircraft, the wing station pylons were smaller than those on the final configuration. The larger center wing station pylon (the one used for drop tanks) appeared on BuNo 134583 and was retrofitted to earlier aircraft except for BuNo 130xxx; the larger inboard and outboard wing stations were available on BuNo 134919 and were retrofitted to earlier aircraft except, again, for BuNo 130xxx. The F4D was also modified to carry Sidewinder missiles on the inboard and outboard wing stations at an early point in its service life.

Early aircraft did not originally have the small fences on the wing leading edge. Although these look like they have an aerodynamic function, their real purpose was to snag the vertical straps on a barrier engagement. Early aircraft did have a sort of spat over the main wheels to engage the barrier system used at that time. The fences appeared and the spats disappeared almost immediately.

Part way through production, the small inlet on the outside lip of each engine inlet was changed from a flush configuration to a bulged scoop. The flush inlet is seen as late as BuNo 134804 but the bulged scoop was apparently retrofitted to all aircraft. The right flush inlet was round while the left was more rectangular.

Finally, there were two different afterburner configurations — a flap type (J57-P-8) or an iris type (J57-P-8A) exhaust nozzle. I would guess that the latter was introduced on the later aircraft and retrofitted to earlier aircraft.

Two more views of 134749. Note the wheel spats which were used on early Fords for barrier engagement. Centerline store is a "NAVPAC" which contains an AN/ARN-14E Omni-range receiver and an AN/ARN-12 marker beacon receiver. (Douglas)

TOP - F4D-1 134752 in 1955. Note original intake without splitter plate. (D.W. Carter via Larkins) MIDDLE - 134752 again in flight with new intakes and splitter plate. Also note NAVPAC. Douglas photo 12-6-55. BOTTOM - Douglas test pilot Walt Harper became the first person to successfully dead-stick a Ford, when he landed this F4D-1 at NAS Los Alamitos, CA. The Ford was written off. (Douglas)

(Douglas) - Completed Fords waiting for test flights at the Douglas El Segundo production Flight Test Facility.

FRONT VIEW
1:72nd SCALE

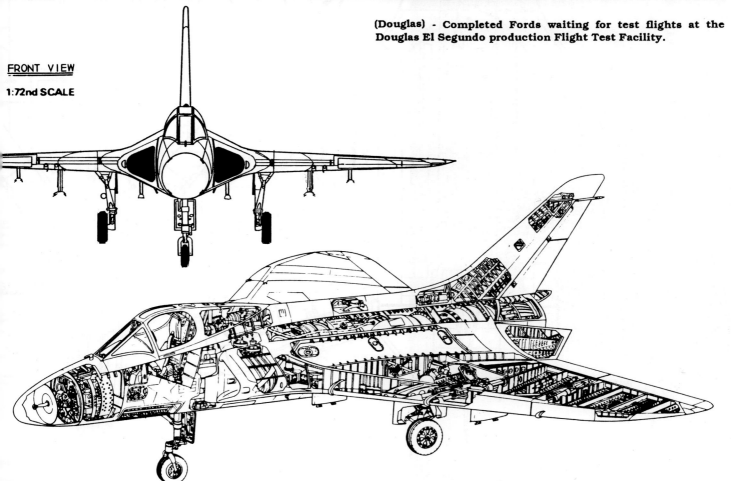

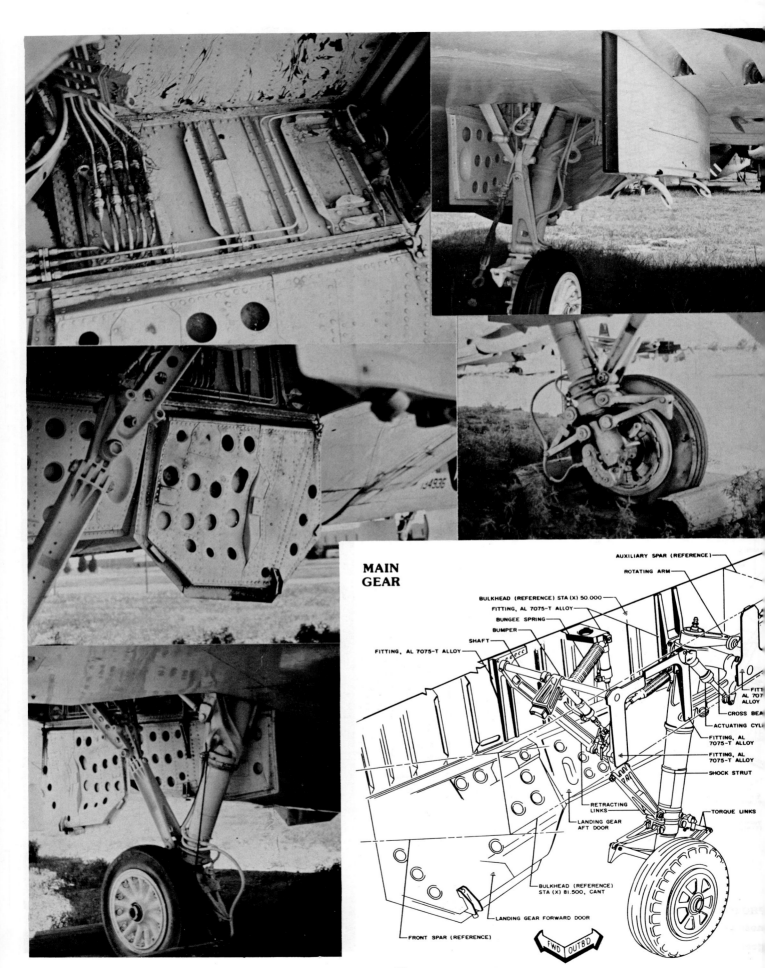

(Douglas) - Completed Fords waiting for test flights at the Douglas El Segundo production Flight Test Facility.

FRONT VIEW
1:72nd SCALE

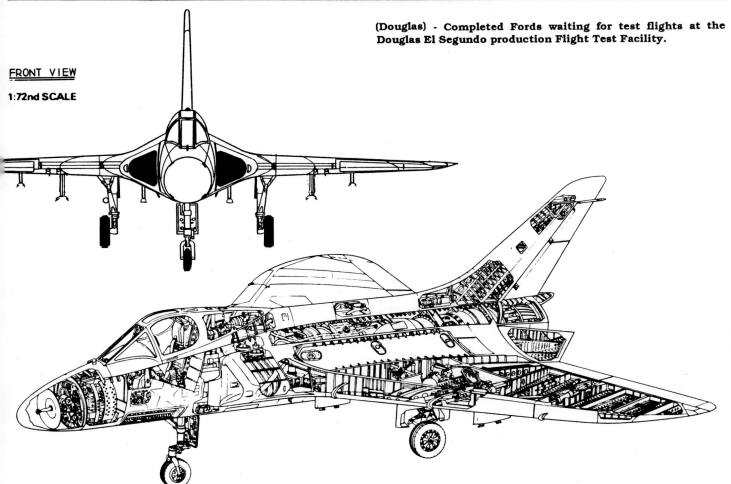

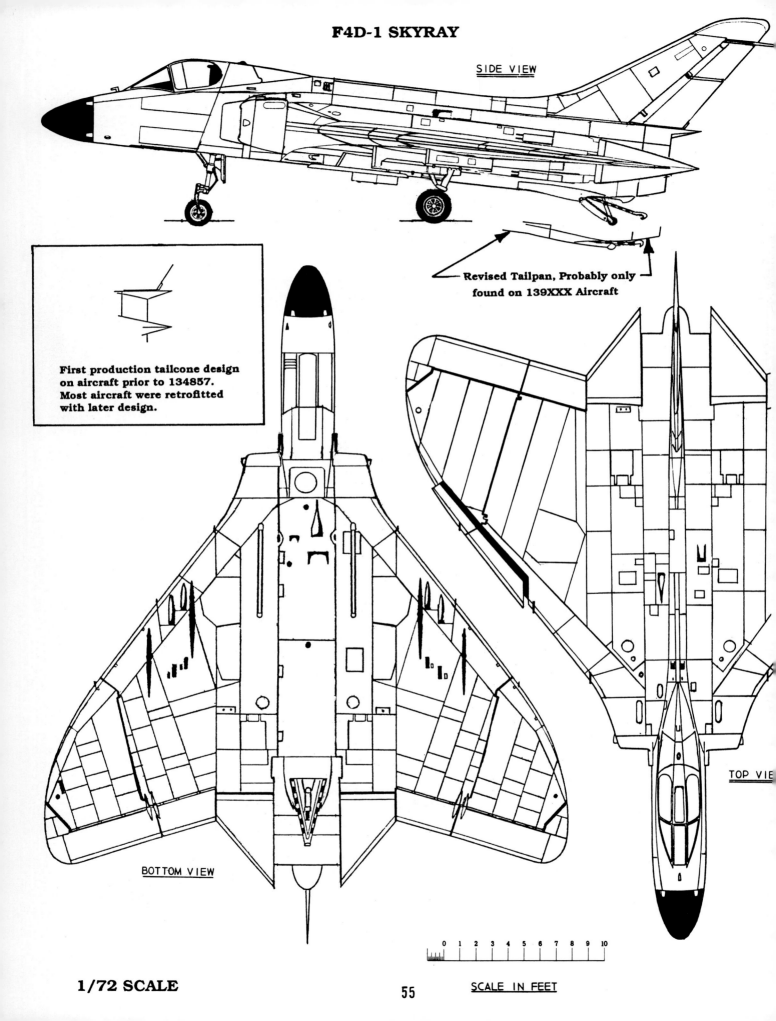

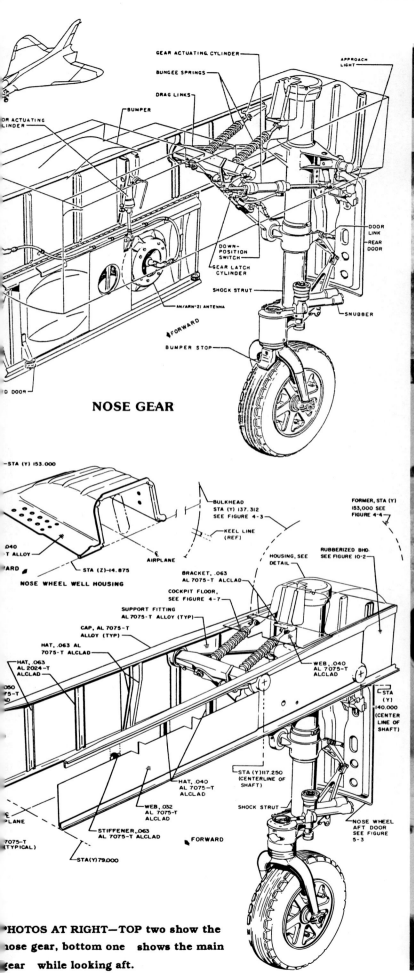

NOSE GEAR

PHOTOS AT RIGHT—TOP two show the nose gear, bottom one shows the main gear while looking aft.

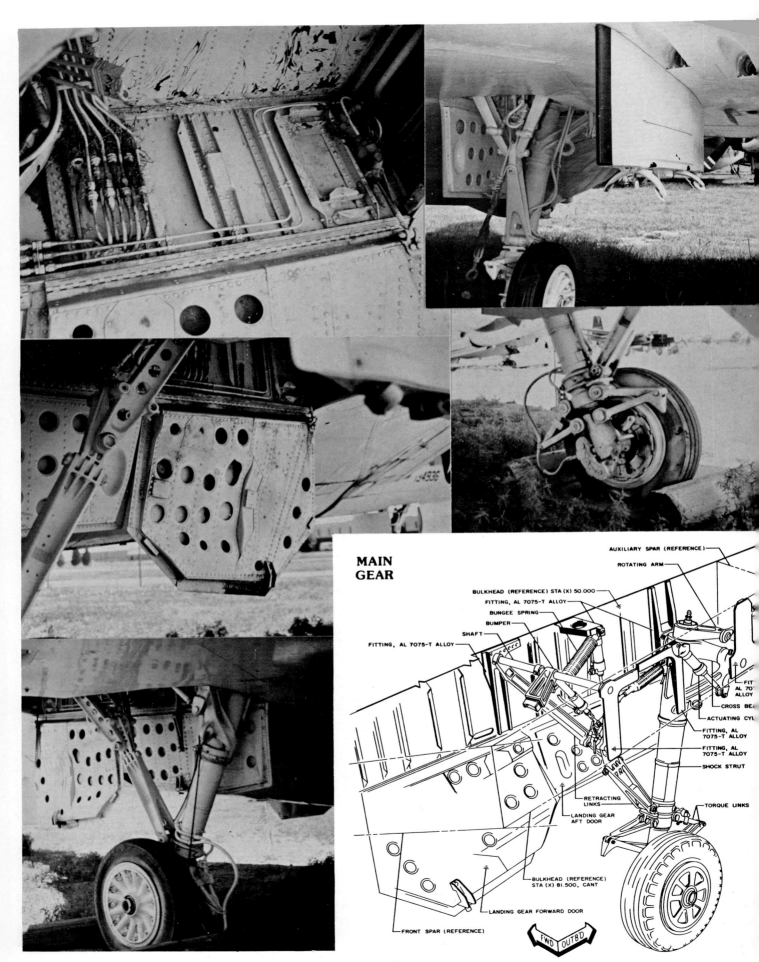

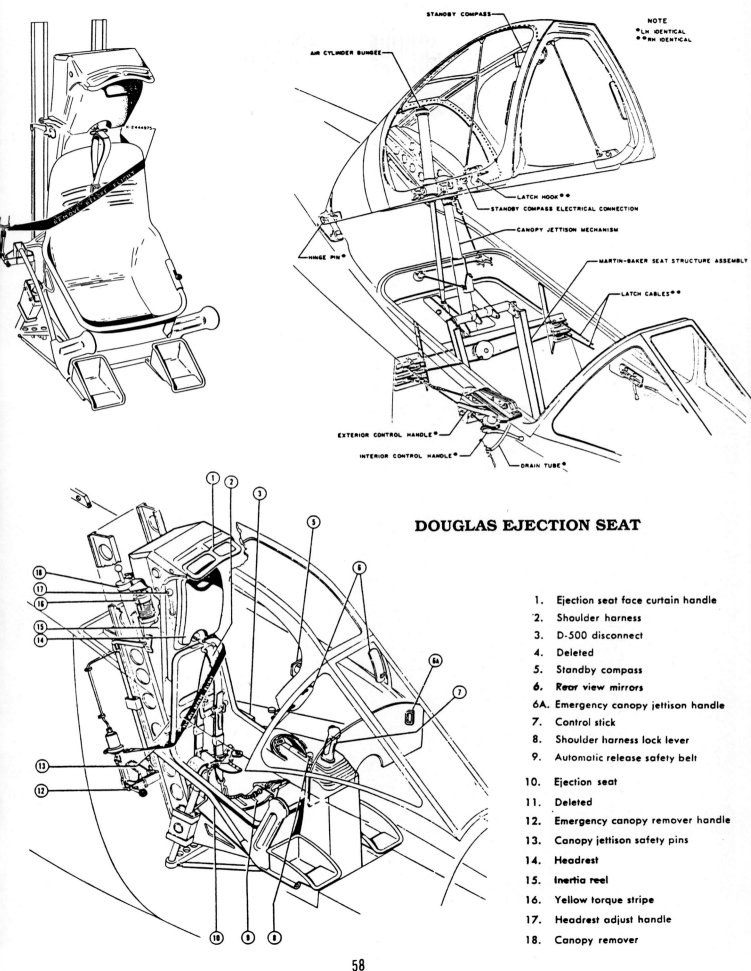

MARTIN-BAKER (MK-P5) EJECTION SEAT

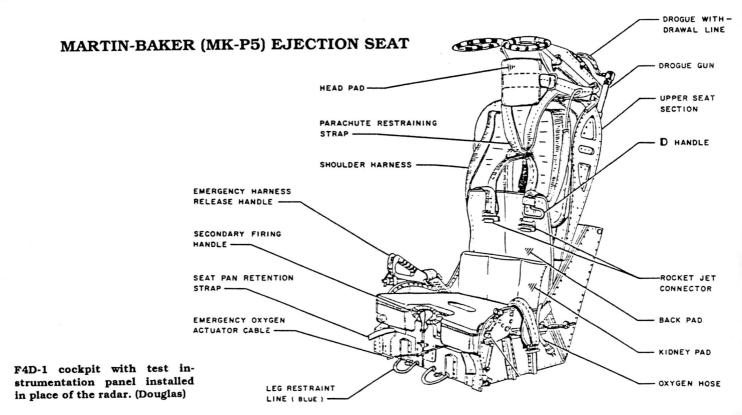

F4D-1 cockpit with test instrumentation panel installed in place of the radar. (Douglas)

FORD
COCKPIT LAYOUT

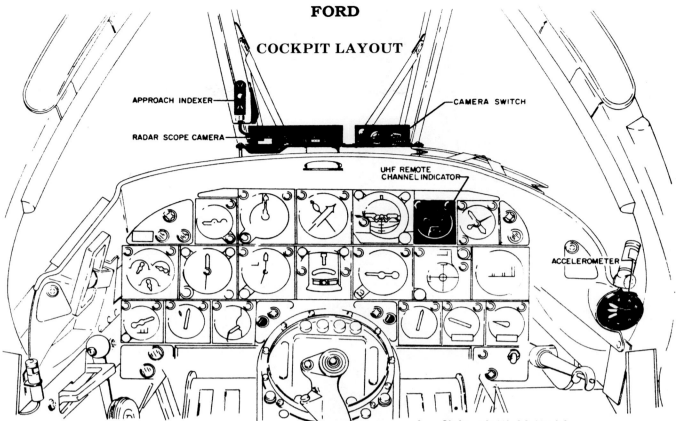

Airplanes BuNo. 134744 and subsequent after service change

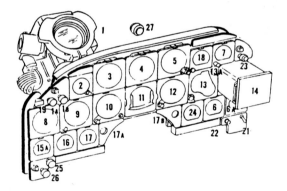

The Douglas seat was painted either black or gull gray. The cockpit instrument and side console panels were black. The side consoles and deck were dark gull gray. You will note that the gun sight is mounted almost vertically behind (forward of) the instrument panel and projects onto the flat windshield. The instrument panel and glare shield permit a better view to the left (where the LSO or mirror landing system would be on a carrier approach) than to the right. The radar scope was partially hidden by the control stick and a periscope was developed by the Navy to provide a better view of the screen. The radar scope was not originally installed in early fleet aircraft due to delays in development of this system, and BuNo 130xxx aircraft never got the radar scope and system. All aircraft were originally delivered with the Douglas ejection seat which was eventually replaced with the Martin-Baker Mk P5 in aircraft BuNo134744 and subsequent. The difference is readily apparent between both the headrests and the rail structure.

1. Sight unit Mk 11 Mod 1
1A. Inverter failure warning light
1B. Boost pump failure warning light
2. Angle of attack indicator
3. Airspeed indicator
4. ID-250/ARN course indicator
5. Gyro horizon indicator
6. Fuel quantity indicator (main tanks)
6A. Fuel quantity indicator (drop tanks)
7. Clock
8. Trim position and mechanical advantage indicator
9. ID-257/APN-22 height indicator
10. Pressure altimeter
11. Turn and bank indicator
12. Rate of climb indicator
13. ID-249/ARN course indicator or ID-351/ARN
13A. Marker beacon indicator
14. ID-310/ARN range indicator
15. Deleted
15A. Pressure ratio indicator
16. Tachometer
17. Tailpipe temperature indicator
17A. Elevon hydraulic pressure indicator
17B. Utility hydraulic pressure indicator
18. ARN/ARC-27A (UHF) remote channel indicator
19. Fire warning light
20. Deleted
21. Drop tank transfer switch
22. Fuel quantity test button
23. Main pump failure warning light
24. Fuel flowmeter
25. Oil pump failure warning light
26. Fuel transfer pump failure warning light
27. On target indicator

LEFT CONSOLE

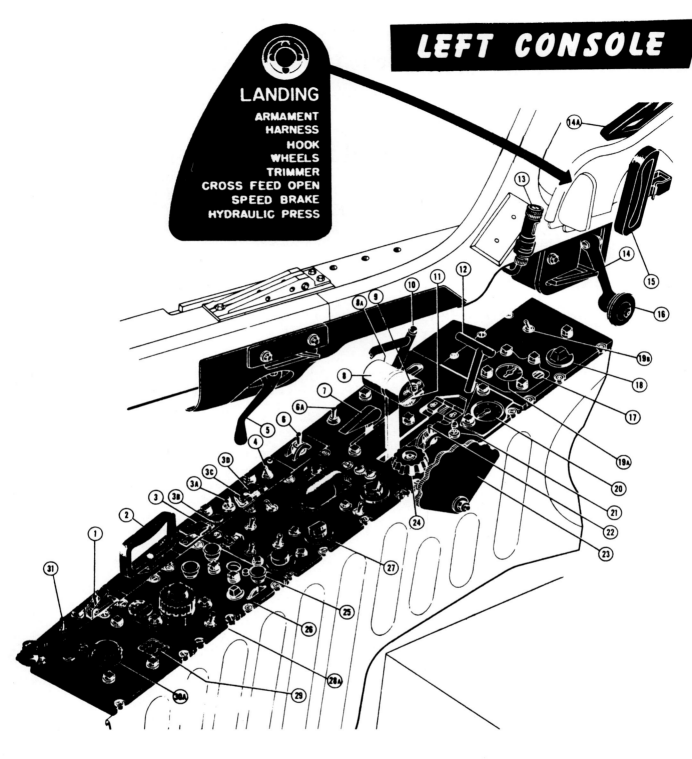

LANDING
ARMAMENT
HARNESS
HOOK
WHEELS
TRIMMER
CROSS FEED OPEN
SPEED BRAKE
HYDRAULIC PRESS

15. Emergency canopy jettison
16. Landing gear control lever
17. Wheels position indicator
18. Wheels position selector knob
19. Oxygen regulator panel[1]
19A. Liquid oxygen indicator[2]
19B. Liquid oxygen "ON"–"OFF" control
20. Cabin pressure altimeter
21. Fuel system selector switch
22. Yaw damper and auto pilot switch
23. Throttle friction control lever
24. Rudder trim control knob

25. Yaw damper control button
26. Auto control panel
26. Auto control panel[3]
27. Radar control panel[3]
28. Oxygen and anti-blackout control panel
28A. Anti-blackout and pressure suit ventilation control panel[2]
29. MACS indicator window
30. MACS control crank[1]
30A. MACS control crank[2]
31. Taxi light switch
32. Cockpit diffuser[4]

[1] Airplanes BuNo. 130740-130750.
[2] Airplanes BuNo. 134744 and subsequent.
[3] Positions interchanged on airplanes BuNo. 139148 and subsequent; BuNo. 134744-134973, 139030-139147 after service change.
[4] Airplanes BuNo. 139030 and subsequent.

Airplanes BuNo. 134744-134973, 139030-139177 prior to service change

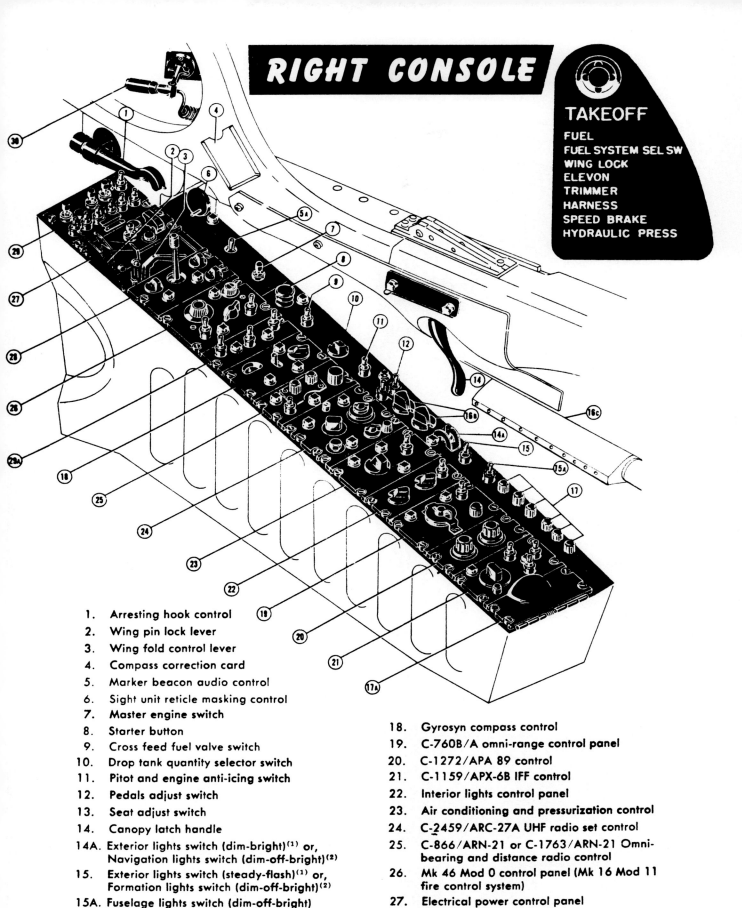

RIGHT CONSOLE

TAKEOFF
FUEL
FUEL SYSTEM SEL SW
WING LOCK
ELEVON
TRIMMER
HARNESS
SPEED BRAKE
HYDRAULIC PRESS

1. Arresting hook control
2. Wing pin lock lever
3. Wing fold control lever
4. Compass correction card
5. Marker beacon audio control
6. Sight unit reticle masking control
7. Master engine switch
8. Starter button
9. Cross feed fuel valve switch
10. Drop tank quantity selector switch
11. Pitot and engine anti-icing switch
12. Pedals adjust switch
13. Seat adjust switch
14. Canopy latch handle
14A. Exterior lights switch (dim-bright)(1) or, Navigation lights switch (dim-off-bright)(2)
15. Exterior lights switch (steady-flash)(1) or, Formation lights switch (dim-off-bright)(2)
15A. Fuselage lights switch (dim-off-bright)
16. Deleted
16A. Defrost-ram air selector switch
17. Interior lights fuses
17A. Spare lamps container
18. Gyrosyn compass control
19. C-760B/A omni-range control panel
20. C-1272/APA 89 control
21. C-1159/APX-6B IFF control
22. Interior lights control panel
23. Air conditioning and pressurization control
24. C-2459/ARC-27A UHF radio set control
25. C-866/ARN-21 or C-1763/ARN-21 Omni-bearing and distance radio control
26. Mk 46 Mod 0 control panel (Mk 16 Mod 11 fire control system)
27. Electrical power control panel
28. Auto control maneuver panel
29. Armament control panel
29A. Aero 13F armament selector panel
30. Instrument floodlight

AN/APQ-50 RADAR

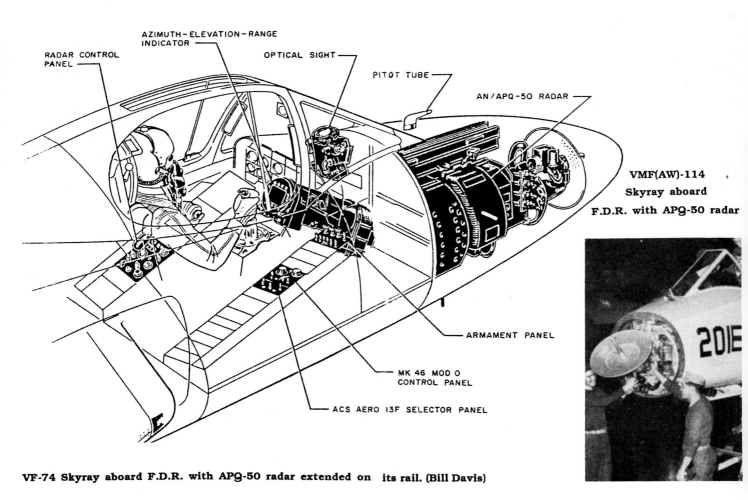

VF-74 Skyray aboard F.D.R. with APQ-50 radar extended on its rail. (Bill Davis)

VMF(AW)-114 Skyray aboard F.D.R. with APQ-50 radar

AN/APQ-50 RADAR

The AN/APQ-50 radar set, located in the fuselage nose section of the airplane, operates as a part of the ACS Aero 13F in conjunction with the Aero 5B armament control director, the Aero 2A flight data unit; and the Aero 2A range adapter. The system is capable of acquiring a target and tracking it automatically, and supplying tracking information to the pilot which will enable him to carry out an effective attack. In addition, the radar set is capable of air-intercept, search, (AI), and mapping, and has provisions for triggering IFF equipment and displaying the IFF response. Major components of the radar set include the AS-629/APQ-50 antenna, the OA-462/APQ-50 radar set group, the C-1181/APQ-50 radar set control, the IP-257/APQ-50 indicator scope, and the C-1182/APQ-50 indicator scope control.

2.75-INCH FOLDING FIN AIR-TO-AIR ROCKET

Ford radar "Lock-on" with "in-range" light on while in flight over Japan in 1963. "In-range" light is located on the platform above the ball. (Jacques Naviaux)

ARMAMENT CONTROL SYSTEM (ACS) AERO 13F

BuNo. 134744 and Subsequent

The Aero 13F automatic fire control system is an all-weather, lead pursuit or lead collision fire control system designed to provide accurate control of fixed, forward-firing 20-mm guns and 2.75-inch folding-fin aerial rockets (FFAR). The equipment is capable of detecting targets at sufficient range to permit successful attacks, tracking targets automatically in range and angle, computing correct lead angles during the attack phase, and presenting steering information and lead angles to the pilot simultaneously on a radar scope and an optical sight. The ACS Aero 13F incorporates both a director system and a distrubed reticle system. The director system uses radar information to provide blind lead-pursuit or lead-collision capability in air-to-surface attacks. The system consists basically of the AN/APQ-50 radar, the Aero 5B armament control director, the Aero 2A flight data unit, the Aero 2A range adapter, and the Mk 16 Mod 11 aircraft fire control system. The radar and Aero 5B director are constructed as a compact, cylindrical package which fits into the nose of the airplane. The cockpit units include the scope, sight unit, and system control panel. The remainder of the units are situated in the main electronics compartment behind the cockpit.

ORDNANCE

28 – 2.75 in. diameter folding fin rockets in 4 external packages, 7 rockets in each package

or

76 – 2.75 in. diameter folding fin rockets in 4 external packages, 19 rockets in each package

or

4 – 20mm M-12 guns mounted in wing, 70 rounds ammunition per gun

or

4 – AAM-N-7 Sidewinders on special launchers.

ELECTRONICS

UHF Comm.	AN/ARC-27A
Nav. Rec.	AN/ARN-21
Radio Altm.	AN/APN-22
IFF	AN/APX-6B
Dir. Finder	AN/ARA-25
NAV PAC, consisting of:	
VHF NAV	AN/ARN-14
Marker Beacon	AN/ARN-12
Fire Control	Aero 13-F System
Consisting of:	
Radar	AN/APQ-50
Arm. Cont. Dir.	Aero 5B
Opt. Sight Syst.	Mk.16 Mod.11

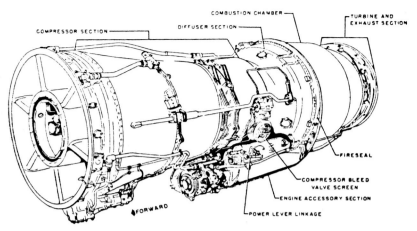

J57 AXIAL FLOW ENGINE

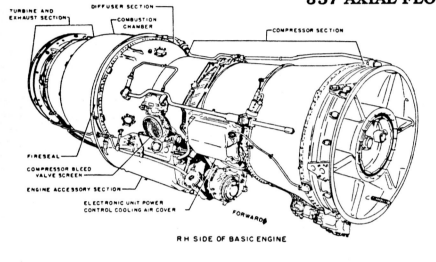

POWER PLANT	
No. & Model	(1) J57-P-8 or -8B
Mfr.	Pratt & Whitney
Eng. Spec.	N-1694B (Rev. 9-15-55)
Type	Turbo-Jet
Compr.	Multi-Stage, Axial Flow
Augmentation	Afterburner
Tail Pipe Nozzle	Two-Position
Length	250 in.
Diameter	40.5 in.

RATINGS

Sea Level Static

	THRUST Lbs.	RPM
Normal	8700	5750
Military	10200	6050
Maximum (with A/B)	16000	6050

STARTER CART

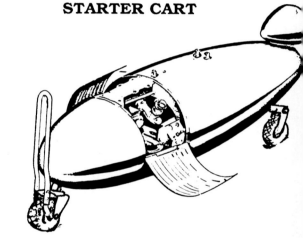

ARRESTING HOOK AND TAIL BUMPER GEAR

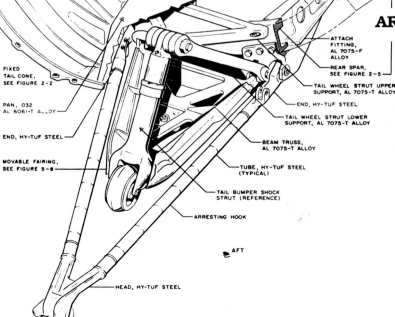

ABOVE - In-flight Ford On 6-26-56 loaded with four rocket pods, two 300 gallon drop tanks and centerline NavPac.

EXTERNAL STORES F4D-1 SKYRAY

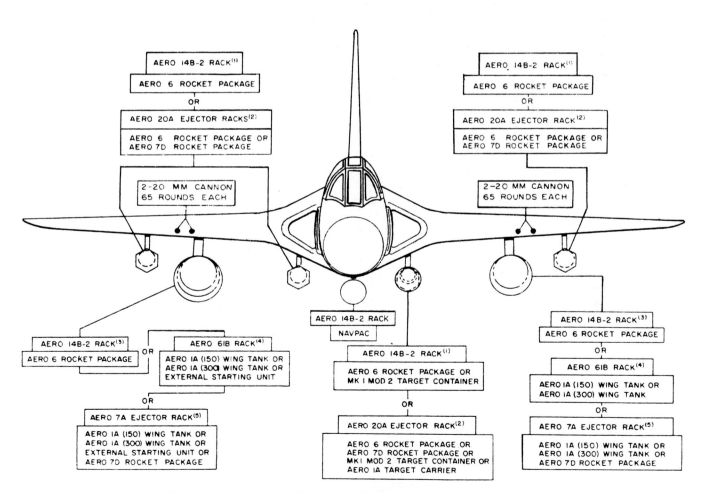

(1) AIRPLANES BUNO 130740-130750; BUNO 134744-134918 PRIOR TO SERVICE CHANGE.
(2) AIRPLANES BUNO 134919 AND SUBSEQUENT; BUNO 134744-134918 AFTER SERVICE CHANGE.
(3) INSTALLATION PROVISIONS ONLY IN AIRPLANES BUNO 130740-130750, 134744-134818.
(4) AIRPLANES BUNO 130740-130744, 130746-130750; BUNO 134744-134852 PRIOR TO SERVICE CHANGE.
(5) AIRPLANES BUNO 130745, 134853 AND SUBSEQUENT; BUNO 134744-134852 AFTER SERVICE CHANGE.

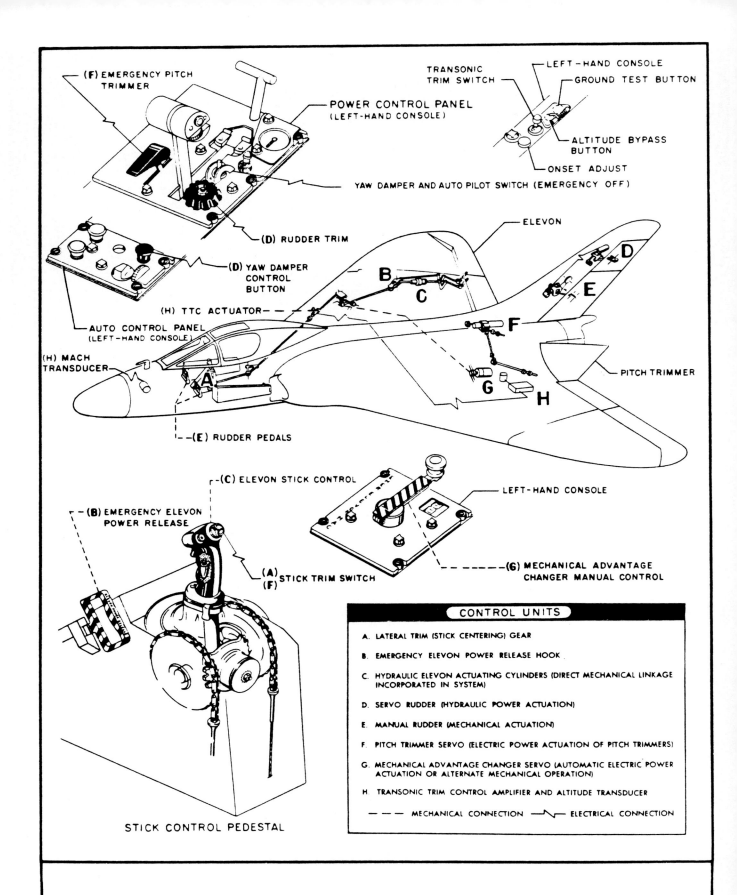

FLIGHT CONTROLS

COMMUNICATION AND ASSOCIATED ELECTRONIC EQUIPMENT

AIRCRAFT INSTALLATIONS

TYPE	DESIGNATION	FUNCTION	RANGE	LOCATION OF CONTROLS
COMMUNICATION				
UHF RADIO	AN/ARC-27A	SHORT RANGE - TWO WAY VOICE COMMUNICATION	LINE-OF-SIGHT	RIGHT-HAND CONSOLE
NAVIGATION				
OMNI-BEARING (1) DISTANCE RADIO	AN/ARN-21	PROVIDES BEARING AND DISTANCE TO A SELECTED BEAM	LINE-OF-SIGHT TO 200 MILES	RIGHT-HAND CONSOLE
UHF HOMING ADAPTER	AN/ARA-25	PROVIDES MEANS OF HOMING ON UHF TRANSMISSIONS	LINE-OF-SIGHT	RIGHT-HAND CONSOLE
IFF RADAR	AN/APX-6B	TRANSMISSION & RECEPTION OF IDENTIFICATION SIGNALS	LINE-OF-SIGHT	RIGHT-HAND CONSOLE
IFF RADAR	KY-81/APA-89	VIDEO RESPONDER	LINE-OF-SIGHT	RIGHT-HAND CONSOLE
ORDNANCE				
FIRE CONTROL	MK 16	VISUAL FIRE CONTROL SYSTEM	2000 YARDS	RIGHT-HAND CONSOLE
RANGE RADAR (2)	AN/APQ-50	SEARCH AND TRACKING	200 NAUTICAL MILES	LEFT-HAND CONSOLE

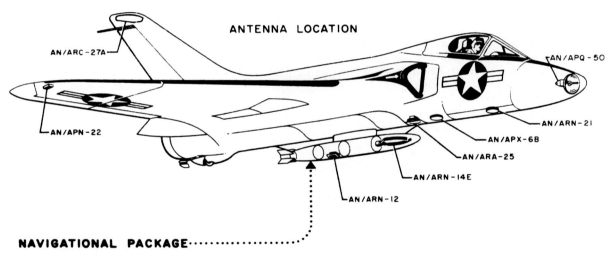

ANTENNA LOCATION

NAVIGATIONAL PACKAGE

TYPE	DESIGNATION	FUNCTION	RANGE	LOCATION OF CONTROLS
OMNI-RANGE RECEIVER	AN/ARN-14E	VOR, VAR & LOCALIZER SIGNALS	LINE-OF-SIGHT	RIGHT-HAND CONSOLE
MARKER BEACON RECEIVER	AN/ARN-12	RECEPTION OF LOCATION MARKER BEACON SIGNALS FROM INSTRUMENT APPROACH STATIONS	WITHIN BOUNDARIES OF FAN MARKER OR Z MARKER	RIGHT-HAND CONSOLE (TONE CONTROL ONLY)

(1) INSTALLATION PROVISIONS ONLY
(2) BUNO 134853 AND SUBSEQUENT

P-5420-1E

Communication and Associated Electronic Equipment

PLASTIC SKYRAYS

There have been at least five different plastic kits of the F4D over the years. They were the Hawk 1/72 scale F4D-1, the Aurora/Addar subscale kit of the first production F4D-1, 130740, the Lindberg 1/48 scale kit of 130740, the Microscale 1/48 manufacturer's display kit and the Airfix/MPC 1/72 scale F4D-1.

The Hawk kit like many 1950 plastic kits, looks fine from across the room, but would require too much effort to make it accurate. The kit has twenty pieces including landing gear. There is no cockpit detail, not even a pilot. Decals are for F4D-1 134833 of VMF(AW)-513. The kit was produced in 1959.

The Aurora/Addar kit has a cast in place pilot figure and landing gear. The kit is made up of six pieces and is fairly accurate. The kit has the nasty 1950 feature of scribed decal placement lines. My kit was an Addar kit produced in 1976.

The Lindberg kit first appeared in the early 1950s and has some toy-like features and bogus rockets. However the general shape and outline are close enough to make an acceptable model with a little work. If you throw out the gear, drop tanks, rockets, cockpit details and engine you would be ready to start. After replacing all of the above with acceptable parts you would focus your attention on the intakes afterburner and tailhook. When finished I'm sure you would have an acceptable addition to your collection. The kit was reissued in 1976 in the same markings as the 1950s kit. It was reissued again in 1984 as a Lindberg Classic in a grey and white scheme.

The Microscale kit was available for a short time in the 1970's. It contained four pieces and had no surface detail. All the detail was provided by the VF(AW)-3 decals which came with the kit.

The Airfix Skyray was a welcome addition to the limited list of injection molded kits of Navy jets of the Fifties. Tommy Thomason tells how to do this kit up right.

The Airfix kit is basically accurate although there are some dimensional problems and many detail errors. The fuselage is slightly too long (about 3/16") and deep. The wingspan is as close as I care to measure but the planform is a little off and is difficult to correct since the vertical fin is correctly located with respect to the tail cone but the tail cone, pitch trimmers, aft end of the main gear wheel well, and wing trailing edge are about 1/8" too far aft with respect to the engine intakes. If you wanted to fix this (and I can't imagine why), you would remove about 1/8" from the center fuselage in the area of the main wheel well and fittle with the wing planform, including rescribing at least some control surface lines.

In an event, the wing fold line is angled too far outboard and the outboard wing slat extends too far outboard. If you go to the trouble to fix this, you might as well fold the wings and extend the inboard slats, which is a typical static pose for the F4D.

If you don't feel up to any of that, two improvements are easy. First, the main landing gear must be moved aft to the position shown on the side view. Second, the engine inlets should be enlarged and reshaped to match the front view. Note that the splitter plates are thinner than the kits and are curved and that the standoff from the fuselage is curved.

The F4D had unusual position lights. These appear on the model as small raised circles on the wing tips and vertical fin. They are realistically depicted by handgrinding a small hole with a drill. After the model is painted, the holes are painted silver and filled in with white glue or Micro Kristal Kleer. The aircraft also had small yellow orange formation lights below the canopy fairing and on the aft fuselage spine. The ones on the aft fuselage were later moved to the vertical fin. There was originally a white light both on the top of the canopy forward of the hinge and on the bottom of the fuselage on the forward engine access door. Upper and lower red anticollision lights were eventually added.

There are several other miscellaneous additions. The small bulges on the outside of the engine inlets were also inlets as noted earlier and need to be opened up. There was a prominent inlet and exhaust on the lower left side of the fuselage. Catapult hooks, pitot and static sources, and other details could be.

Microscale Decal Sheet No. 72-186 "F4D-1 Skyrays" provides for some alternatives to the kit markings, including one for the distinctive VF(AW)-3 aircraft:

VMF(AW)-114	10EK
VMF-115	10VE
VF(AW)-3	12PA
VF-74	110AF
VF-213	310NP

Microscale No. 72-329 includes a VF-162 F4D, 102 AF which has black control surfaces covered with gold stars.

For the 1/48 scale kits, Microscale No 48-22 includes the following:

VMF-115	10VE
VMF(AW)-114	10EK
NATC	0743
VF-213	310NP
VF-74	110AF

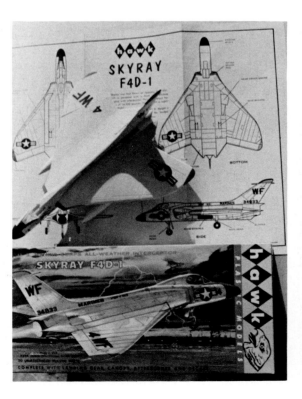

PLASTIC SKYRAYS

(MODEL BY T. THOMASON)

71

THE DOUGLAS SKYRAY IN FLEET COLORS

While each unit is covered in an arbitrary sequence, the story actually begins and ends at NAS Patuxent River, Maryland, with the first assignment of a production F4D-1 to the Naval Air Test Center in 1955, continuing to the disposal of the last flyable Skyray at Pax River's Naval Test Pilot School in 1969.

The Douglas F4D-1 Skyray was a remarkably adaptable airplane. In eight short years, from the first "Factory-to-Fleet" delivery in April 1956, to the retirement of the last "Ford" in an operational Fleet squadron in February 1964, the Skyray served in the colors of no fewer than 35 separate Navy and Marine Corps squadrons, shore facilities, and civilian agencies.

During this period, consistant squadron markings displayed by these Skyrays very often were short lived, as many schemes changed in detail from year-to-year. Within each squadron, a markings evolution usually progressed from elaborate schemes to more simplified ones over the two to eight year span of each unit's operation of the F4D-1.

Several related factors account for this difficulty in maintaining consistant squadron markings. Each airplane's rotation through its progressive maintenance cycle occasionally resulted in its re-assignment to a different squadron. The high cost of repainting these aircraft caused a hesitancy on the part of many squadrons to retain elaborate schemes. The Marine Corps' policy of rotating squadron personnel on foreign deployment, leaving the aircraft for the replacement unit, also caused the eventual reduction of Marine squadron markings to simple tail Modex letters and little else.

These and other considerations resulted in what has been described as a "running battle" between the squadrons and their parent commands. This battle was more like a family feud between the squadron fighter pilots, who enjoyed flying colorfully painted aircraft and appreciated the special spirit they evoked, and their Navy or Marine Corps command organizations, who had difficulty in justifying the time and expense involved in maintaining these flamboyant schemes.

Mention should be made of several operational peculiarities of the Skyray which affected its markings. The design's large J-57 engine coupled with a small internal fuel capacity made drop tanks a practical necessity. The Skyray rarely flew without them. Installation delays with the Skyray's APQ-50 radar resulted in the airplane's early use within a carrier air group as a day fighter only. Hence, it initially appeared in the fleet in yellow markings with 200-series nose numbers, rather than with the red markings and 100-series numbers often associated with many all-weather fighter aircraft. Finally, the F4D-1's detachable fiberglass vertical stabilizer cap, which housed the UHF antenna, was a convenient location to add squadron markings. However, when it was left unpainted, its basic gray, black or white coloring can be confused to day in black and white photographs for the intended tail markings.

The following is not intended to be a definitive "markings article," for complete official information on unit colors, histories, insignia and even squadron nicknames had often been nonexistent or contradictory. Likewise, the surviving photographic record is surprisingly small, considering that less than 25 years have ellapsed since the events covered in this article took place. In any event, it is hoped that the historian and modeler alike will find interest in this account of a somewhat neglected era in the colorful history of naval aviation.

F4D-1s, 134936 and 139065, of VF-102 on 5-4-61, while flying from the USS Forrestal, CVA-59. CVG-8s "AJ" tail code is carried. Spine, tail stripe and drop tanks of "065" are red with white diamonds. "936" has white drop tanks. Note the sidewinders on the outer rail. (USN)

NAVAL AIR TEST CENTER

As the Navy's main aeronautical testing facility, the Naval Air Test Cent (NATC) as NAS Patuxent River, Maryland, has the responsibility for determining a new aircraft's suitability for use with the fleet. In the 1950s, NATC project pilots and engineers were divided among four test divisions: Flight Test concerned itself with airplane and engine performance, stability and control, and carrier suitability; Service Test evaluated operational and tactical suitability, emphasizing maintenance; Electronics Test reported on all avionics equipment; and Armament Test conducted an evaluation of the airplane as a weapons platform.

Additionally, the NATC supplied an evaluation team to the contractor's plant for a Navy Preliminary Evaluation (NPE), a formal series of test with the prototype models prior to the production aircraft's arrival at Patuxent River. The Board of Inspection and Survey (BIS), while independent of the NATC, also conducted fleet suitability evaluations using the test center's aircraft. Finally, Service Test Division aircraft and personnel later were involved in the Fleet Introductory Program (FIP), which trained the first squadron pilots and ground crews scheduled to operate a new airplane in the fleet.

In all, the Naval Air Test Center flew over two dozen Douglas Skyrays beginning in July 1952 when an NATC three-pilot team evaluated one of the XF4D-1s. NATC pilots tested the updated prototype in November 1952 and again in July 1953 when Carrier Suitability Trials were conducted with XF4D-1 124586. In November 1954, an NATC Navy Preliminary Evaluation team began testing the early production F4D-1s, while a second NATC NPE was run in June 1955 and the BIS trails were accomplished at the NATC between November 1955 and January 1956.

The first Skyray actually attached to the NATC, F4D-1 130746, the seventh production airframe, arrived in March 1955. During the remainder of the year an additional six Skyrays joined 746 at the test center, while approximately nine were gained in 1956, six in 1957, two in 1959, and one at late as 1962. The early-arriving aircraft were painted gloss white undersides. However, beyond the standard "NATC" painted on their tails in block letters, and "FT", "AT", "ET" or "ST" painted on each airplane's nose (denoting the particular test division to which each aircraft was attached), these aircraft seem to have appeared in a wide variety of often colorful markings. Also, a small number of aircraft apparently served at the NATC while retaining their previous Douglas Testing Division paint schemes.

Over the many years the NATC flew the Skyray, tests were conducted on virtually every facet of its operations: performance and flight characteristics, catapult and arresting phases, barrier engagement, external stores, and so forth, as well as utilizing them for drone control, chase aircraft and target tugs. While problems with various components would plague the design throughout its service life, the Skyray's NATC project pilots helped mold the airplane into a successful fleet fighter.

NATC test pilot Tim Wooldridge offers an "outsider's view of the Skyray and its idiosyncracies: "I flew the Skyray from 1956 to 1959 while attached to the Electronics Test Division. My primary project there was testing the radar and weapons system of the F3H-2 Demon. However, my boss at the time, Cdr. Jerry O'Rourke, had the F4D-1

weapon system project and we used to frequently swap aircraft just to keep each other honest. I was a proponent of the Hughes radar in the Demon and Jerry liked the Westinghouse system in the Ford, so there was considerable good-natured rivalry about the merits of the aircraft and the radars.

"I did like the Demon better than the F4D. The F4D-1 had a very short control stick which, for me anyway, felt very awkward and made it difficult for me to fly the airplane the way I wanted to. I am tall, with long legs and arms, and I never really felt comfortable in the F4D. The radar scope was located right in front of the control stick at the bottom of the instrument panel. It was impossible to see the scope because of the stick! Jerry had a smart young ensign named Al Morris who was not a pilot. Al took one look at the problem, went home and stole two mirrors out of his wife's purse, glued some cardboard boxes together with the mirrors inside, and the next day installed this periscope in the airplane. It worked. It was possible to see the face of the radar scope over the top of the stick. We went on from there to get the old Navy gun factory in Washington to come up with fine precision mirrors. We found a craftsman who could do wonders with plastic molds, and Al finally came up with a very professional periscope which became standard equipment in the fleet."

As successful as the Skyray turned out to be one might assume that these NATC test pilots would feel satisfied for a job well done. For some, however, memories of the Skyray program are filled with regrets for a task left uncompleted. George Watkins, a former NATC test pilot intimately involved with the Skyray's testing program, expresses some misgivings regarding the airplane's deficiencies: "I think it's important to understand a couple of different things about an engineering test pilot. He has a responsibility to the Naval Air Systems Command— and to the Navy— to insure that any new model airplane not only meets the contract specifications and guarantees submitted by the airframe contractor, but also to insure that the fleet pilot is getting a damn good flying machine that performs its assigned fleet mission in a superb manner. The test pilot has an equal responsibility, as a given model project pilot, to report all deficiencies found in stability and control, handling characteristics, performance, carrier suitability and serviceability of that new model airplane before it goes to the fleet as an acceptable production model. The F4D-1 had very poor transonic trim change characteristics, right in the Mach range where the airplane would be expected to be engaged in air-to-air combat. It also had very poor lateral/directional/roll characteristics, among other things. This is one of the main reasons why I was against production and even further testing of the

BELOW - The first two Skyrays assigned to NATC, 130746 and 130747, during catapult tests in Jan. and Feb. of 1956. Colors are blue overall with black radome, anti-glare panel and fin tip. Wheels are natural metal. Note both have white right drop tank and 746 has a white NavPac and 747 has blue rocket pods. (National Archives)

F5D-1 model. This airplane, in December 1956, exhibited the same poor flying qualities as did the 'Skyray'. I wasn't really an F3H fan, but it did have good flying qualities and handling characteristics, and was a good stable platform in the carrier approach. I enjoyed flying the F4D very much, but like the F8F-1 'Bearcat' before it, it just didn't provide the fleet with a good stable-platform, high-performance fighter in the air-to-air role. And back in 1955 when we were flying the XF8U-1 at Edwards AFB and getting level flight Mach numbers of 1.5 and higher with essentially the same engine as the F4D, it was a little difficult to get too pumped up over the 'Skyray's' subsonic performance limitations and capabilities."

Jerry O'Rourke, now a retired Navy Captain, expresses what seems to be the majority opinion among ex-NATC test pilots regarding the Skyray's qualities (see "The

Flight Test F4D-1 130746 launches from XC-7 steam catapult at NATC on 2-15-56 (Douglas/National Archives)

Douglas Navy F 4D Ford," by Jerry O'Rourke, JAAHS summer 1979): "I once had respect and admiration for the Ford. After years of restrospect, however, I feel that it was a pretty bad airplane which should have been bypassed in favor of either a better F3H or an F5D version. Myself, Tim Wooldridge, John Glenn, Tony Nollet, George Watkins and a few others were Patuxent River test pilots at a time when we could have forced the issue. We did not, for one reason or another. I feel we were either wrong or lazy on the matter, and we should have demanded a long series of fixes and improvements which would probably have resulted in scrapping of the Ford in favor of the F5D."

Only a handful of Skyrays remained at the Naval Air Test Center in 1960. These gradually were disposed of until the last NATC F4D-1, 134778, was retired in February 1965.

THE FORD: A STRANGE BUT FUN AIRCRAFT

Captain Robert Dreesen, USN, Ret., first flew the F4D at NATC Patuxent in late 1955 as part of the airplane's Board of Inspection and Survey trails. (For his reminiscences on the Cutlass, the FJ-2 Fury, and the Demon, see Naval Fighters Numbers Six, Ten, and Twelve respectively.)

BACKGROUND AND FLIGHT CHARACTERISTICS:

The fleet scuttlebutt during the '53-'53 period was that Fleet introduction would be in 1953-1954. Actual first squadron use was delayed until 1956 by the problems caused by the Westinghouse J-40 engine. Had it made it to the fleet when originally scheduled, the F4D would have represented a quantum improvement over fighters in use at the time, particularly in the all-weather role then filled by the Skyknight and the dash-three and dash-four Banshees.

The J-40 was to have been designed to deliver 10,000 lbs. thrust, with a 50% augmentation to 15,000 lbs. in afterburner. As installed in the F4D it yielded only about 7,000, with about 10,000 in burner. Although the F4D which set the speed records in 1953 had a J-40 engine, Dreesen noted that it was specially tuned and treated. He said that the pilots at Pax River joked that they must have given the engine the old Civil War cannon treatment—wrapped it in wire to keep it together. (Those records, set by then LTCDR Jim Verdin, were 753.4 MPH over a 3 kilometer course at Salton Sea on October 3 and 728.11 over a 1000 Kilometer 12-pylon course at Edwards AFB on October 16. They were topped by Frank Everest on October 29, flying at YF-100A at 755.15 MPH at Salton Sea.)

The aircraft did not have to be substantially redesigned to accommodate the replacement J-57, but there were some unexpected problems. As an example, the J-57 had been designed to be used as a flat-plate, even-pressure distribution engine—in other words, ideal for installation in a nacelle. The J-40 had been designed for a bifurcated duct setup. As installed in the Ford, the J-57 required a series of rods in each intake to generate a turbulent flow, in order to even out the pressure flow across the face of the engine. Of course, putting all those rods in there caused a small loss of thrust, so the J-57 as installed produced a little less thrust than it would have in a nacelle-type installation.

Because of the engine problems, they didn't get an F4D at Armament Test at Pax River until the fall of 1955. Ironically, although they'd waited two years, the one they got didn't have a fire control radar installed. Since they couldn't work with the fire control system, they concentrated on other specification qualification tests. One example was to fly to 35,000 feet, hold it there for half or three quarters of an hour, and then use the afterburner to go to 50,000 feet and test-fire the guns—Dreesen called it "cold-soaking" the guns.

At Pax River they flew it completely clean, and he recalled that it was "fun to fly" clean. In mid-altitudes it would do slightly over Mach 1 in afterburner. With only about 4,000 pounds of internal fuel, afterburner takeoffs further limited the already short flight time. But Dreesen described a hot takeoff in a clean F4D as "a real kick...you just barely started rolling before the airplane was airborne in a burner takeoff."

The main aerodynamic problem they encountered was that the airplane would go into a terrific nose-down pitch at about Mach .87 or .88. It was controllable, but required a lot of stick force to keep the nose level. It petered out by Mach .92 or .93 and the airplane returned to normal trim condition. There were no ailerons or elevators, but large "elevons" on the wings. Longitudinal trim was handled by two trimmers in the form of big spikes on the aft fuselage, where the fuselage joined the wing. They weren't very useful in dealing with this pitch-down phenomena, partially because their movements were so large that they couldn't move very quickly and partially because pilot response tended to be somewhat slow. The pilots at Pax River decided that either a major redesign of the aircraft would be necessary or pilots would simply have to pressure it on through. Once Dreesen, as an experiment, trimmed his F4D carefully so that it would fly hands-off in the pitchdown airspeed region; then he reduced power, and as the aircraft decelerated out of the pitchdown region it went into a 4-G pitchup.

The Douglas people dealt with the pitch-down problem by installing a pair of Mach-controlled, electrically actuated screwjacks which would force the elevons up at the onset of pitchdown and then ease them down as the aircraft flew out of the critical speed range. By Mach .92 or .93 the screwjacks would be back in the home position and you'd be flying normally. The procedure reversed itself when decelerating. According to Dreesen, the problem was that it was almost impossible to keep the screwjacks in electrical and physical balance. In one F4D the system might be a roll to the left. In a second it might be a roll to the right, and on a third it might work as designed. As a result many Fleet pilots kept the system off and flew through the pitch with hand and elbow power on the stick—the same way they did at Pax in 1955.

In Armament Test they weren't particularly concerned with carrier suitability or instrument flight conditions, but they did note that both lateral and directional stability were touchy at landing speed.

In the fleet the F4D was not flown clean. With the extra 4,000 pounds of fuel the drop tanks gave you, there was enough fuel to fly comfortably for 90 minutes to two hours, providing you didn't use too much afterburner. But flying it with wing tanks and other underwing stores made the low-speed stability problem worse. Dreesen commented that "It just flew differently from almost anything else you were used to at carrier approach or GCA speed. It had a peculiar double-rudder arrangement. In moderate to high speed flight, only the lower half was used for rudder control, while the upper rudder was an independent yaw dampener. As the landing gear went down, the upper half was tied back into the system, and you needed all of it. It liked to fly slightly sidways at low speed...slightly in yaw, or slightly wing-down. The most interesting characteristic was low-speed turns. Once down to landing speed, you'd start turning with the elevons, then bring them back to neutral and continue the roll with the rudder; elevons and rudder had to be worked together. To stop the roll, you'd use upper rudder, hold it, and then use heavy rudder and a little elevon to level the wings. This was completely the antithesis of the way all other jets flew then and now. Jet aircraft have very little adverse yaw with ailerons—you throw in a lot of aileron and maybe think about stroking the rudder pedal just a little. With the F4D at low speed, it was just the opposite—stroke the elevon and throw in a lot rudder. At high speed, in terms of lateral directional control, it flew extactly like every other jet aircraft—lots of elevon and a touch of rudder."

The F4D was one of the last aircraft with a direct mechanical control system. Normally it flew totally on a hydraulic boost system with an automatic mechanical advantage changer which worked off dynamic or "Q" pressure. (Q is the measurement of pressure due to motion, and is the product of one-half the air density times the velocity squared.) For example, at low speeds a one-inch stick movement would cause a certain movement of the elevons—say, for example, 10 degrees. At high speed the mechanical advantage would change so that the same one-inch stick movement would give you only three degrees of elevon movement. This was a safety feature, since a stick movement that would be OK at low speeds might cause the airplane to tear itself to pieces at high speed. One nice characteristic was that if the hydraulic system failed, you could still fly it with the stick. Hydraulic pressure kept the mechanical control system disengaged, and it only engaged when hydraulic pressure fell. The pilot would then remove the radar hood and push a button on the stick which would allow him to pull it up higher into the cockpit, lengthening it. It was normally a very short and stubby stick—right at leg level, so that you could see the radar-scope hood above it. when flying it under mechanical con-

Tail of 130747 in May 1955, showing the YF4D-1 designation it carried for a short time. (Picciani)

trol, the pilot used the longer stick with its greater mechanical advantage and also adjusted the mechanical advantage gears. The mechanical advantage changer was a small rotating handle on the lower left console. Dreesen flew it mechanically both in simulators and in practice, but never had to resort to it for real.

All these strange flight characteristics resulted in carrier squadrons adopting a sort of two-tiered setup. The junior officers did all the day flying and the senior people with two or more tours did all the night work. Good first-tour pilots might work their way up to some night work, but only on clear and bright nights. "It was simply not a good carrier aircraft."

130747 takes a wave-off on 6-14-56. Note off-white radome and white drop tanks. (Douglas)

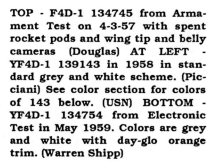

TOP - F4D-1 134745 from Armament Test on 4-3-57 with spent rocket pods and wing tip and belly cameras (Douglas) AT LEFT - YF4D-1 139143 in 1958 in standard grey and white scheme. (Picciani) See color section for colors of 143 below. (USN) BOTTOM - YF4D-1 134754 from Electronic Test in May 1959. Colors are grey and white with day-glo orange trim. (Warren Shipp)

The most colorful Skyray of all, BuNo. 130743 on 5-13-60 at Andrews AFB. (Besecker) Colors are blue fuselage with yellow wings and drop tanks and day-glo red tail and wing stripe. Fin tips is medium grey with black leading edge. Radome, wing-walk and anti-glare panel are varying shades of flat black. Leading edges are natural metal and gear is white.

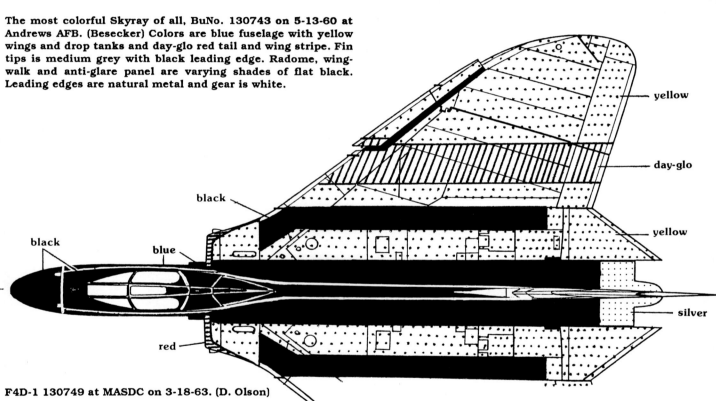

F4D-1 130749 at MASDC on 3-18-63. (D. Olson)

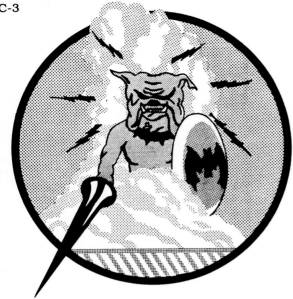

VC-3/VF(AW)-3

Fleet Composite Squadron Three, base at Moffett Field, Calif., had the distinction of being the first operational unit to receive the F4D-1. In the first Skyray "factory-to-fleet" delivery. BuNo 134777 was formally accepted by the squadron at El Segundo on April 16, 1956.

The Douglas-applied markings on this airplane were spartan: a black tail band with three white stars, a large "NP" tail Modex, "VC-3" on the fin, and the squadron's emblem on each side of the canopy. Although Douglas gave 777 nose number "21," this was later changed by the squadron to "22."

Within a month, VC-3 accepted at least three additional Skyrays, using them to provide fleet pilot instrument training and indoctrination training for fleet replacement pilots and maintenance personnel.

On July 1, 1956, VC-3 was redesignated VF(AW)-3, presumably due to its acquisition of the all weather Skyrays. However, its mission remained unchanged, and VF(AW)-3 Skyray's retained their "NP" tail code and the original VC-3 insignia for some time. At a later date these Moffett-based Skyrays acquired a new tail code: a smaller, stylized "TT." As far as is known, Skyrays with this code did not display VF(AW)-3's squadron insignia.

In any event, VF(AW)-3 continued to fly their Skyrays until May 2, 1958, when the squadron was decommissioned and its duties taken over by VF-124.

FAWTUPAC/VF(AW)-3

The history of Fleet All Weather Training Unit. Pacific begins in 1944, when NACTUPAC was commissioned at Barber's Point, Hawaii to provide training in night operations for combat pilots in the Pacific area. Through several redesignations (NightDevRon, Pac; VCN-1) FAWTUPAC emerged in 1948 with the mission of providing all weather training for fleet pilots.

The unit moved to NAS North Island in Feb, 1955, and in December of that year assumed the supplementary mission of air defense, being assigned to the Continental Air Defense Command, 27th North American Air Defense Division (NORAD).

When the squadron assumed their air defense role they functioned as a "split unit," one element continuing in all weather training, and the other element under Air Force control, flying for NORAD. As FAWTUPAC had been maintaining "Detachment Bravo" at Moffett Field since Oct. 1953, it is assumed that this unit supplied the all weather part of the squadron's mission, while the North Island unit was used exclusively for air defense.

At the time of this unique assignment, FAWTUPAC had been flying Douglas F3D Skynights, but the squadrons began supplementing these with F4D-1 Skyrays by the summer of 1956.

For some time, FAWTUPAC Skyrays carried only their unit name, a nose number, and their tail code "PA" in large letters. Early in 1958, however, at least one FAWTUPAC Skyray was painted in one of the most spectacular schemes to be applied to any aircraft of the era. This consisted of a dark blue spine and tail with various sizes of yellow stars scattered randomly about. The unit's "PA" Modex was changed to white letters superimposed over a large yellow lightning bolt on the tail. Similar treatment (yellow stars on a blue field) was given each wing tip and 300 gal. drop tank.

An additional FAWTUPAC Skyrays carried what appears to be a "one off" special paint scheme applied for the Third Annual Naval Air Weapons Meet, held as NAAS El Centro in April 1958. The aircraft, BuNo unknown, featured a red spine, wing tips, and drop tanks. Little is known about this variation as it appeared only during this occasion.

On May 2, 1958, the same day that Moffett Field-based VF(AW)-3 was decommissioned, San Diego-based FAWTUPAC was redesignated VF(AW)-3! The squadron was relieved of its all weather training duties, Detachment Bravo was disbanded, and the unit assumed the full time role of air defense.

As the only Navy unit in NORAD, All Weather Fighter Squadron Three became one of the most unique of Navy outfits, in more ways than one. They not only continued to fly their F3D's well into the 1960s, but were equipped with anywhere from 25 to 31 Skyrays, most probably making them the largest non-training squadron in the Navy.

In nearly five years of VF(AW)-3 operations with the F4D-1, usually only Skyrays with nose numbers up to 18 carried their full paint scheme. The remainder displayed

only the unit's "PA" modex, with nose numbers reaching into the 50s. The original FAWTUPAC scheme was modified somewhat over the years as the Air Force Air Defense Command shield was often carried on the canopy, although this was sometimes partially obscured by the blue spine paint. At least one Skyray was decorated with white stars on the Blue field, although the lightning bolt remained yellow.

The pilots of VF(AW)-3 were as colorful as the aircraft they flew. The squadron, nicknamed the "Blue Nemesis," was split into four flights, with each flight trying to outdo the other by adopting nicknames, non-standard headgear (beret, derby hats, etc.) to promote a special espirit de corps.

VF(AW)-3 racked up an impressive list of achievements, among these two consecutive Air Force "A" awards for 1959 and 1960, winning the "Top Gun" competition at the Fourth Annual Naval Air Weapons Meet at Yuma in 1959, a flight safety award in 1960, and final Navy Unit Commendation in March 1963.

The squadron deployed a detachment of F4D-1s to NAS Key West during the 1961 Cuban alert. By 1963, however, the Skyrays had long been obsolete and the squadron was decommissioned on March 4 of that year, bringing an end to one of the most colorful of Navy Skyray squadrons.

TOP - F4D-1 134777 taking off from Los Angeles International Airport in the first "Factory-To-Fleet" delivery to VC-3 at NAS Moffett Field, CA., on 4-16-56. (Douglas) Note squadron insignia on canopy, black tail stripe, medium grey radome and dark grey anti-glare panel. (Douglas) BOTTOM - F4D-1 134777 with a new nose number 22. Note that main wheel spats have been removed (Balogh via Menard)

Side view of 777; note small missile pylon. (Balogh via Menard)

F4D-1 134786. (Larkins)

ABOVE - F4D-1 134757 at Moffett on 5-19-56, note crudely applied NP and 20 and absence of squadron tail band and designation. (Larkins) BOTTOM F4D-1 134780 with VFAW-3 replacing VC-3 on the spine (Besecker)

Three Moffett-based VF(AW)-3 Fords and the FAWTUPAC line at North Island. TOP - 134794. (Harry Gann) MIDDLE - 134850 and 134849 with new TT tail code on 5-18-57. (Larkins) BOTTOM - 134788 in the foreground in Aug. 1956

TOP - Two FAWTUPAC Skyrays leave the squadron's line at NAS North Island in Aug. 1956. MIDDLE- Same two Fords 134784, number 31, and 134796, number 33, in flight (National Archives) BOTTOM - The only FAWTUPAC Skyray to be painted in this red trim leaves the runway at NAAS El Centro, CA. during the Naval Weapons Meet on 4-18-58. See the back cover for color. (Douglas)

TOP - Two FAWTUPAC Fords prior to launch in Aug. 1956: 134790, number 35, and 134796, number 33. (National Archives) MIDDLE - 134905 in flight; note tail code PA is now slanted. (Via Kaston) BOTTOM - FAWTUPAC F4D-1 134908 over El Centro on 4-14-58 during the Air Weapons Meet. New scheme is dark insignia blue spine, tail, and drop tanks with yellow stars and lightning bolt and white lettering on the tail. (USN) See color Section.

VF (AW)-3: MISSION AND OPERATIONS

Dreesen reported to VF(AW)-3 at NAS North Island in January 1959—the only Navy West Coast squadron attached to the Air Defense Command. It was established with two missions in mind. One was the air defense role, in which they were tied in completely with the NORAD system, working under the 27th Air Division with nearby F-101B and F-106 units. The second mission was to provide fighter detachments to go aboard the newly converted ASW carriers-13 Essex and Oriskany class carriers such as the Lake Champlain and the Intrepid. The idea was to put 4-6 plane F4D detachments on these CVS's. When Dreesen got his orders to report to VF(AW)-3, the squadron was getting ready to stand up the CVS detachments. But by the time he reported, someone had gotten around to reading the carqual reports from Pax River, which said that the F4D was totally incompatible with the Essex and Oriskany CVS class carriers. (He had left Pax before the carquals took place and wasn't aware of the results.) Those Essex and Oriskany class carriers that retained the CVA role and designation had been upgraded—steam cats instead of hydraulics and heavier arresting gear with larger and stronger wires. Those which became CVS's retained the hydraulic cats and older arresting gear, and the Pax reports clearly showed that the arresting gear wire size couldn't handle the F4D. According to Dreesen, there was an attempt to put F4D's on the Hornet, but a pilot was killed on one of the first landing attempts when a wire broke. The CVS fighter concept was realized later, but with A4's from special "VSF" squadrons and from detachments of regular Marine VMA squadrons.

VF(AW)-3 was, in Dreesen's words, "a very peculiar squadron." One advantage was that at a time of relative austerity and lowered flight hours for pilots, the squadron was able to convince the Navy that they needed extra money to meet the Air Force air defense syllabus requirements and then to convince the Air Force that they required more flight authorization to keep current by Navy standards. As a consequence they wound up with more flying than the other Pacific Fleet fighter squadrons and more than most west coast Air Force fighter units as well. Dreesen found in looking over his logs that he accumulated more jet time in a short period with VF(AW)-3 than during any other fighter squadron period in his career.

VF(AW)-3 flew the F4D in a fully loaded configuration— two wing tanks and four 7-short FFAR rockets pods or two rocket pods and two Sidewinders. The rockets weren't very accurate; they all went forward, but you could only count on one being in the vicinity of the target and the others spread around it. That was usually the result when firing at towed targets—one on and the other six in the general area. The squadron also carried NavPacs on their aircraft. The F4D's carried TACAN for carrier use, and all the West Coast NAS's had TACAN, but most of the Air Force bases and civilian airfields they operated from still used VOR. All this "junk" made it a considerably different aircraft from the one he'd flown at Pax, with the effects on stability noted above.

The F4D's rather small high-pressure tires tended to hydroplane when landing on wet runways, and this caused a problem at North Island, since the runway lined up with the GCA was only 7,000 feet long. Anytime you landed on that runway with any cross wind and a wet runway, it was nip and tuck whether you'd get it stopped without taking the arresting gear. The SOP for landing on a wet runway without wind was to kill the engine, since it produced 600-800 pounds of thrust at idle, and that reduced your stopping margin. If everything looked OK after rollout, you would then relight the engine at 30-40% RPM, then taxi in to the squadron line. Since the electrical generators ran off the engine, during the time when your engine was off the pilot had only the minimal light supplied by the battery. It became a matter of pride in the squadron to never take the arresting gear when the runway was wet—you cut the engine but had the aircraft well enough controlled to relight it towards the end of the roll and taxi in.

Dreesen described the AN/APQ-50F radar as "very good, only a little below that installed in the early Phantoms." There were four scope ranges— 12, 24, 100, and 200 miles. The standard intercept flight against a big aircraft (B-47/707 Neptune size) would be to pick up the target between 80 and 100 miles, track it to the 24 mile scope range, and then do a fire control lock-on. The fire control solution was a locked radar and a circle/dot presentation and a single line showing distance to target. The outer circle had a little notch which indicated the closure rate-clockwise movement of the notch around the circle meant an increasing closure rate, and vice versa for counterclockwise movement. As the firing range was approached, the circle decreased in size and a dot would appear. The idea was to arrive at the firing position with the circle closed up tight and the dot dead center. If this sounds complicated, it was. Assuming you were flying a barrier patrol at loiter speed when you received the intercept assignment, you were trying to center a dot in a shrinking circle around which a notch is moving—and just as you're accelerating to fight speed you have to deal with the tremendous longitudinal pitchdown already mentioned. Dreesen wryly noted that flying an intercept under these conditions "required a little more headwork than usual by both the pilot and the GCI (or CIC) operator."

The standard intercept run was to try to set up a lead collision course from 135 degrees and slide back to 90 degrees, but trying to fire with at least a 90 degree angle— that is, 45 to 90 degrees lead collision firing from the 12 O'clock position. If the target was too fast or if the pilot got sucked on the run, they'd slide back and convert it to a lead pursuit Sidewinder run.

VF(AW)-3 kept two aircraft on alert and four more on a standby alert. Their primary GCI site was in the mountains east of San Diego. The established procedure was that if there hadn't been an actual alert flight by the end of an 8-hour watch, the alert pilots going off duty would get a practice alert launch as soon as their relief came on. They'd go out and "butt heads"— the wingman would make runs on the leader for the first half hour, and then they'd switch. It made for lots of flight time.

Toward the end of his time with VF(AW)-3 , the squadron underwent the same kind of Operational Readiness Inspection (ORI) done to the Air Force interceptor units. During the actual intercept portions of the ORI, the F4D's were observed by Air Force pilots flying F-104s. They found the F-104s had a hard time staying with them at the loiter speed at which they flew while waiting for intercepts. In order to stay with them the Starfighters would have to wallow around or fly in circle at high speeds— they couldn't duplicate the F4D's low-speed capability. The standard joke was that once the Ford started chasing something the F-104 would go to burner but then have to throttle back to stay behind the F4D.

Dreesen noted that for new pilots straight from Training Command or for those with little fleet time, the VF(AW)-3 training syllabus was "so long as to be economically unsupportable—justifiable only in the sense that it was such a damn strange airplane." The transition time was much greater than for a standard squadron.

He saw the F4D's main problem as timing. It was to have been a second generation jet, but didn't really get to the fleet until the third generation (Crusader and Phantom) came along. "The delay made it a one-tour airplane—most squadrons had it for only one or two cruises." VF(AW)-3, in contrast, flew it for almost five years, keeping it until the squadron was decommissioned in March of 1963.

"With all its peculiarities, it was a fun aircraft to fly."

TOP - CDR. Gene Valencia, CO of VF(AW)-3 (Douglas) BOTTOM - Typical PR photo showing a VFAW-3 Ford armament and its support team. (Douglas)

TOP - F4D-1 134802 on 8-19-61, note NORAD insignia on canopy and three Western Air Defense Force flags on nose. (Harry Gann) MIDDLE - 134772 in flight. Note wing code, (Douglas) BOTTOM - VF(AW)-3 line with 134893 in foreground, then 139080 and 139107. (Douglas)

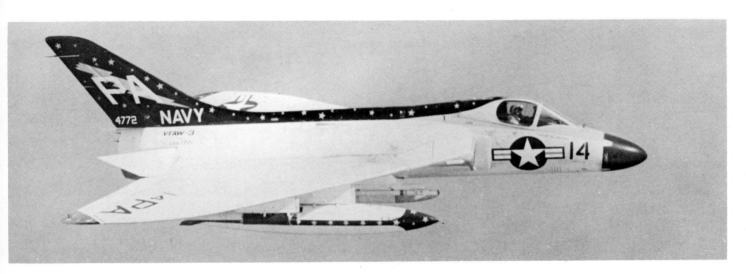

TOP - 134898 with red and white NavPac and unusual natural metal intake leading edges at Moffett on 4-29-61. (Larkins) MIDDLE - 134954 used as a target tug at the Air Gunnery Meet. Note Del Mar device. (Bulban) BOTTOM - 139164 at North Island. (via Wiliams)

NAVY LIAISON OFFICER

The Navy Liaison Officer, Edwards AFB, Ca., was assigned F4D-1 134769 as seen here in 1957. All markings are black with "RAY II" written on the nose. (R.N. Cooper)

The Navy Liaison Officer, Edwards AFB, California, was assigned F4D-1 134769 from August 1956 to April 1958. The airplane was painted in a somewhat unusual scheme with a broad black band high on the tail, a black radome tapering rearward to a point just forward of the national insignia, black drop tank noses (except for the tips) tapering rearward, "769" painted in very large numerals on the drop tanks, and the inscription "Ray II" painted on the nose below the windscreen.

COLOR PAGE AT RIGHT
TOP - XF4D-1 124587 in flight. (Douglas) ABOVE LEFT - XF4D-1 124586 landing (USN) ABOVE RIGHT - XF4D-1 124587 with gear doors closing on takeoff. (USN) AT LEFT - XF4D-1 124586 at China Lake in 1962 prior to its destruction (Via Jim Sullivan) BOTTOM - F4D-130745 that set five time-to-climb records on May 22-23, 1958.(USN)

TOP - F4D-1 130747 from NATC Flight Test on a carrier deck edge elevator (Via Kasiuba) MIDDLE - F4D-1 134938 of the Naval Air Development Unit in May 1957 (Candid Aero Files) BOTTOM - VU-3 F-6A 139143 at NAS North Island on 5-2-64 (Swisher)

TOP - 139143 from Flight Test Division of NATC at moment of launch. (USN) MIDDLE - F-6A 134806 from the Test Pilot School in slow flight in Oct. 1966 (Phil Oestricher) BOTTOM VF(AW)-3 F4D-1 134756 firing 2.75" rockets. (Douglas)

TOP - Yellow tails of VF-2? Fords on 8-10-75. (Larkin? MIDDLE - VF-102 F4D with fuel tank refueling probe at the Paris Airshow on 5-25-6? (Via Nicolau) BOTTOM - V? 74 F4D at MCAA's Yuma o? 12-3-59. Note red painted US? INTREPID below tail on the rear fuselage. (Swisher)

TOP - Naval Air Test Facility F4D-1 134854 being readied for launch from the XRE-1 expeditionary catapult in 1963 (USN) MIDDLE - NAS Olathe Reserve F-6A 139083 at MCAS El Toro during two week ACDUTRA of VMF(AW)-215 on 7-24-64. (USN) BOTTOM - NMC F4D-1 134856 at Point Mugu in April 1961. Rig under wing is for aerial target towing. (Douglas Olson)

TOP - VF(AW)-3 F4D-1 at NAS North Island on 8-22-59. (Swisher) MIDDLE - VMF(AW)-115 F4D-1 at Ping Tung (North) Formosa in June 1958. (Harold Caldwell via R. Picciani) BOTTOM - VMF(AW)-114 F4D-1 at MCAS Cherry Point in 1958. Note open engine door and sway brace for drop tank pylon. (Jack Gagen)

TOP - VMF(AW)-542 F4D-1 over Mount Fuji in 1963. (Jacques Naviaux) MIDDLE - Lt. Naviaux in his Ford's cockpit over Japan (Naviaux) BOTTOM - VMF(AW)-513 F4D at El Toro. (Douglas)

TOP - VMF(AW)-114 F4D-1 lands aboard the USS Franklin D. Roosevelt in Dec. 1958 with a day-glow trimmed VMF(AW)-513 Ford in the foreground. (Jack Gagen) BELOW - FDR flight deck in 1957 with VF-74 F4Ds on deck. Note squadrons insignia on the rear portion of the canopy and CVG-17s "AL" tail code. (Bill Davis)

TOP - VF(AW)-3 line showing 14 Fords with 12 in full markings. (Douglas) MIDDLE - VF(AW)-3 F4D-1 scrambles with sidewinders and rocket pods (Krause) BOTTOM - Squadron line with 26 Fords, 16 in full markings, note USAF F-102s at right. (via Williams)

VX-3

Air Development Squadron Three was formed on November 20, 1948, by merging two squadrons of CVLG-1, VF-1L and VA-1L, and was placed under the operational control of Commander Operational Development Force. VX-3's main mission was threefold: to evaluate new and already existing naval aircraft, airborne equipment and methods; recommend methods for the most effective tactical employment of aircraft and equipment; and to recommend training procedures and countermeasures for these aircraft and methods. Base at NAS Atlantic City, New Jersey, VX-3 boasted some of the Navy's most experienced aviators, and from 1948 until decommissioning flew nearly every new model of carrier-based aircraft in the fleet.

The squadron received its first Skyray on January 8, 1957, and began an extensive operational evaluation program with the F4D-1, its weapons and equipment. In April 1957, VX-3 took the Skyray aboard the USS Roosevelt (CVA-42) for carrier qualifications and advanced work on the TACAN project (OP/V175), and in June moved aboard the USS Saratoga (CVA-60) for carquals and all-weather evaluations on the TACAN project. By the fall of 1957, VX-3 operated seven Skyrays on its various projects.

VX-3 pilots spent two weeks aboard the USS Forrestal (CVA-59) in April 1958 for carrier qualifications with the F4D-1 and more TACAN project flights. IN May 1958, VX-3 transferred operations to NAS Oceana, Virginia Beach, Virginia. Still more carrier qualifications with the Skyray were flown by squadron pilots aboard the USS Independence (CVA-62) in August 1959.

Initial markings carried on VX-3 Skyrays consisted only of the unit's "XC" tail code, "VX-3" on the spine, and a squadron identification number on the nose. In mid-1957, the squadron's tail code was changed to "JC." As far as is known, the squadron's insignia was never carried on their Skyrays. This insignia, approved in April 1949, featured a gray sundial (an instrument of time denoting progress and growth), gold wings (denoting flight), a light-blue aircraft with red exhaust (denoting fast progress over time), and black Roman numerals on a black background with red outer circle.

VX-3 planned to move operations to NAS Roosevelt Roads, Puerto Rico, in February 1960. The squadron instead was decommissioned on March 1, 1960, and its Skyrays were transferred elsewhere in the fleet.

VX-3

VX-3 Ford with "JC" tail code at NAS Chincoteaque, Va. on 9-4-58. Note sidewinder mounted on outer wing. (USN)

F4D-1 134865 in early 1957 with initial XC tail code, note nose number duplicated on tail. (Bowers collection)

A VX-3 F4D-1 with the later "JC" tail code in April 1958 aboard the USS Forestal (CVA-59) (Tailhook photo service)

VU-3

Utility Squadron Three was commissioned in December 1948 at NAS Santa Ana, California, and assigned the mission of furnishing radio-controlled drone aircraft for fleet target practice. After moves to NAS Miramar in 1950, NAAS Ream Field, Imperial Beach, in 1951, and NAAS Brown Field, San Ysidro, in 1956, VU-3 settled in at NAS North Island, San Diego, in 1961.

When the squadron's aging KDA jet targets and FJ-3D2 control aircraft were unable to keep pace with modern fleet missile requirements, they were replaced by the high-performance Q2C pilotless aircraft targets, with the F4D-1 serving as the new drone control and chase aircraft. The first Skyrays began arriving early in 1962, and were reconfigured to provide airborne drone control capability. Due to these modifications, the Skyrays were redesignated as DF-6As, although this change was not painted on the aircraft. In addition to drone control, these VU-3 Skyrays were used "to provide Air Intercept Controller training for personnel on board fleet destroyers, cruisers, carriers, and personnel in training at the Fleet Anti-Air Warfare Training Center."

At the time of VU-3's acquisition of the Skyray, the squadron insignia was that originally approved in March 1949: a yellow drone bee with black stripes on its back, red wings and tail, and brown feet, operating a white control box. This insignia was replaced in October 1962 with a design "based on the consideration that manpower is the predominant asset even in a technological climate. The reservoir of knowledge of the trained manpower is represented by the book. The trustworthiness and dedication of these men is depicted by the Nordic fidelity symbol in the left hand. The scope of the mission of UTRON-3 includes such task assignments as the operation of five types of pilotless aircraft targets, high-performance intercept services, and the Fleet Introduction of the DASH

VU-3

weapons system; therefore, the large red "V" denotes the Versatility of Utility." This squadron insignia was often displayed on the Skyray's aft canopy surfaces. Markings carried on VU-3 Skyrays included orange da-glo tail, outer wings and nose band, and da-glo designs on each wing tank nose and tail, although these markings varied considerably on each of the squadron to use the F4D-1s.

As the last operational Navy squadron to use the F4D-1, VU-3 performed an honorary retirement ceremony for the Skyray on October 16, 1964. After flying one last operational mission, squadron pilots ferried the aircraft to NAF Litchfield Park, Arizona, for a well-earned rest.

TOP - Five VU-3 Fords in Jan 1964. BuNos (bottom to top) are 139153, 139143, 139137, 139161 and 139166. (USN) See 139143 in the color section. MIDDLE - Closer view of 131961 with day-glo tail, outer wings and area behind canopy. Fin tip is red and drop tanks are trimmed in day-glo outlined in black. Note squadron insignia behind canopy (USN) BOTTOM - F6A 139047 at NAF Litchfield Park on 3-23-64. Note day-glo band behind radome and black fin tip.

TOP - F-6A 139122 at North Island on 5-2-64. (Clay Jansson) MIDDLE - 122 again at the Douglas Long Beach plant. Day-glo nose stripe and tail show up well in this photo. Note that this seems to be the only VU-3 F-6A with a white rudder instead of day-glo. Drop tanks and NavPac have day-glo noses. (Harry Gann) BOTTOM - F-6A 139153 also at Long Beach with day-glo tail, outer wings, nose stripe and bar above National insignia. Note day-glo area behind cockpit with insignia on it. Radome and fin tip are off-white and leading edges are natural metal. Both Skyrays were at Long Beach as demonstrators for the government of India, to whom Douglas was attempting to sell them aircraft. (Harry Gann)

EARLY VU-3 INSIGNIA

Naval Air Missile Test Center insignia

Naval Missile Center

The U.S. Naval Air Missile Test Center, Pt. Mugu, California, received its first Douglas Skyray in February 1958 when F4D-1 134752 was used for five months after being transferred from the Douglas Testing Division. Over the following four years the renamed Naval Missile Center operated at least four additional Skyrays, 130748, 134763, 134856 and 134875, using them as missile launch platforms, target tugs, and chase aircraft. One of the more unusual NMC missions with the Skyray began in July 1961 when 134856 launched the first of 10 Sparroair unguided sounding rockets. Powered by two Sparrow air-to-air rocket motors, the Sparroair eventually succeeded in reaching a height of 64 miles.

Generally, these Naval Missile Center Skyrays were painted nearly identically in a standard gull gray/gloss white scheme with an orange da-glo nose and lower forward fuselage, wings and tail surfaces, with "Naval Missile Center" stepped back on the tail in large block letters. The first insignia of the original Naval Air Missile Test Center, approved in December 1948, featured a stylized missile and aviator's wings in a circular design. In September 1961 the renamed U.S. Naval Missile Center adopted a triangular insignia.

While most NMC Skyrays were flown by the center for less than a year, F4D-1 134856 lasted at least until 1962. It is assumed that the difficulty of maintaining the Skyray by this late date in the airplane's service life precluded its continued use with the Naval Missile Center.

F4D-1 134856 in colorful white and day-glo markings at NAS Point Mugu on 5-19-62 (Swisher) see color section.

TOP - 134856 with prototype Sparrow II. Note "Moon" racing eyes on radome. (Wyckoff) MIDDLE LEFT - 856 with Sparroair air sampling vehicle in June 1961. Good view of wing fold. (USN) MIDDLE RIGHT - Grey and white 134875 with prototype Crow missile. (USN) BOTTOM - 875 again with added day-glo nose stripe, tail and outer wings and carrying an AQM-37 target. Note white canopy. (USN)

Two views of 875 being thawed out after being frozen inside the climatic chamber at Pt. Mugu at -20 degrees F. (USN) BOTTOM - 875 today after being repainted blue and left to rot in a park in Oxnard, Ca. (Williams)

AIR DEVELOPMENT SQUADRON FOUR

VX-4

Air Development Squadron Four was commissioned on September 15, 1952, when the Commander Naval Air Force, Pacific Fleet directed Cdr. James G. Sliney to form and command the squadron at the Naval Missile Center, Point Mugu, California. The squadron's mission was to conduct projects dealing with the evaluation of air-launched guided missiles, namely the Sparrow I. VX-4's mission evolved into the development of a missile or missile component and its best use as a weapon, to conduct tests and evaluations of aircraft weapons systems and support systems in an operational environment, and to develop all-weather intercept tactics for air-launched guided missiles.

The Vanguards of VX-4 initially were equipped with the F7U and F3D, but with the advent of the Bullpup and Sparrow III missiles, the squadron acquired the FJ, A4D, F3H, F8U and F4D-1 for advanced missile test programs. The first Skyray arrived at VX-4 late in June 1959, repor-

ABOVE - VX-4 F4D-1 134952 in a near vertical climb on 4-18-60. Colors are standard grey and white with black lettering (USN) BELOW - 134963 at Pt. Mugu in 1959, note unknown store on NavPac pylon (Wyckoff)

tedly being used "to evaluate new weapons and missiles, and to develop new methods of attack." VX-4 apparently never operated more than two Skyrays, serial numbers 134952 and 134963. These aircraft carried only the squadron's "XF" tail code, "VX-4" on the rear fuselage, and nose numbers 12 and 15 respectively. Although exact dates of the retirement of VX-4's Skyrays are not known, it is assumed that these aircraft did not last with the squadron beyond 1961.

Naval Air Facility, China Lake

The U.S. Naval Air Facility, China Lake, California (U.S. Naval Air Facility, Inyokern prior to July 26, 1955), provides support to the U.S. Naval Ordnance Test Station (NOTS) China Lake, for research, development, test and evaluation of guided missiles, aircraft weapons delivery systems, aircraft rockets and rocket launchers, aviation fire control systems and underwater ordnance. Since its establishment in 1944, NAF China Lake has conducted virtually all of the flight testing of NOTS-developed ordnance, including the 5" HVAR, Tiny Tim, Mighty Mouse, Zuni, Shrike and Sidewinder missiles.

By the mid-1950s, NAF China Lake maintained approximately 20 different models of aircraft, including a total of at least five F4D-1 Skyrays. The first NAF F4D-1, 130747, arrived at China Lake in August 1956 after serving duty with the Douglas Testing Division. This airplane, along with another ex-Douglas Testing Division Skyray, 130745, were used during 1958 as satellite launch platforms in a unique NOTS-sponsored program, the Naval Observational Television Satellite project.

During the four years NAF China Lake operated the F4D-1, these aircraft appeared in both the earlier overall glossy blue paint scheme and later gull gray and gloss white markings. As far as is known, the only distinguishing markings carried on the aircraft were the words "China Lake" painted high on the tail, with the last three digits of the airplane's serial number displayed on the nose.

In any event, five Skyrays (130745, 130747, 134762,

134765 and 134853) flew for varying periods under the NAF China Lake banner. Their last F4D-1, 130745, was stricken at China Lake in October 1960 after accumulating only 137 flight hours while in service at the Naval Air Facility.

F4D-1 130747 assigned to China Lake in June of 1957 while testing "Fat Boy." Note medium grey radome and white pylon and pitch trimmer. The chase plane is an FJ-4B; note the two VMCJ-3 Skynights and the JD-1. (USN)

Naval Air Facility, China Lake

TOP - Douglas Testing Division F4D-1 134752 on loan to China Lake on 5-11-56. Colors are standard grey and white with red wing and tail stripes and two inch stripes on speed brakes and main gear doors. Note Testing Division insignia on the tail (USN) MIDDLE - F4D-1 134762 is representative of several ex-Douglas Testing Division Skyrays which flew for China Lake. Overall white with red markings as above plus a red stripe on the aft canopy surface and "China Lake" painted in black on the tail band. (Douglas via Colapietro) AT RIGHT - F4D-1 134853 at Litchfield Park on 3-18-63. (Swisher)

NIGHT CAPPERS

VF-13

The "Night Cappers" of VF-13, based at NAS Cecil Field, Florida, began transitioning from the F9F-8 to the F4D-1 in January and February 1959. Less than four years later VF-13 was the last Navy squadron to make an operational carrier deployment with the Skyray.

The squadron went aboard the USS Randolph (CVA-15) in April 1959 for carrier qualifications as part of Carrier Air Group 10. The following month VF-13 boarded the USS Essex (CVA-9) for training operations before a planned Mediterranean deployment. From August 1959 until February 1960 the Essex joined the Sixth Fleet in the Mediterranean. This cruise marked the first successful deployment of the F4D-1 aboard a carrier equipped with the outdated hydraulic catapults.

The markings VF-13 Skyrays carried at this time were rather elaborate. The entire upper elevon surface of each wing was painted with seven red and six white stripes, with a small black star centered in each stripe. The lower half of the rudder was painted to represent the squadron's emblem: black and red fields separated by a diagonal "bar sinister" in black. This was used to indicate the squadron's "outcast" origin when it was formed in September 1948 by taking personnel and aircraft from VF-11 and VF-12 to provide another fighter squadron for Carrier Air Group One. The squadron motto, "Potentia et Potestias" means the "will and the might."

Essex-based VF-13 Skyrays carried the tail code "AK," indicating Carrier Air Group Ten, and their squadron insignia was placed behind the cockpit window. Although VF-13 Skyrays used the CVG-10 "AK" modex throughout their career, the emblem was infrequently displayed on their aircraft subsequent to this deployment aboard the Essex.

VF-13 carried this colorful paint scheme at least until early 1961, but it was subsequently altered (by eliminating

TOP - VF-13 F4D-1 134827 aboard the USS Shangri La (CVA-38) in Aug. 1960. Note odd size serial number on tail. BOTTOM - The last two digits of nose number of F4D-1 139204 is repeated on the upper and lower wing-tips. (Robin Walker)

the elevon stripes and stars) due to the maintenance involved. After this date VF-13 Skyrays carried only the rudder insignia and a small red band on the fin.

The squadron returned from their Med cruise aboard the Essex in February 1960, but three months later left Cecil Field for operations off Guantanamo Bay, Cuba aboard the USS Shangri-La (CVA-38). VF-13 continued to fly aboard the Shangri-La in August and September 1960 during NATO exercises in the North Atlantic. In November 1960, VF-13, aboard the Shangri-La again as part of CVG-10, was sent to the Caribbean as part of a deterrent force there to "preserve peace."

In February 1961, VF-13's Skyrays were equipped with drop tanks fitted for in-flight refueling, and the squadron again deployed to the Mediterranean aboard the Shangri-La as part of the Sixth Fleet.

The Dominican Crisis forced the Shangri-La into an early return to Mayport in May 1961. Three weeks later VF-13 and the Shangri-La were on station in the Caribbean as part of the emergency force during the crisis. VF-13 returned in mid-June and spent the remainder of 1961 alternating between operations aboard ship and ashore for carrier qualifications, VIP cruises, and an Operational Readiness Inspection.

VF-13 deployed aboard the Shangri-La in February 1962 for its third Mediterranean cruise with the F4D-1s. The last operation carrier flight by a Navy Skyray took place aboard the Shangri-La in August 1962 with Cdr. Hjalmer E. Swanson, VF-13 Executive Officer, at the controls.

The squadron returned to Cecil Field in early September 1962, and on the 14th of that month began transitioning to the F3H-2 Demon.

TOP - VF-13 F4D-1 on final for landing aboard the USS Essex (CVA-9) on 1-8-60 (USN) BOTTOM - Three VF-13 Fords lay damaged aboard CVA-9 after a cart wheeling fighter crashed into them on its way over the side. (via Williams)

TOP - 139120 taking waveoff from CVA-38 on 1-12-61. (USN) MIDDLE - 134874 launches from CVA-38 on 1-12-61; elevon stripes are red and white with black stars. (USN) BOTTOM - Four VF-13 Skyrays over Cannes in June of 1962. Rudder is red below and black above and the nose number is repeated on a red stripe below the fin tip. (USN)

VF-13

TOP - Two VF-13 Fords over the Med with refueling probes on the left drop tanks. (USN) BOTTOM - 139117 and 134919 at Litchfield Park on 3-18-63. Note VF-13 F4D-1 with nose numbers repeated on the drop tanks. (Swisher)

VF-23

NAS Moffett Field's VF-23 began its association with the F4D-1 Skyray in December 1956, having returned three months earlier from an Air Task Group Four Western Pacific cruise aboard the USS Yorktown (CVA-10). The squadron began replacing its F2H-3s with the F4D-1 on December 11, and soon painted the Skyrays' tails yellow (except for the fin cap) with ATG-4's "ND" tail code in black bordered by two horizontal black bands. In a unique departure from other Navy Skyray outfits, each airplane's entire serial number was painted in large black numerals below the lower black band. The squadron insignia, a white skull with a flaming dagger in its mouth, superimposed over blue electron rings, had been adopted in June 1955, but was not carried on the Skyrays.

VF-23 spent the next year in a hectic training schedule before a planned February WestPac cruise. Thirteen squadron F4D-1s were brought aboard the USS Hornet (CVA-12) on September 20, 1957, for carrier qualifications with ATG-4. VF-23 returned to Moffett Field on October 11, and on the 29th was detached from ATG-4 and transferred to Carrier Air Group 15. The squadron was at NAS Miramar from November 3-7 for practice firing of the Sidewinder missile, aboard the USS Hancock (CVA-19) on December 3-13 for further carrier qualifications, again aboard the Hancock from January 7-24, 1958, for night carquals, and finally spent Jan. 26-31 at NAAS Fallon, Nevada, for gunnery practice.

On February 15, 1958, VF-23 began its first— and last— deployment with the F4D-1 when it sailed westward aboard the Hancock. Their Skyrays now were colorfully painted with two yellow "rays" bordered in black on the tail, CVG-15's "NL" tail code in slanted black letters, and two similar black-bordered yellow rays on each drop tank, which also sported black noses. The area separating each pair of yellow rays was painted gloss white. The last four digits of each airplane's serial number was painted in large numbers at the base of the tail and rudder, and 200-series nose numbers were carried.

While aboard the Hancock, VF-23 participated in a weapons demonstration for Asian military leaders from May 20-23, 1958, and "Knockout," a one-week exercise

from June 9-17 in which fleet units simulated conventional and nuclear warfare in the Western Pacific. On July 2, VF-23 Skyrays provided convoy and task force Combat Air Patrol (CAP) to defend against strikes launched from the USS Shangri-La (CVA-38) during exercise "Rex 58 Oscar." Finally, the F4Ds of VF-23 acted as Combat Air Patrol and sweep aircraft on July 12 and August 9 in "Blue Sky," a joint U.S.-Nationalist Chinese exercise. After returning to NAS Moffett Field on October 3, 1958, VF-23 received a commendation for outstanding performance during the cruise by the Commander of Carrier Division One, Rear Admiral Paul H. Ramsey.

Upon its return, VF-23 almost immediately began transition training to the F3H-2. By January 1959 the squadron had ceased operations with the Skyray. VF-23 was redesignated as VF-151 in mid-February, and began preparing for another WestPac with its new Demons.

134786 at NAS Miramar, Ca. on 8-10-57. VF-23 Fords had yellow tails with black stripes, see color section. (Larkins)

TOP - 134817 on 8-10-57 with ATG-4's "ND" tail code. (Larkins) MIDDLE - 134794 on the taxiway at Miramar. (NASM) BOTTOM - 134891 on board the USS Hancock (CVA-19) in 1958. Note CVG-15's "NL" tail code and yellow rays bordered in black. (Tailhook photo service)

VF-51

Located some 60 miles south of El Toro, home of the longest-lived F4D-1 squadron. NAS Miramar provided the home base for one of the shortest-lived Skyray units: VF-51.

The Screaming Eagles of VF-51 returned in October 1958 from carrier qualifications with their newly acquired F11F-1s but wasted little time in exchanging their Tigers for Skyrays. As the F4D-1s began to arrive in January 1959, the squadron applied few markings to the aircraft: "NF" on the tail, "VF-51" on the fuselage, a nose number, and red tail caps containing the last digit of the nose number in white.

These markings were carried at least into mid-1959. However, the pilots of VF-51 felt that these colors were a little drab for an outfit nicknamed the Screaming Eagles, and a new set of markings were designed and quickly applied to their Skyrays. Three stylized red talons were now carried on each side of the fuselage and drop tanks. Satisfied with their new-found identity, VF-51 operated their Fords with this scheme for several months.

However, a "running battle" between the squadron and COMNAVAIRPAC developed over the markings. Roy Johnston, Commanding Officer of VF-51 at the time, comments. "Our markings were not spectacular, but in those days COMNAVAIRPAC considered even that little bit of color too flamboyant and we were requested to revert to standard gray with normal markings."

The squadron reluctantly complied and, in October 1959, boarded the USS Ticonderoga (CVA-14) for carrier qualifications, sans talons.

On March 5, 1960 VF-51 embarked aboard the Tico again for their only WestPac with the Skyrays, attached to CVG-15. The squadron returned to San Diego on October 11, and by November 1960 had begun to convert to F-8 Crusaders.

SCREAMING EAGLES

VF-51 F4D-1 139147 aboard the USS Ticonderoga (CVA-14) during its only carrier deployment with the Skyray in 1960. Note red fin cap with white number 4. (USN)

TOP - 139058 and 139089 sporting the Screaming Eagles' stylized red talons on the fuselage and drop tanks on 12-3-59. (Swisher) MIDDLE - 139160 in flight with fuselage talons removed, although talons are still present on drop tanks. (USN) BOTTOM - 139192 about to be washed by its pilot after he landed at the wrong field and grafitti had been applied to his Ford. Note FAGU emblem below wind screen and 192 repeated on drop tank(USN)

VF-74

The "Be-Devilers" of Fighter Squadron 74 was one of the most active of Navy Skyray squadrons, operating the airplane for five years on three Mediterranean cruises. The squadron also was instrumental in the development of in-flight refueling procedures with the F4D-1.

VF-74 became one of the first fleet units to receive the F4D-1, as a small number of officers from the squadron had participated in the Fleet Introduction Program early in 1956. These men served as a nucleus for further training of VF-74 pilots. The first Skyray arrived at the squadron facilities at NAS Oceana, Virginia, on April 17, 1956. For several months, VF-74 Skyrays carried only the "C" tail code of Carrier Air Group Six. By the fall of 1956, these aircraft were given red rudder surfaces with six white stars (signifying CVG-6), a black-bordered red lightning bolt streaking downward across the forward fuselage, and 100-series nose numbers.

In April 1957, VF-74 went aboard the newly commissioned USS Saratoga (CVA-60), for carrier qualifications. Lt. Bill Davis, a pilot with the squadron now flying Boeing 737s, remembers, "President Eisenhower came down to Mayport, Florida, to view the Fleet [on June 6]. The Saratoga was tied up alongside the pier with the bow out, and with two VF-74 Skyrays stationed on the deck. The Columbine landed at Mayport and taxied right up to the pier. As Eisenhower left his airplane, the Navy band played 'Hail to the Chief,' and the two Skyrays were launched from the Saratoga. It was quite impressive!"

On July 9, 1957, VF-74 deployed aboard the USS Roosevelt (CVA-42) for a Mediterranean cruise with the Sixth Fleet. As part of Carrier Air Group 17, these 12 VF-74 Skyrays carried CVG-17's "AL" tail code, a black-bordered yellow tail band, a black-bordered yellow lightning bolt on the fuselage, and 200-series nose numbers. As this was the Skyray's first deployment with the Sixth Fleet, and its all-weather capabilities were untested, this change in color and nose numbers signified VF-74's status as the Air Group's "day fighter" squadron. The squadron's insignia of a purple devil's head squinting through a target sighting grid was carried on the rear portion of the canopy.

The Skyrays of VF-74 participated in many exercises while deploying aboard the Roosevelt to the Atlantic and Mediterranean. As part of NATO exercise "Strikeback," the squadron took part in exercise "Counter Punch" on September 19-21 and "Deepwater" on September 25-28. Further NATO operations included participation in exercises "Flip-Flop" from September 29 to October 30, and "Red Epoch" from October 31 to November 2. Final CVG-17 exercise "Ascendex" on January 22 and 27 and "Strikex" on February 10 required the squadron to from the Air Group's HI-CAP, High Altitude Combat Air Patrol. Bill Davis recalls, "During these CAP exercises, we would fly on a radial out to 100 miles from the ship in 10 or 20-mile racetrack patterns, in flights of two at 35,000 feet. One was outbound all the time so that we could effectively extend the ship's radar coverage. Once during exercises over Crete, I was sent out to investigate a bogey. He was a high flyer, a British Vulcan bomber. I was on trail with a couple of FJs. We had a chain behind him, so I stroked it into burner, which got me past the FJs. I got under the bogey enough to do a pitch-up to his altitude. The air is pretty thin up there and the sudden rotation was enough to disrupt the airflow, and I got compressor stalls. I eased out to

VF-74 insignia

let the air go straight in and she motored on up to the Vulcan, which was cruising at about 54,000 feet.!"

The Roosevelt and CVG-17 returned to port on February 28, 1958, and VF-74 settled in at NAS Oceana. The squadron was reattached to Carrier Air Group Six on March 3, when it participated in "Intex," a simulated ballistic missile attack on NAS Norfolk.

On February 13, 1959, VF-74 embarked aboard the USS Intrepid (CVA-11) for its second Med cruise. As part of CVG-6, the Skyrays carried the air group's "AF" tail code in small letters, a red rudder with six white stars, a yellow-bordered red lightning bolt on the forward fuselage, 100-series nose numbers, and, somewhat unusually, "USS Intrepid" on the rear fuselage in red block letters. During this time period, some VF-74 Skyrays carried red lightning bolts pointing rearward on each drop tank, with six white stars within each bolt.

From February 25 to March 1, VF-74 participated in "Big Deal," a combined Second Fleet-Six Fleet exercise conducted in the western Mediterranean Sea. Other exercises in which VF-74 Skyrays participated were "Top Weight" (April 13-16), when VF-74 flew CAP missions against opposing NATO bombers; "Greenswing" (April 20-22), where VF-74 flew CAP during a combined Sixth Fleet-Italian Armed Forces exercise; an unnamed exercise on May 7-8 when VF-74 flew CAP missions over the landing area for a U.S. Marine amphibious landing on Crete; and "White Bait" (June 21-26), a combined American, British and Libyan amphibious exercise on the coast of Libya, where VF-74 flew CAP against opposing NATO bombers over the force and landing area.

VF-74 returned to NAS Oceana on August 30, 1959, and began intensive training in all-weather air-to-air intercepts. During January and February 1960, a detachment of VF-74 Skyrays went aboard the USS Forrestal (CVA-59) for air defense exercises. After a short carrier qualification cruise in May, and participation in "Lantflex 60" in July, the Be-Devilers boarded the Intrepid on August 4 and departed Norfolk once again for a Sixth Fleet Med cruise with Carrier Air Group Six. Sporting the same colors as

TOP - VF-74 F4D-1 134756 on 5-19-56 (Clay Jansson)
MIDDLE - Poor but interesting twilight photo of early VF-74 Ford on an afterburner takeoff in 11-56. Red lightning bolt with black outline and red rudder with white stars added to CVG-6's "C" tail code. (USN) BOTTOM - Another poor but interesting photo of a VF-74 Ford, 134816, in the same scheme as above. (Tailhook photo service)

their previous deployment, VF-74 Skyrays participated in the NATO exercise "Flashback-Strikeback" from September 19-26, 1960, providing all-weather interception of simulated attacks, and night and day Combat Air Patrol.

This last Med cruise provided a Navy "first" for VF-74 Skyrays, as the first operational inflight Skyray refueling was made on August 13. The squadron maintenance officer had earlier proposed to ComNavAirLant a simple, inexpensive air refueling system for the F4D-1. The proposal was approved, and an A4D probe was attached to an F4D drop tank by O&R Jacksonville. Although only two test flights could be made with the new tank before deployment, by October all squadron pilots had qualified in aerial refueling, and the system was subsequently approved for use in the fleet.

In January 1961, VF-74 provided all-weather fighter support for the Sixth Fleet in exercise "Right Hook." The Be-Devilers of VF-74 returned from their last Med cruise with the F4D-1 on February 17, 1961, and, on July 8, the squadron received its first F4H-1 Phantom II.

TOP - 134868 aboard the USS Roosevelt (CVA-42) in 1957-58 with yellow lightning bolt and tail band, both outlined in black, and sporting CVG-17's "AL" tail code. Note Del Mar target. See color section. (Bill Davis) MIDDLE - 139150 with CVG-6's "AF" tail code. Note absence of drop tanks. (via Williams) BOTTOM - 139200 on 7-2-60. (R.T. O'Dell)

VF-74

TOP - 139113 at Norfolk, Va., on 4-15-61 with red lightning bolt with yellow outline and red rudder with white stars. Note squadron insignia on canopy and gull grey upper portion of drop tank. "Sexy Six" is written on the splitter plate with "USS Intrepid" on fuselage in red. AT RIGHT, TOP - 139184 over the Intrepid (via Williams) AT RIGHT, BOTTOM - VF-74 Skyray landing aboard CVA-11. (S. Krause) BOTTOM - VF-74 134860 at the Naval Air Weapons Meet. (via Williams) See color section.

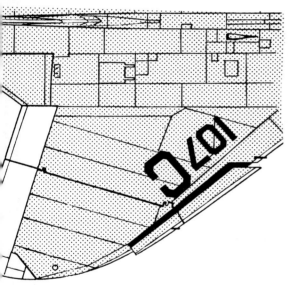

VF-101 Ford carrying a tow target and the squadrons first tail code, "J" for Air Task Group 201. (Joel Griggs)

VF-101

The Grim Reapers of VF-101 operated the Skyray in a variety of functions from 1956 to 1962. Commissioned at NAS Cecil Field, Florida, on May 1, 1952, VF-101 adopted the nickname and insignia of the famous WWII-era VF-10, while flying the F2H-3 Banshee.

The unit's F4D-1 Skyrays began arriving at Cecil Field in August 1956. Familiarization check-out flights began immediately, followed by an "intensive program in all-weather tactics such as broadcast control." The eventual arrival of radar-equipped Skyrays enabled the squadron to develop radar intercept procedures and practice early in 1957. In May 1957, while aboard the USS Roosevelt (CVA-42), VF-101 became the first Atlantic Fleet Skyray equipped squadron to completely day qualify, while night qualifications were completed aboard the USS Saratoga (CVA-60) in July.

These early VF-101 Skyrays carried only a "J" tail code, signifying Air Task Group 201, and 100-series nose numbers. The squadron apparently did not add any color until early 1957, when their F4Ds were given a small red tail band with four white stars, and red drop tanks markings also with four white stars, the four stars probably signifying the unit's permanent attachment to CVG-4.

VF-101 made its only carrier deployment with the Skyray when it departed aboard the Saratoga on September 3, 1957. Now carrying ATG-201's two-letter code, "AP," the squadron participated in a joint NATO exercise, "Operation Strikeback," while in North Atlantic waters. During this operation, VF-101 Skyrays joined in crossdeck exercises with the british carrier HMS Ark Royal. One F4D-1, piloted by Lt. Max K. Morris, landed on the Ark Royal after having lost its catapult holdback fitting during the previous launch. By using afterburner with internal fuel only (and 580 feet of deck space!), Lt. Morris made the first free deck launch of a Skyray when he departed the Ark Royal off the coast of France on October 13. The Grim Reapers returned to NAS Cecil Field on October 22, 1957. From November 1-16, the squadron was deployed on the USS Forrestal (CVA-59) for a VIP cruise, during which they participated in exercise "Lantflex 257."

In April 1958, VF-101 moved to NAS Key West, Florida, and on June 10 the squadron merged with the Fleet All Weather training Unit, Atlantic. The new squadro, while retaining its VF-101 identity, combined the combat readiness training of the old VF-101 with the all-weather intercept procedures developed by FAWTULANT. Its new mission was to train replacement pilots for duty with fleet units, using the F3H Demon and F4D Skyray to provide training in all-weather intercept tactics. VF-101 now boasted a total of 36 squadron aircraft: 11 each of the F3D Skynight and F3H Demon, and 14 F4D Skyrays, although by spring 1959 this total would reach a high of 64, including two Lockheed TVs and an Douglas R4D.

VF-101's first class of fully qualified all-weather pilots completed their day and night carrier qualifications in the first week of December 1958. From January to March 1959, VF-101 pilots participated in a series of "Big Blast" exercises, intercepting Air Force B-47 raids coming through their warning area.

VF-101 was instrumental in developing many training aids used in all-weather interceptor practice with the Skyray: the Dart target one-way tow reel, the Del Mar target tow rig, a four-shot reusable rocket pod, radar optic scorer recording camera installation, and a Sidewinder adaptor on the Skyray's Aero 20-A bombrack. The target towing services provided by VF-101 were an important part of the squadron's mission. For example, from June 4-6, 1959, three VF-101 Skyrays were used to tow the Del Mar target for a CVG-3 Operational Readiness Inspection (ORI) aboard the USS Saratoga, and on June 24-25, a similar service was provided for an ORI for the USS Independence (CVA-62). In August, squadron pilots tendered Del Mar towing services and officated as ComNavAirLant judges for various squadron gunnery competitions and the competitive shootoffs, in preparation for the annual Naval Air Weapons Meet. Finally, from November 25 to December 4, 1959, VF-101 Skyrays provided Del Mar tow services for the F3H competition during Operation Topgun at NAS Pt. Mugu, California.

VF-101 Skyrays continued to be used in the training of all-weather replacement pilots throughout 1960-1961, the unit maintaining several carrier qualification detachments aboard the carriers Independence and Forrestal. As part of Replacement Carrier Air Group 4, VF-101's F4D-1 displayed the RAG's "AD" tail code and the traditional squadron insignia of a winged skeleton carrying a scythe was displayed on the rear portion of the canopy of some Skyrays. By 1962, the Grim Reapers of VF-101 had transitioned to the F4H Phantom II, ending their relatively long use of the F4D-1 Skyray.

TOP - VF-101 134824 in late 1956. Note location of wing code and red fin tip. (Tailhook photo service) BELOW - VF-101 Skyrays operating on the HMS Ark Royal during crossdeck exercises with the USS Saratoga (CVA-60) in Sept. - Oct. 1957. Aircraft now carry ATG-201's two-letter "AP" tail code and red stripe with four white stars on the tail. (via Williams)

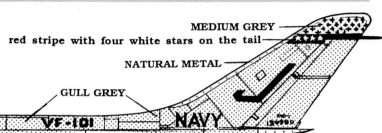

Fighter Squadron One Hundred One

GRIM REAPERS

VF-101 was instrumental in developing many training aids used in all-weather interceptor practice with the Skyray: the Dart one-way tow reel as seen on 134876 below, the Del Mar target tow rig as seen at right, and the four shot reusable rocket pod seen above. TOP - 134925 with extended air brakes at Master Field, Miami on 1-25-58. (Swisher) AT RIGHT - (Joel Griggs) BOTTOM - Note wing code and red drop tank markings with four white stars. (USN)

TOP - 134917 carrying the RAG's "AD" tail code at NAS Sanford on 5-17-58. (Swisher) AT RIGHT - Number 113 with NavPac. (Barry Miller)   BELOW - 134861 over NAS Key West, Fla. note censored squadron insignia on the aft cockpit. (USN via J. Griggs) BOTTOM - The end of the line: NAF Litchfield Park on 3-18-63. (D. Olson)

VF-101 GRIM REAPERS

FLEET ALL WEATHER TRAINING UNIT (FAWTULANT)

Fleet All Weather Training Unit Atlantic (FAWTULANT) operated several Douglas Skyrays at NAS Key West, Florida, with F4D-1 134861 being acquired in September 1957, 134860 a month later, and 139050 in February 1958. By March 1958, FAWTULANT operated five F4D-1s as well as 14 F3D Skyknights, three TV-2s and an R4D. It is not known whether these FAWTULANT Skyrays carried the squadron's "LA," or only the post-1958 "HG" tail codes. FAWTULANT merged with VF-101 in June 1958. A new squadron was formed with the primary mission of training replacements pilots for duty with fleet units.

BELOW—FAWTULANT Fords 134861, 134860 and 139050, no unit colors were carried except the "HG" tail code. Photo is blown-up from the background of VF-102 photo of 134929 as seen on page 127. (Barry Miller)

TOP - Excellent 1959 photo of a VF-101 Ford. Engine bays were very often left open, and to do that with the NavPacs attached the NavPac's tail fins would have to be removed. Note drop tank sway brace on the pylon. (USN) AT RIGHT - A VF-101 Ford that didn't make the runway. (Joel Grigs)

VF-102

The history of VF-102 begins with an event understandable perhaps only to the Navy. On July 1, 1955, VF-102, located at NAS Cecil Field, Florida, was redesignated VA-36 and assigned F9F-5 aircraft.

On the same day at the same field, however, another VA-36 was commissioned and immediately redesignated VF-102! The nucleus of this new squadron, comprising four officers and fifty enlisted men, chose the rattlesnake for their new unit emblem, and called themselves the "Diamondbacks." They were assigned the F2H-4 Banshee, which they flew for nearly two years.

The squadron began the transition to F4D-1s in the early spring of 1957, and spent the next nine months in training with the Skyrays. VF-102 was assigned to Air Task Group 202 in Nov. 1957. Little is known about the group's operation, although it appears they were aboard a carrier for part of their existance.

At this time VF-102 Skyrays were painted in a distinctive diamondback scheme, which they carried nearly unchanged for the following four years. Each Skyray featured a red spine with white diamonds spotted along its length, with similar markings on the fin and drop tanks. Air Task Group 202's tail code, "AQ," was carried on the tail in block letters, although, as with all later tail codes on VF-102 Skyrays, these apparently were not carried on the upper right wing.

Early in 1958 VF-102 went aboard the USS Ranger (CVA-61) for carrier qualifications. When these had been completed in March, the squadron travelled to NAS Key West for advanced ground controlled intercept training and high altitude rocket firing.

In April 1958, the Diamondbacks' Skyrays were chosen to represent the Atlantic Fleet in the All Navy Weapons Meet at NAAS El Centro, Cal. Two VF-102 pilots took a second and third place in the first air-to-air all weather event, VF-102 being one of two teams selected to blind fire their missiles in the contest. Displaying Carrier Air Group 10's "AK" tail code in large, upright block letters, VF-102 Skyrays placed second overall in the meet.

VF-102 next joined Carrier Air Group 10 for a Mediterranean cruise aboard the USS Forrestal (CVA-59) in the fall of 1958, Departing Norfolk on Sept. 2, their F4D-1s carried the group's "AK" modex during the six month cruise. After their return in March 1959, the squadron spent the following three months in electronic countermeasure training with VAW-33 and VCMJ-1.

To prepare for upcoming carrier exercises, VF-102 moved to NAS Oceana, Virginia on June 1, 1959, and began four months of intensive training in field carrier landing practices, carrier controlled approaches, and high

VF-102 Diamondbacks 134968, 134959 and 134929 with distinctive red with white diamond patterned spines, fin flashes and drop tank markings. (Tailhook photo service)

DIAMOND BACKS

altitude rocket firing runs. These weapons evaluation exercises, dubbed "Operation Wexval-9," were held aboard the USS Forrestal during October and November 1959.

VF-102 again boarded the Forrestal in January 1960 for a Med cruise as part of CVG-8. A squadron operations record was set on this cruise when their F4Ds were flown for a total of 538 hours during the month of June. The Diamondbacks returned to Norfolk in August 1960, but boarded the carrier again briefly in November for further carrier qualifications.

On February 9, 1961, VF-102 began its final Mediterranean cruise with the F4D-1 aboard the Forrestal, again carrying CVG-8's "AJ" tail code. Although the squadron pilots broke their own operations record by flying 540 hours in 15 days, several accidents marred the tour. Weakness in the Skyray's tail hook assembly were becoming common during carrier operations, and caused at least one VF-102 Skyray to have its lower fuselage ripped out upon engaging a wire.

VF-102 returned from this last cruise in August 1961, and almost immediately began transition training in VF-101's Det. A. By December 1961, the Diamondbacks of VF-102 had relinquished their F4D-1 Skyrays for McDonnell Phantom IIs.

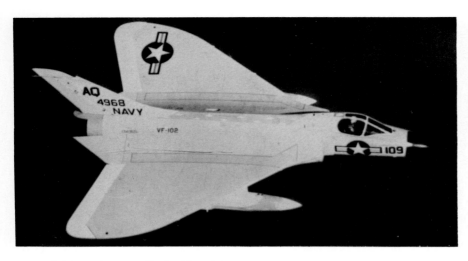

TOP - 134968 off Florida with Air Task Group 202's "AQ" tail code in 1957. (National Archives) UPPER MIDDLE - 134929 with Carrier Air Group 10's "AK" tail code in late 1957. (Barry Miller) LOWER MIDDLE - 139099 after trapping aboard the USS Forrestal in Nov. 1958. (LCDR Shinnholser) BOTTOM - 134927 with Del Mar target over NAAS El Centro while competing in the Third Annual Weapons Meet on 4-14-58. (USN)

ABOVE - 134923 from VF-102 is launched from the USS Ranger (CVA-61) on 2-1-58. (USN) BELOW - VF-102 pilots coming on deck in Mark IV pressure suits and air-conditioning units. Note white diamonds on red trim on 134936. (USN)

TOP - Lt. Don Kough in VF-102 139069 with sidewinder on 10-11-58. (USN) MIDDLE - CO. CDR. Keyworth Jr. in 134870 aboard CVA-59 on 4-7-60 with CVG-8's "AJ" tail code. Note medium grey anti-glare panel and wing-walls. (USN) BOTTOM - 134959 at MCAAS Yuma on 12-3-59. Note change in drop tank diamonds from 5 to 4. (Swisher)

TOP - VF-102 134803 AND 134841 ON 4-25-60. Note squadron insignia on canopy of 134803. (USN) MIDDLE - VF-102 Skyrays with used rocket pods and extended tailhooks. 134921 in the background carries. a Del Mar target. 7-28-60. (USN) BOTTOM - Catapult crew hooking bridle to VF-102 F4D-1 134959 aboard CVA-59 in July 1961. Note white drop tanks and refueling probe, sidewinder and black fin top. (USN) See color section.

VF-141

NAS Miramar's VF-141 began transition training from F2H-3s to the F4D-1 after returning from a WestPac cruise aboard the USS Kearsarge (CVA-33) in May 1956. The squadron's first Skyray arrived on June 26, and over the next year VF-141 underwent three carrier qualification cruises aboard the carriers Essex, Lexington, and Bon Homme Richard. The squadron's Training Officer, Capt. Bob Haxlett, an Air Force exchange officer, recalls one frightening incident during carquals aboard the Lexington: "One of the men in the squadron, Lt. Sothan, made the first successful underwater ejection from an F4D. As he taxied forward he hit the brakes— not knowing he had lost his right brake— and taxied off the port side. The F4D hit the water inverted. Lt. Sothan was sinking in the inverted F4D, and at an estimated depth of 70 feet he ejected. He pulled the emergency oxygen and was surfacing mostly butt first, as his seat pack retained a lot of air. He saw what he thought was the ship's prop and tried to swim down, but was pulled up by the seat pack. Luckily, what he thought was the prop was actually foam in the wake of the carrier, and he surfaced about 1000 feet aft of the ship. He was unhurt, but decided he no longer wanted to fly F4Ds."

For these cruises, squadron F4D-1 appeared in Carrier Air Groups 5's "S" tail code contained within a large yellow pennant painted on their tails, and with 200-series nose numbers. VF-141's insignia, the Iron Angel, was the same as adopted by VF-14 during World War II, but apparently this was never carried on the squadron's Skyrays.

On July 12, 1957, VF-141 embarked aboard the USS Bon Homme Richard (CVA-31) for a WestPac cruise. While aboard the Bonnie Dick, some VF-141 Skyrays carried their "S" tail code and some CVG-5's new two-letter tail code, "NF" in a black-bordered yellow pennant with 200-series nose numbers. As this was the first deployment of a West Coast F4D-1 equipped squadron, the Iron Angels experienced the usual headaches of introducing a new aircraft into the fleet, although losing only one Skyray with no fatalities. Carrier life is not all humorless, as Bob Hazelett relates: "On a night flight during our WestPac deployment, Lt. Berringer made seven unsuccessful passes at the deck. We thought we might have to shoot him down, but on the eighth attempt he landed. However, he stuck a main gear through the teakwood deck, and put a six-inch dent in the steel panel under the teak. The F4D received minor damage...a real tough airplane! The deck was patched with a zinc chromated steel panel.

"Mr. Berringer wanted to fly again right away, so he was launched as soon as the deck was repaired. He made three passes at the deck before landing on his fourth pass. He again punched a hole in the teakwood deck with minor damage to the F4D. When the deck was repaired this time, someone painted on the repair panel: 'Where will the Phantom strike next?' On Mr. Berringer's next flight, he blew a nose tire on launch. He stayed in the 'dog' pattern until everyone else had recovered. Mr. Berringer was not noted for his sense of humor, but called in the pattern as 'Phantom at the 180.'"

Upon its return to NAS Miramar on December 9, 1957, all but three of VF-141's pilots were ordered elsewhere, and the process of reforming an almost completely depleted squadron fell to these three "old timers" who indoctrinated the "new blood." Squadron training progressed rapidly; in March 1958 alone VF-141 pilot flew 507 hours

with only nine aircraft available. When called upon for Joint Exercises in May, 100% of the assigned missions were completed, although the squadron was only in Phase I of its training cycle. The first three weeks of June were spent at NAAS El Centro, when 10 F4D-1s were flown during the Phase II firing portion of the weapons syllabus. In July, VF-141 practiced intensively on day and night mirror landings in preparation for carquals, in addition to its normal all-weather training missions. The unit participated in "Bluebolt" from July 9-11, 1958, making several successful day and night intercepts.

The Iron Angels of VF-141 were assigned to Carrier Air Group 14 on August 29, 1958. On September 8-13, the squadron participated in "Phibex" as Combat Air Patrol, making two successful intercepts out of two assigned. During this period, it is believed the squadron adopted a short-lived markings scheme for its Skyrays: CVG-14's "NK" tail code painted in slanted white letters within a black-bordered orange ray on the tail, and 200-series nose numbers. Although photos do exist showing these markings, virtually nothing has been uncovered concerning their use.

From September 21-27, 1958, VF-141 went aboard the USS Ranger (CVA-61) for day carrier qualifications, the squadron making 154 traps in 3½ days. Iron Angel Skyrays operated aboard the Ranger twice again, on October 11-17 and November 7-14, 1958, for day and night carquals. Finally, on December 28, the squadron left aboard the Ranger for their second WestPac with the Skyray. For this cruise, VF-141 Skyrays carried only the Air Group's "NK" tail code in large letters, a thin yellow tail stripe, and 200-series nose numbers.

VF-141 completed night carquals aboard the Ranger from January 9-14, participated in CVG-14's operational readiness training from January 26-30, and the final Operational Readiness Inspection from February 9-13, 1959. The squadron spent March 16-28 at NAS Atsugi, Japan, boarding the Ranger once again on the 28th for operations at sea. On June 25-30, VF-141 Skyrays participated in exercise "Granite Creek" as a CVG-14's day, night and all-weather fighter squadron. The VF-141 Iron Angels returned to NAS Miramar on July 27, 1959, and immediately relinquished their F4D-1 Skyrays for the F3H-2 Demon.

TOP - VF-141 F4D-1 134806 aboard USS Essex in 1956. CVG-5's "S" tail code is on a yellow pennant. (Fairley) **MIDDLE** - 134904 with new CVG-5 "NF" tail code trapping aboard USS Bon Homme Richard (CVA-31) on 12-31-57. (USN) **BOTTOM** - 134866 aboard CVA-31. Note wing code and black and grey radome (Tailhook photo service)

TOP - VF-141 F4D-1 134875 is about to launch from the USS Ranger (CVA-61) BOTTOM - Briefly used or possibly one-off color scheme of 134809 in the second half of 1958. CVG-14 "NK" tail code is carried on an orange ray outlined in black. (via Williams)

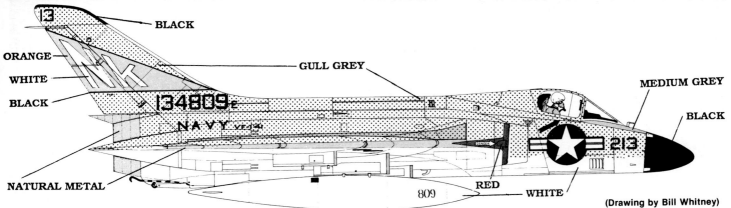

F4D-1 134809 carried a little-known color scheme of VF-141, believed used during 1958. Tail ray is orange with white CVG-14 "NK" tail code.

TOP - 1348880 with CVG-14 "NK" tail code and thin yellow fin stripe at NAS Miramar on 12-12-58. (Tailhook photo service) MIDDLE - 134866 sans tail code on CVA-61's elevator; note wing codes. (Douglas) BOTTOM - The Ranger's deck with many VF-141 Skyrays in view. (USMC)

VF-162

The "Hunters" of VF-162 have the distinction of being the shortest lived carrier based Skyray unit in the Navy. In a grand commissioning ceremony held on September 1, 1960 at NAS Cecil Field, Florida, VF-162 was established along with VF-161, VA-163, VA-164, and VA-165, as well as the parent organization Carrier Air Group Sixteen.

Congress had granted the Navy permission to organize the Air Group for one year only, and its existence beyond this time was in doubt. The other units of CVG-16 were formed to fly the AD Skyraider, A4D Skyhawk, and the F3H Demon, all of these aircraft still in wide use throughout the fleet. However, as there had been no specific procurement measures to equip these units, the building up process was a slow job.

VF-162, on the other hand, had no problems in finding surplus Skyrays with which to equip itself. The F4D-1 had already been phased out of the Pacific Fleet, and reduced in favor of the F3H in the Atlantic Fleet. The advent of the F4H Phantom II was at hand, and ComNavAirLant knew that in the process of introducing the Phantom into the fleet, an additional all weather fighter squadron would be needed to fill in the gaps left by squadrons temporarily taken out of service for retraining. Consequently, VF-162 was built up rather quickly and began a period of intense training.

The first F4D-1 arrived at Cecil Field on October 10, 1960. By the end of the year the unit had a full complement of aircraft and nearly a full complement of pilots, the rest of the Air Group having few of either.

During the winter of 1960 and into the spring of 1961, several detachments from VF-162 were dispatched to NAS Key West, Florida to stand alert watches during the Cuban Crisis. In these deployments, VF-162 Skyrays replaced F4D-1s flown by VF-101, the all weather Replacement Air Group (RAG) for AirLant, as these air defense duties interfered with the RAG training program.

At this time VF-162 Skyrays carried CVG-16's modex "AH," a "200" series nose number, and an elaborate marking scheme consisting of black upper elevon and rudder surfaces with gold stars of various sizes scattered randomly about. Their unit insignia also was carried on each

VF-162 Skyrays 134795 and 134836 with 200 series nose numbers and CVG-16s "AH" tail code on 2-9-61 over Cecil Field, Fla. (USN)

side of the cockpit behind the window: Orion, "The Mighty Hunter" poised on a black field with a club and shield in hand superimposed over the constellation Orion. A small gold stripe on the fin also displayed each aircraft nose number in black. The nose of each drop tank carried similar gold stars on a black field, with the left tank's refueling probe painted in a gold and black spiral pattern.

In the spring of 1961, VF-162 transferred to Carrier Air Group Six, changed its modex to "AF," and replaced VF-74 aboard the USS Intrepid (CVA-11). Between April 15 and August 1, 1961 the squadron made four deployments. During the first two of these VF-162 qualified for day and night carrier operations while cruising off of Norfolk. The third came when the squadron received a phone call at Cecil Field at 3 p.m., giving notice that the assassination of the dictator Trujillo had caused a crisis situation in the Dominican Republic. By midnight, the entire squadron was aboard the Intrepid and was underway by six the next morning. The fourth deployment was made during an Atlantic Fleet exercise off the coast of New York. For each of these deployments it was necessary to airlift the squadron to Norfolk, as VF-162 was based at NAS Cecil Field while the Air Group was headquartered at NAS Oceana, Virginia.

On August 3, 1961, VF-162 departed for an extended Mediterranean cruise aboard the Intrepid. The squadron returned to Cecil Field on February 28, 1962, and almost immediately prepared to move to NAS Miramar, as CVG-16 had been shifted to the Pacific Fleet.

On April 2, 1962, VF-162 began painting out their squadron markings on the Skyrays, and by the 4th most of their personnel had left for VF-124's "Crusader College" at Miramar. On that date, fifty-nine squadron personnel were left at Cecil Field to launch the last of VF-162's Skyrays for the short flight to NAS Jacksonville's Overhaul and Repair depot.

TOP - 134795 in July 1961. VF-162 Fords went against Navy doctrine by not using red as required by 100-series squadrons. Rudder, elevons, refueling probe and drop tank noses are black with gold stars. Fin tip radome and anti-glare panel are black. Stripe on fin is gold (USN) MIDDLE - 134757 aboard the USS Intrepid (CVA-11) in 1961. Note that pilot's helmet is black with gold stars. (USN) BOTTOM - 134946 at Litchfield Park on 3-18-63. Note squadron insignia on canopy and VMF(AW)-115s drop tank. (via Clay Jansson)

VF-213 F4D-1 134967 on 8-20-58. (USN)

VF-213

The "Black Lions" of VF-213 based at NAS Moffett Field, Cal., began transitioning from F2H-3 Banshees to Skyrays in Feb. 1957. With only ten F4D-1s on hand, the squadron entered into Phase I training in instrument and tactics flying throughout the summer an fall.

The squadron deployed to NAAS Fallon, Nevada twice in the fall of 1957: from October 11 to 26 and December 6 to 20, achieving the best scores to that date in aerial gunnery with the F4D-1.

From March 2 to 22, 1958, VF-213 deployed to NAAS El Centro for three weeks of rocket firing practice. Squadron pilots concentrated on perfecting their lead collision intercept skills, which enables an interceptor to meet an inbound bomber or missile at head-on angles with a high percentage of kills.

This practice paid off the following month at the Third Annual Naval Air Weapons Meet at El Centro. From April 14-18, 1958 VF-213 competed against other all weather squadrons winning the air-to-air event. The Black Lions also were awarded the James V. Forrestall Memorial Trophy, Navy League Champions Trophy, Team Championship Trophy, Individual Champions Trophy, and 52 other winners trophies.

VF-213s marking on their Skyrays remained unchanged for nearly the entire time they flew the F4D-1: light blue and white checkers on the tail bordered by light blue stripes top and bottom; a light blue arrow running from the cockpit to the tail; and light blue designs on the drop tanks. Their Carrier Air Group 21 tail code "NP" was blended in over the checkered design on the tail. At some later date, VF-213 Skyray markings were reduced to a small band of blue and white checks carried above their tail code, with standardized markings on the drop tanks absent.

Shortly after returning to Moffett Field, VF-213 boarded the USS Lexington (CVA-16) for three periods of carrier qualifications: May 19 to June 3. June 24 to 30, and July 1 to 11. On July 15 the squadron embarked aboard the Lexington for a West Pacific cruise with CVG-21. During this cruise, VF-213 participated in "Operation Blue Skies," 7th Fleet exercises in the Taiwan Straits. VF-213 Skyrays conducted fighter sweeps of the area and provided Combat Air Patrol for these Fleet maneuvers.

VF-213 returned to Moffett Field on Dec. 17, 1958, travelling to NAAS Fallon once again from Jan. 31 to Feb.

20, 1959 for weapons training VF-213 spent the spring of 1959 in another series of carrier qualifications aboard the USS Lexington. In two short cruises from March 8-20 and April 6-17, 15 pilots accumulated over 1000 hours during day and night carrier qualifications flights.

On April 25, 1959, a week after returning to Moffett Field, the Black Lions of VF-213 boarded the Lexington for their last WestPac cruise. Once in Hawaii, the squadron received a score of 94.48 for their Operational Readiness Inspection.

At sea once again, VF-213 spent the summer of 1959 in three exercises, conducting simulated strikes on Taiwan and the southern coast of Japan, and providing CAP for the Lexington during these operations. From July to December, the 14 pilots of VF-213 amassed over 1000 hours during these training flights. Upon their return to NAS Moffett Field on Dec. 4, 1959, VF-213 had set a deployment record for F4D-1 squadrons by flying 1934 hours and 1123 carrier arrestments aboard the Lexington. Ten VF-213 pilots were designated Centurions during this cruise for making their 100th arrested landing aboard the Lexington.

The Black Lions of VF-213 received their first replacement F3H-2s on December 14, 1959, and by January had ended their association with the F4D-1 Skyray.

TOP - 134911 on 8-10-57 at NAS Miramar. Check mark on spine is light blue and tail markings are light blue and white checks. Note early small wing pylon (D. Olson via Swisher) MIDDLE - 134796 on 8-10-57. Note white around "NP" on tail. (Swisher) BOTTOM - VF-213 Fords aboard the USS Lexington (CVA-16) on 7-7-58. (Larkins)

TOP - 139058 (307) and 139060 (306) over NAAS El Centro, Ca. on 4-14-58 during the Third Annual Air Weapons Meet. Note drop tank, light blue check marks, and wing codes. (USN) MIDDLE - 11-3-59 photo shows tail markings were reduced to a small band. Note drop tank markings on 312. (USN) BOTTOM - VF-213 Ford readied for launch aboard CVA-16 on 1-28-59; note absence of checked tail markings. (USN)

Fleet Air Gunnery Unit, Pacific

The Fleet Air Gunnery Unit Pacific, was commissioned on May 22, 1952, at NAAS El Centro, California, to provide aerial gunnery training for Navy and Marine pilots. By the late 1950s, FAGU operated a small number of Skyrays as target tugs and gunnery aircraft, in addition to the F8U-1, FJ-4B, and A4D-2.

During the five-week postgraduate course, each student spent 60 hours in the classroom and 40 hours in the cockpit, flying all-weather, air-to-air and air-to-ground training missions in weapons delivery and tactics. The FAGU Skyrays, which began arriving in January 1958, were painted in the squadron's distinctive scheme: the unit's "TR" tail code superimposed over a red and white checkerboard pattern, and two black bands encircling the airplane's nose and drop tanks with a diagonal red lightning bolt arcing forward on each, the latter being clever reproductions of the squadron insignia. At some later date the checkerboard tail design was reduced to a small band running horizontally, high on the tail. The squadron's insignia, a black and white target circle with a lightning bolt stabbing the bull's eye, apparently never was carried on FAGU Skyrays. It is interesting to note, however, that this insignia has appeared below the windshields of other squadron's F4D-1s [VF-51 and VF(AW)-3], probably indicating the pilot's graduation from the FAGU course. FAGU continued to operate the F4D-1 at NAAS El Centro until the unit moved to MCAAS Yuma, Airzona, in the summer of 1959. By the end of the year, the Skyrays were replaced by more modern equipment.

TOP - FAGU F4D-1 on 4-14-68. Markings consisted of a red and white checkerboard pattern on the tail, black "TR" tail code, black and grey target circles on nose and drop tanks with red lightning bolts.(USN) BOTTOM - 134802 firing a FFAR rocket from its rocket pod on 2-10-58. (via Clay Jansson)

Fleet Air Gunnery Unit, Pacific

TOP - A FAGU F4D-1 with a Del Mar target takes off from NAAS El Centro during the Naval Air Weapons Meet on 4-18-58. (Douglas) MIDDLE - The red and white checkerboard pattern on FAGU Skyrays was eventually reduced to a narrow band on their tails as seen here on 134749. (USN) BOTTOM - 134790 without nose or drop tank stripes or lightning bolts. Note spent rocket pod and "FAGU" painted on the spine. 12-3-59 (Swisher)

Naval Air Development Unit

The Naval Air Development Unit, located within the old blimp hangar at NAS South Weymouth, Massachusetts, was commissioned on September 1, 1953. Its primary mission was to evaluate the effectiveness of experimental and prototype detection, tracking and interception functions in air defense systems. To accomplish this the NADU operated a variety of aircraft types including the F4D-1, F2H, F3H, P2V, WV-2 and ZPG airship.

The NADU's first Skyray, 134825, arrived in August 1956. Within two years the unit operated at least four additional F4D-1s, 130748, 134748, 134930 and 134938, most of these painted in identical gull gray and gloss white schemes with extensive areas of da-glo on the nose and lower forward fuselage, wings and tail, with "NADU" painted in black block letters on the fin and rudder surfaces. By 1962 the NADU had ended its use of the Skyray, employing more advanced fighter aircraft in its test programs.

ABOVE - 134802 banks away on 4-14-58 over El Centro. (USN) See back cover.

ABOVE - NADU F4D-1 134938 at Litchfield Park on 3-18-63 in a later scheme than is shown in the color section. Nose and tail - as was well as the aft half of the wing are day-glo. (Swisher) BELOW - 134930 in a white and day-glo scheme on 4-23-60. (Jim Burridge)

Naval Air Development Center

The Naval Air Development Center, NAS Johnsville, Pennsylvania, was established on August 1, 1949, superseding the Naval Air Development Station established two years previously. By 1956 the NADC had expanded to include seven laboratories and departments with the primary missions of providing design and development of aircraft electronics, aviation armament and pilotless aircraft.

The NADC operated at least two Douglas Skyrays, 134763 and 134966. F4D-1 134763 was transferred from the Douglas Testing Division to Johnsville in August 1957 and flew with the NADC until September 1959, accumulating approximately 60 flight hours.

While contemporary photographs of NADC Skyrays are lacking, F4D-1 134966, more recently on display at the Bradley Air Museum in Windsor Locks, Connecticut, carried a white NADC arrow design containing "NADC" in black letters painted on the airplane's tail, with a glossy blue overall paint scheme. Unfortunately, neither the Skyray's serial number nor its NADC insignia are authentic to this particular airplane, having been applied when the F4D-1 was displayed aboard the USS Intrepid (CV-11) in 1976.

While this Skyray shown on display at the Bradley Air Museum carries the serial number 134966 and the insignia of the Naval Air Development Center, NAS Johnsville, Pennsylvania, neither is authentic to this particular airplane.

F4D-1 134748 was bailed to the Raytheon Company in 1961 while in custody of the Bureau of Naval Weapons Representative, Waltham, Massachusetts, for development work with the company's Sparrow III missile. The airplane, shown here at NAS South Weymouth, Massachusetts, in September 1961, retained its original Douglas Testing Division paint scheme: a red tail band and stripe on canopy. (Jim Burridge)

A surprising variety of shore-based units or organizations had custody of single F4D-1s. Utility Squadron 7(VU-7) at NAAS Brown Field, California, normally equipped with the FJ-4 as well as several utility types, borrowed an F4D-1, 134772, from nearby VF(AW)-3 from June to August 1959 for an unnamed project. The Naval Aviation Ordnance Test Station (NAOTS) at NAS Chincoteague, Virginia, flew F4D-1 134754 for over 100 hours from June 1957 to March 1959 before transferring the airplane to NATC Patuxent River. Interestingly, it appears that the airplane retained its initial Douglas Testing Division paint scheme while serving with NAOTS Chincoteague.

F4D-1 134748, after brief stints with the Douglas Testing Division and the NADU, flew several hundred hours while in the custody of both the Inspector of Naval Material (INM), Boston, Massachusetts, from October 1957 to February 1961, and the Bureau of Naval Weapons Representative (BWR), Waltham, Massachusetts, from February 1961 until the airplane's retirement in October 1963. This airplane also retained its original Douglas Testing Division paint scheme during its subsequent use with the INM Boston and BWR Waltham. It appears that the Skyray was bailed to the Raytheon Company at this time for flight testing of their Sparrow III air-to-air missile, probably flying it from NAS South Weymouth, Massachusetts.

Miscellaneous Units

Ex Douglas Testing Division Ford assigned to NAOTS Chincoteague is shown on 8-28-58 while conducting a Dart pick up. (USN)

Naval Air Test Facility

The Naval Air Test Facility (Ship Installations) was established at NAS Lakehurst, New Jersey, on October 1, 1957. Utilizing 11 test sites, including what was the longest military runway on the East Coast, the Test Facility was given the primary mission of research, development, testing and evaluation of shipboard and shore-based catapult and arresting systems. To conduct these evaluations a small fleet of contemporary fighter and attack aircraft was maintained by the NATF, including at least two F4D-1s, 134854 and 134931.

These NATF Skyrays were employed from 1959 through 1964 on numerous test projects. The first of these encompassed a three-week period beginning on December 11, 1959, when the Bureau of Naval Weapons requested that the NATF determine the Skyray's compatibility with the MK7 Mod 2-3 arresting gear system (shipboard barricade). A total of 63 F4D-1 arrestments were made with this system, the aircraft being declared compatible with minor limitations. From May 16 to July 31, 1960, an NATF F4D-1 was launched 19 times during an evaluation of the TC13 steam catapult, while F4D-1 134931 made 46 arrestments during the year in a lengthy evaluation of the M4-1 Expeditionary Arresting Gear located at NAS Patuxent River, Maryland. A Skyray was again used (along with six other NATF aircraft types) during a further evaluation of the MK7 Mod 2-3 arresting gear system when some 44 arrested landings were made by the F4D-1 between April 14 and August 28, 1961. The TM-20 Expeditionary Arresting Gear was tested by an NATF Skyray in June and July 1961, while the NATF F4D-1/F-6As were used throughout 1962 to test the XRE-1 Expeditionary Catapult System, molybdenum coated arresting hook points, MK-7 Mod 1 arresting gear system, and the RE-1 Expeditionary Catapult gear.

Naval Air Test FAcility F4D-1 134854 first appeared in standard gull gray upper and gloss white lower surfaces with "NATF" painted on the tail in block letters. A distinctive red-orange NATF colored band design bordered on each side by thin white and black bands was painted high on the airplane's tail, with the nose number "1" displayed above it on the fin cap. By 1963, 854 had been repainted

NATF F4D-1 134854 launches from NAS Lakehurst. Colors are white with day-glo tail, nose, lower forward fuselage and upper and lower forward wing halves. Tail band is red-orange bordered by thin white and then black lines. Radome, fin tip and anti-glare panel are black. (via Williams) See color section.

Naval Air Test Facility insignia

glossy white overall with red da-glo nose and lower forward fuselage, wings, tail, and wing tanks and pylons. The NATF tail design had been enlarged and moved further down on the airplane's tail.

The last known test assignment for an NATF F-6A occurred during the initial aircraft compatibility demonstration of a single E-27 emergency arresting gear when eight arrestments were made on August 2 and 21, 1963. The NATF Skyrays were finally stricken from the record in 1965, while the Naval Air Test Facility itself later was disestablished on March 10, 1977, and consolidated into the Naval Air Engineering Center.

Naval Air Test Facility

AT LEFT TOP - First scheme of 134854 was standard gull grey and white with red-orange tail band bordered with white and black. (USN) AT LEFT BOTTOM - 134854 in its later scheme as seen on the XRE-1 Expeditionary catapult. (USN) BELOW - 134854 on 5-13-61 with white drop tanks and pylons. (R.T. O'Dell) BOTTOM - All white 134763 seen at NAS Lakehurst in Nov. 1967, reportedly used for barrier tests. (Robert Esposito)

F-6A 134828 takes off from NAS Olathe Kansas on 4-20-63. Drop tank design, tail and outer wings are day-glo. (USN)

VF-881 insignia.

VF-881/882 and VMF-113/215

By 1962 the F4D-1 Skyray (F-6A after multi-service standardization in 1962) was nearing the end of its usefulness with front-line Navy and Marine Corps fighter squadrons. On the West Coast only NAS North Island's VF(AW)-3 continued to fly the Douglas interceptor for the North American Air Defense Command, while at NAS Cecil Field, Florida, VF-13 and VF-162 were preparing to relinquish their Skyrays within the year. Six Marine Corps squadrons, VMF(AW)-114, -115,-314, -513, -531, -542, were still operating the airplane, but all would transition to more modern equipment within two years.

Although it had quickly become outdated by the latest generation of fighters, the supersonic Skyray still represented a quantum jump in performance over the various models of the F9F Cougar then being flown by many reserve fighter units. In the spring of 1962 these surplus Skyrays replaced the F9F-8/8Bs being shared by four squadrons at NAS Olathe, Kansas: VF-881 and VF-882, part of the Navy's Reserve Air Wing 88, and VMF-113 and VMF-215, operating as components of the Marine Air Reserve Training Detachment (MARTD) Olathe, Marine Air Reserve Training Command (MARTCOM).

The first of approximately 18 Skyrays began arriving at NAS Olathe in May 1962 from various fighter outfits, and from temporary storage at NAF Litchfield Park, Arizona. The aircraft soon were given fluorescent red-orange (da-glo) markings: a da-glo fin continuing onto the airplane's dorsal, curving to form a point several feet forward of the tail, and da-glo outer wing panels excluding the elevon surfaces. Each airplane carried the station's "7K" reserve tail code, both "Navy" and "Marine" on the lower fin and fuselage, and 100-series nose numbers repeated high on the fin. The drop tanks were given da-glow noses tapering rearward to a point just forward portion of the tanks, Eventually, this scheme changed with the addition of a da-glo nose band between the radome and the national insignia, and by the deletion of the drop tank markings and the tapered da-glo point on the dorsal spine. At times, however, some Olathe F-6As were seen in the standard Navy gull gray and gloss white scheme with no da-glo whatsoever.

As one might expect, individual squadron insignia were not applied to these aircraft. What did appear on the rear portion of the canopies of some aircraft was the Naval Air Station Olathe insignia: a blue triangular emblem with the yellow Kansas sunflower at its center containing the black silhouette of a jet aircraft. Only the two naval squadron insignias are known at this writing. VF-881 chose the wild goose as its emblem because of its endurance in flight as well as for its discipline in maintaining excellent formation in flight. This black and white insignia appears to be an early one dating from the early 1950s and may not be representative of the squadron's Skyray era. VF-882's insignia features a dark blue and white shield separated into quadrants within a light blue circle. The four quadrants contain a pair of naval aviator's wings, a stylized jet airplane, a missile, and a beaver symbolizing the squadron's mission.

While the arrival of these Skyrays presented some relatively minor logistics problems, the Olathe reserve units adapted quickly to their new mounts. Each squadron flew, or "drilled," with the Skyrays one weekend per month, with two weeks of active duty training scheduled each summer. During this two-week active duty training period, the two Navy or two Marine squadrons combined for deployment to a fleet activity, usually operating with the fleet units to which they would be assigned if mobilized. In July 1962, the Commanding Officer of VMF-215, Lt. Col. P.D. Suddarth, and his Operations Officers, Lt. Col. L.J. Perina, made their qualification flights in the Skyray becoming the first Marine aviators in the Corps' Air Reserve program to fly supersonic, afterburner-equipped aircraft.

But, as with all "new" aircraft entering a squadron, some problems did occur, as related by Cdr. Dudley Gillaspy, a former Ford pilot with VF-882.

"Most of the 'Skyray's' bugs had been worked out by the time we received the 'Fords'. About the only problems we had were supply of parts, lack of technical maintenance, and of course the problem of pilot ability you get in any reserve squadron. We had several pilots who had never flown operational jets, consequently learning to fly 'Fords' with a total of only 300-400 hours of jet time in 'Cougars'. This made for some 'hairy' situations in itself.

"First impressions of the 'Fords' after flying the 'Cougars' were good. It was an extremely maneuverable aircraft at high speed, had good climb specs, and was a good aircraft at altitude as long as you kept the afterburner in above 35,000 feet.

"We always carried two drop tanks, and these really cost on high-altitude performance. But without them, range and endurance were nothing, especially below 30,000 feet.

"The all-weather weapons system was fine when it worked, but with the limited technical maintenance we had in reserve squadrons we were lucky to have 10 percent of our aircraft in an 'up' condition on weapons systems. The airplane's radar was very good when working. We used to make one-minute takeoff intervals with three aircraft and join up in the soup when the radar was working. It gave a very good presentation both for range and altitude, but we usually left it off of autopilot and flew the intercept with an eyeball on the scope. We had trouble with the servos in the autopilot system, and in later years couldn't get all the replacement parts we needed, so we finally quit even trying to keep the autopilots in operating status."

Ralph Saunders, an engine mechanic with the Naval Air Station, points out that Olathe base personnel also were trained on the Skyray in order to teach the four groups of reserve squadron members. He remembers one unusual incident during their early use of the airplane: "One of the station pilots, Cdr. 'Shorty' Bell, normally had the job of chase pilot for new pilots in the F4D. Their first flight in the 'Skyray' was made without the afterburner, but the second flight was a different story. One of these new pilots was a Lt. Boyd, who was taking off on his second flight—using the afterburner—when he reported a fire warning light. Bell flew up below and behind Boyd's airplane and confirmed a fire in the aft fuselage. Boyd proceeded to return to the field with the crash crew standing by, but was waved off because he had forgotten to lower his landing gear, while all this time the rear of his aircraft was in flames. He came back for a second try and made a successful landing, hooking the field arresting cable with no injury to himself but with major damage to the aircraft. It turned out that the fuel lines on the afterburner had hairline cracks, and when the afterburner was activated raw fuel was sprayed on the outside of the afterburner, creating a fire in the wrong place. As luck would have it, all aircraft with the J57 with afterburners were grounded for inspection of these lines and many were found bad. The incident was written up by [Naval Aviation News'] Grandpa Pettibone."

Unfortunately, another recurring problem with the Skyray's automatic yaw damper system is thought to have caused the crash of an Olathe Skyray on January 6, 1963, producing the only known fatality with the reserve airplanes. The pilot, Lt. Donald K. Cauble, made an afterburner takeoff into a rainy, 300-500-foot ceiling. The aircraft entered the low overcast properly, but approximately four seconds later emerged from the base of the clouds inverted, still in afterburner, impacting a half mile from the station. Although vertigo was the suspected cause of the crash, the airplane's rudder was soon found to be the culprit. "We had some problems with the yaw stabilizer rudder kicking over 'full throw' on several occasions," recalls Cdr. Gillaspy. "Research showed [Cauble's] yaw stab rudder in full throw, which simply rolled the aircraft to the inverted position from which the pilot didn't have sufficient altitude to recover."

Despite these mishaps the four Olathe-based reserve squadrons soon became proficient in the F-6A (F4D). In May 1963, one year after receiving the Skyray, VMF-215 was redesignated as an all-weather unit, becoming the first all-weather squadron in the Marine Corps Air Reserve Training Command. In September 1963, the Olathe Marines were awarded the MARTD Proficiency Trophy for fiscal year 1963, "the first time a trophy was awarded to a detachment for its role in supporting the Marine Air Reserve Program." For both 1963 and 1964 VMF-113 and VMF-215 earned MARTCOM awards for flight safety, and in October 1964 VMF-113 also was redesignated as an all-weather squadron, giving the Marine detachment two operational all-weather units.

The Navy reserve squadrons ended their association with the Skyray in August 1964 when VF-881 and VF-882 converted to the A-4B Skyhawk. VMF-113 and VMF-215 continued to fly their F-6As until approximately April 1965, when the first of 18 F-8A Crusaders began replacing the Marine Skyrays.

Three different schemes appeared on Olathe Fords. TOP - Grey and white 134936 on 3-18-63. (Swisher) MIDDLE - 134815 with day-glo tail, outer wings and drop tank markings. (Dickey) BELOW - 134945 and 134826 with day-glo tail, nose band and outer wings and white drop tanks in June 1964. (J. Geer)

TOP - F-6A 139080 being readied for a VMF(AW)-215 training mission on 7-24-64 with Lt. Col. W. Shanks Jr. (USMC) ABOVE - F-6A 134936 on display in 1972. AT RIGHT - 134936 today at Pueblo, Co. Historical Society Museum. (Spencer) BOTTOM - F-6A on display at Olathe in 1977. (Williams)

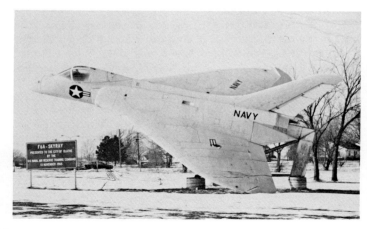

Skyray 134950 in bogus markings of VA-64 at NAS Oceana on 9-20-64. (Paul Stevens) 134950 today in markings of VF-102 (Joel Griggs)

F4D-1 134759 being accepted by NACA in April 1956 with standard grey and white scheme with yellow tail stripe bordered in black. (Harry Gann)

NACA/NASA

While not a fleet unit, the National Advisory Committee for Aeronautics acquired a single F4D-1 to conduct a flight test program for the Navy. This Skyray, serial number 134759, was flown from the El Segundo plant to NACA's Ames Research Center at NAS Moffett Field, California, in April 1956. The flight program included evaluations of the Skyray's handling qualities at low speeds, and investigations into high-altitude roll coupling and reductions in transonic trim changes.

During its initial use with NACA, the Skyray carried the organization's traditional yellow tail band with black borders, featuring the winged NACA shield in black, "Ames" on the tail in large letters, the "TEST" in even larger letters on the upper and lower wing fillet surfaces. When NACA became the National Aeronautics and Space Administration in October 1958, the F4D-1 was repainted in a striking da-glo scheme, retaining the black-bordered yellow tail band but now featuring the letters "NASA" within the band and "Ames" in smaller letters below this on the tail. Skyray 759 remained with NASA until approximately September 1959, when the airplane was transferred to NAS Patuxent River's research and development facility for additional test assignments.

134759 with test probe added and "AMES" in black on tail as well as "TEST" in black on upper and lower fuselage. (NASA)

H&MS-15 AND H&MS-24

In the Marine Corps aviation hierarchy, the Headquarters and Maintenance squadrons provided training, administrative and logistical support to their parent Marine Aircraft Groups (MAG), with squadron detachments often accompanying MAG tactical squadrons on weapons training deployments. In theory, each H&Ms (at one time referred to as "HAMRON") operated at least one example of every major aircraft type flown by the squadrons belonging to the MAG.

It appears that of the several H&MS units which had custody of Douglas Skyrays (including H&MS-11 at NAS Atsugi, Japan, and H&MS-30 at MCAS Kaneohe, Hawaii), only H&MS-15 of Marine Air Group 15, MCAS El Toro,

134759 on 5-16-59 with day-glo tail, spine, forward fuselage and wings. "NASA" has replaced "NACA" on yellow tail band. (Larkins)

California, and H&MS-24, MAG-24, MCAS Cherry Point, North Carolina, flew the airplane for a significant length of time or in any great numbers. H&MS-15 had custody of at least four F4D-1s (134795, 134804, 134851 and 139111) during the latter part of 1959, giving them their "YV" tail code as the only apparent squadron markings. H&MS-24 applied an "EW" tail code to the three F4D-1s (134789, 134823 and 139085) known to have been flown by the squadron during 1961-1962.

BELOW - HAMRON-15 F4D-1 134851 at NAF Litchfield Park on 3-18-63. Note black fin cap and drop tank noses and white rudder. (Olson via Jansson)

TOP - HAMRON-15 F4D-1 134804 at MCAS El Toro, Ca.; note open fuselage door and black tipped drop tanks. (Clay Jansson) MIDDLE - HAMRON-15 F4D-1 134744 on 9-15-62 at El Toro. (Swisher) BOTTOM - H&MS-24 F4D-1 134823 at Litchfield Park, AZ on 3-18-63 with black fin tip. (D. Olson)

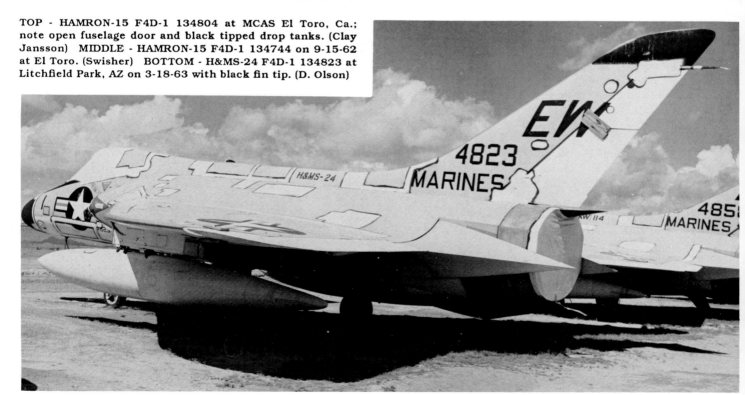

VMF(AW)-114

The Death Dealers of VMF(AW)-114 flew the F4D-1 Skyray for six years in an amazing variety of colorful paint schemes. Originally commissioned at MCAS El Toro in 1943, VMF(AW)-114 operated throughout the war flying F4U Corsairs as a day-fighter squadron, being transferred to MCAS Cherry Point, North Carolina, in February 1946. Between August 1947 and June 1953, the squadron operated as a night-fighter unit, and on May 1, 1957, VMF(AW)-114 was redesignated as an all-weather outfit and began converting from the F9F-8 to the F4D-1.

VMF(AW)-114 received its first Skyray at Cherry Point in June 1957, and applied the squadron's "EK" tail code as part of the 2nd Marine Aircraft Wing, Fleet Marine Force, Atlantic. Early markings were an "EK" tail code with red rudder and upper surfaces, a red spine, and elevons and red designs on the drop tanks. After undergoing extensive training ashore and aboard ship for carrier qualifications, VMF(AW)-114 sailed aboard the USS Roosevelt (CVA-42) on February 13, 1959, for a Mediterranean cruise with Carrier Air Group One. For this deployment, VMF(AW)-114's Skyrays carried CVG-1's "AB" tail code in slanted black letters over a yellow tail band, the motto "Primus Principles" in black letters painted within a yellow scroll on their tails, and 200-series nose numbers. The squadron participated in several Sixth Fleet exercises, finally returning to MCAS Cherry Point on September 1, 1959. During the Med cruise the squadron lost two aircraft and pilots, as well as one airplane and pilot a month before the cruise. Curiously, despite the above incident, in November 1959, VMF(AW)-114 received the Marine Corps Commandant's Annual Aviation Efficiency Trophy, given for flying efficiency and safety. During this time the unit became the only 2nd Marine Aircraft Wing squadron to become day and night carrier qualified.

Phil Oestricher relates the following. Our flying schedule embarked was very heavy as the other all-weather squadron aboard flew F3H-2 Demons which were not scheduled when weather conditions were such that they

Photo above shows the two schemes originally used by VMF(AW)-114 from above in 1958. 5/EK has its spine, rudder, elevons and drop tanks designs in mandarin red. VMF(AW)-114 on spine is black outlined in white. 15/EK has no other markings except the black codes. (USMC via Barry Miller)

would have to fly in visible moisture. At this time, at least, the Demon was plagued with engine seizures while flying in clouds. VMF(AW)-114 picked up the moisture-scrubbed Demon missions and this resulted in a rather busy cruise.

VMF(AW)-114 Skyrays remained at MCAS Cherry Point throughout 1960, sporting a new paint scheme of a bright flourescent red-orange design on the spine and lower tail and fuselage, and the squadron's "EK" code carried high on the tail. This design was the same as that carried on VMF(AW)-115 Skyrays, but there is no evidence that VMF(AW)-114's Skyrays carried any similar markings on their drop tanks, as did their sister squadron. The Death Dealer insignia also was carried on the rear portion of the canopy: a gray skull over crossed black and white bands, which had the black spade and club and red heart and diamond designs.

In February 1961, VMF(AW)-114 was attached briefly to Provisional Marine Aircraft Group 10 at NAS Roosevelt Roads, Puerto Rico, in support of 24th Marine Expeditionary Unit amphibious operations in Vieques Island, Puerto Rico. The unit's Skyrays became the first jet aircraft to land on the island's Short Expeditionary Landing Field on February 6, 1961.

VMF(AW)-114 remained at MCAS Cherry Point throughout the remainder of 1961, but by the summer of 1962 the squadron had deployed to NAS Atsugi, Japan, where they were attached to Marine Air Group 11, 1st Marine Aircraft Wing, Fleet Marine Force, Pacific. Some evidence indicates that the squadron aircraft initially carried the tail code "EK" in large block letters, as was the Marine Corps custom at the time. However, VMF(AW)-114 quickly painted its Skyrays in markings representative of its Death Dealer nickname: each rudder was given a slanted white strip bordered in black showing the four card suits of a black spade and club, and red heart and diamond. Also, each drop tank nose was given a red lightning bolt, often with a dark blue or black anti-glare upper surface blended in above the bolt.

VMF(AW)-114 remained based at NAS Atsugi from 1962 to 1963, while making short deployments to NAF Naha, Okinawa, and Ping Tung, Taiwan. On July 1, 1963, the squadron was disbanded at Atsugi.

TOP - Gull grey and white VMF(AW)-114 F4D-1 at MCAS Cherry Point in 1958 with USAF exchange pilot Joe Guth. Note engine and upper wing access doors are open. (Jack Gagen) BOTTOM - VMF(AW)-114 Ford in 1958 with the mandarin red spine, rudder, elevons and drop tank design. "VMF(AW)-114" and the "K" on the tail are outlined in white. (Harry Gann)

VMF(AW)-114 Fords over the Med in Feb. 1959. Note squadron insignia on the canopy (via Williams)

THE FORD AND VMF(AW)-114

AS RELATED BY COL. JACK GAGEN

Col. Gagen started his career as a NAVCAD and completed his first tour of duty with VMF(AW)-114 and the F4D-1. Subsequent duties were; MAG-24 (S-3); Selection Officer; VMFA-314; USAF 12th Fighter Wing, Vietnam, VMF-513, 2nd Mar Div (Asst. Div. Air Officer), VMA-542, Vietnam, MAG-11 (G-3 Asst. Ops. Officer), USMC Staff College, Senior Aide-de-camp and Asst. XO to the Dep. Commander-in-Chief European Command, CO VMFA-531, MAG-11 (S-3), CO VMFA-531, CO VMFAT-101, XO MCCRTG-10, and CO MCCRTG-10.

Jack Gagen accumulated over 600 hours in the F4D while assigned to VMF(AW)-114. He participated in a cruise to the Mediterranean in 1959 aboard the USS Franklin D. Roosevelt. What follows are a few of his sea stories from that period.

F4D FLIGHT CHARACTERISTICS

I'd classify the old Ford as a going machine, even after going on to fly Phantoms for some seventeen years after I left Skyrays. I thought the old J-57 with afterburner really put out the thrust, as I was able to prove on many a test hop. You see, I was the VMF(AW)-114 post maintenance test pilot for the squadron. I'd release those brakes at the end of the runway at Cherry Point and I'd be going through 40,000 ft. in 4½ minutes. This was a timed test, and if the old bear didn't make it in the 4½ minutes, we would bring it on back and correct it.

I would also classify the plane as "stability-n-instability." It wasn't a bad machine while flying at anywhere from 5,000 to 40,000 ft., however it did get a little wobbly above 35,000 ft. But down in the old landing pattern is where the Ford really got your attention. I have to admit that it took me a good fifty hours in the machine before I really felt comfortable entering the break, lowering the gear and making an on-speed approach. When we first received the Ford we didn't have an angle of attack indicator so we flew the on-speed approach. We did finally get the angle of attack gauge midway through our carrier cruise in 1959. I became a real believer in it and flew the angle of attack in every aircraft from there on in.

Coming into the break with the Skyray, I would bend that bear around and get to the 180 position, lower the gear and one gear would always come down before the other, which would of course put you into a skid. Until you got used to this the aircraft really got your attention. The same thing would also happen on takeoff when you were raising the gear. Here again, one always came up faster than the other and you would always go into a slight skid. Of course, after you got about fifty hours in the bird you wouldn't even notice it because you just naturally compensated for it with rudders every time it happened.

Making a section takeoff was not that hard either because you didn't do that till you had proper experience in the aircraft. An experienced pilot could make as good of a section takeoff in the old Skyray as you could in any aircraft.

We had a Mechanical Advantage Changer in the Ford that we would set at 3 to 1 for takeoff. If you had a hydraulics failure, you would pull an emergency handle, which would disengage the hydraulics from the control surfaces. You would then flick a switch and pull the stick up about another foot to a foot and a half, 'til it was just under your chin. Now with the MAC set at 3 to 1 it was like flying an old piper cub: direct mechanical linkage to the control surfaces. It was not that stable, but I flew it that way more than once on test hops, and it certainly was a lot better than having to eject. You would set up a straight in approach from five miles out and control your descent with power, moving the stick as little as possible.

Since the Ford did not have a RAT (ram air turbine) you never buzzed around the sky too long when you lost your hydraulics or electrical systems, because you were operating on battery power only, and it would only last about 20 minutes.

ARMAMENT SYSTEMS

For the all weather intercept task, the F4D radar was super for its day. Especially when you think that it was built in the mid 50's. The radar had a 24 mile capability and we would generally get 18 mile pickup and 12 mile lock-on. Well F/A-18 jocks of today would laugh at me,

VMF(AW)-114 Fords parked on the angle deck of CVA-42 in 1959. Note wing fold braces and tow bars. (Jack Gagen)

but I'll tell you that was some radar in those days. The only thing the Ford lacked was a weapon to tie in with the radar. All we had was the sidewinder, which of course wouldn't tie in with the radar, and the unguided 19 shot rocket pods. We trained firing the rocket pods against a Del Mar target at altitudes between 30,000 and 35,000 ft. We would pump off those 19 shot pods and you would see 38 rockets going every way but backwards. We never did hit the target with a rocket.

The Ford was not built for the air to ground, close air support or interdiction type of mission. The wings had a very thin skin which was easy to overstress in this environment. It was very easy to overstress while going in on a dive bombing run as you were pulling up after pickeling a bomb. On top of that the Ford was not equipped with a good bombsight. One of our squadron-mates on a bomb run in Puerto Rico overstressed one pretty badly and we weren't able to fly it home, we had to barge it.

I was the assistant maintenance officer aboard the "fruity roo" during our Med cruise. One of our Fords had an engine problem while in flight and had to divert into Decimamond Airfield on the island of Sardinia off of Italy. I had to take my maintenance team over in the COD (carrier onboard delivery aircraft) and we had to change the engine there on the field. The engine change was completed in less than eight hours and during this time I got to talking to some Canadians who had a CF-100 squadron on the base. Well these Canadians thought we were nuts to fly a single engine aircraft aboard a carrier in the daytime, let alone at night. So being the bright, flashy, young Marine pilot that I thought I was, I took off to show them what a crazy Marine and a Skyray could do. After I finished the test hop, I came back over the field for a couple of flybys and a mini-airshow. The Canadians who were living in tents off the end of the runway were really impressed with the Skyray's performance.

While back in the states our squadron was asked to provide some young Marine bachelors to escort some Remington Rand Secretaries in New York City. So four of us from MCAS Cherry Point went to New York in our Fords to impress the ladies. We were requested to put on a little flyby at Floyd Bennet NAS which we did in a diamond formation. I then came around solo and did a slow flyby, sucked up the gear, doulbe clutched it into afterburner and took it straight up. Remington Rand got its money's worth that day.

One day I was sitting on the end of the runway at Cherry Point getting ready for a test hop. I had completed my checklists and everything was "go." Just prior to launch I looked up and saw these contrails not far from Cherry Point proper, so I figured I'd go up and see who was there and have a little fun with them. I launched and did my maximum afterburner takeoff, and was pushing through 15,000 ft. before I realized that the contrails were only at 20,000 to 22,000 feet. That was puzzling because 30,000 feet was usually the lowest altitude for contrails. So I joined up and found two Fords from our sister squadron VMF(AW)-115. One of the Fords was spitting fuel, which explained the contrails. What had happened was that the pilot had tried to light the afterburner and it had failed to light. Well, if you then left it in AB detent you would be in basic engine with the AB fuel dumping overboard. By the time I had told them what was wrong, it was too late. He was setting up for a (flame-out) landing at Cherry Point and was down to 800 lbs. of fuel. He was set up well at 20,000 feet above Cherry Point. At Cherry Point we had about 18,000 feet of runway if you took what we called the "jog." If you took it you had about 9,000 ft. coming in and then you would go across the jog and you had 9,000 ft. more. So rather than eject he took it on in and did a flame out approach, which in the Ford was not recommended. He did a beautiful job except he landed about 300 ft. short of the runway, in the approach lights. He then took one bounce and was up on the runway and stopped within 9000 ft. with only minor damage to the plane. The pilot, an old friend of mine who had all of about 20 hours in the aircraft, did a super job.

ABOVE - While aboard the USS F.D. Roosevelt (CVA-42) in 1959 VMF(AW)-114 displayed CVG-1's "AB" tail code over a yellow band, and the motto "Primus Principes" within a yellow scroll on the tail. 134953 in first in line under the bridge. (Jack Gagan) BELOW - VMF(AW)-114 Fords preparing to launch from CVA-42 on 2-23-59 during operation "Big Deal"

TOP - 139045 with day-glo spine and tail flash as used on VMF-(AW)-115 aircraft in May 1960. (USN) ABOVE - 131958 on 8-2-62 at NAS Atsugi with large "EK" tail code (T. Matsuzaki) LEFT - 139158 on 8-2-62 in the squadron's final markings. Each rudder had a slanted white strip bordered in black showing the four card suits of a black spade and club, and red heart and diamond. Drop tank lightning bolt is red. (T. Matsuzaki) BOTTOM - 139197 with dark blue or black anti-glare panel on the drop tanks. (T. Toda)

VMF(AW)-115

VMF(AW)-115, whose personnel had participated in the Fleet Introduction Program with VC-3, began receiving its Fords shortly after the first delivery to this unit. Not only did VMF-115 have the dubious distinction of being the first Marine unit to receive the supersonic Fords, they also became the longest lived Skyray outfit, flying their F4Ds until early 1964.

Based at MCAS El Toro, California, VMF-115 received its first F4D-1 in mid April 1956. This aircraft, BuNo 134758, carried only the squadron's tail Modex "AE" and "1" on the nose to indicate that it belonged to the CO. Lt. Col. J.S. Flickinger.

In short order 758 became the first Marine Corps Skyray to crash, when, on May 8, Lt. Col Flickinger was killed while trying to dead stick the airplane on final approach to El Toro. This accident was the first in a series of Skyray accidents in VMF-115 that occurred over the next year-and-a-half. Major problems centered around a balky fuel transfer system, compressor stalls, and structural weaknesses in the wing stores. Several hundred modifications and service changes made during this period slowed the unit's training schedule considerably, as the Fords were grounded for several weeks.

On December 31, 1956, VMF-115 became VMF(AW)-115 to reflect their acquisition of the all weather Skyrays, and their Fords were repainted accordingly. During 1956 and into mid-1957 the squadron applied distinctive markings to their Skyrays. These consisted of red, white, and blue bands on the wing tips, drop tanks, and near the top of the fin and rudder. During this time period, the squadron insignia featured a diving eagle superimposed over a large capital "A." This insignia was supposed to depict the squadron modex letters "AE" through the use of the "A" and the eagle.

By April 1957, the squadron was ordered to change its tail code to "VE." This repainting job occurred gradually, the squadron flying its Skyrays with both codes for some time afterward. With this modex change came a second trio of red, white, and blue bands carried below the tail code, the colors of these being reversed from the top tail bands. A revised squadron insignia was approved on April 30, 1958. This emblem, still in effect with the squadron, featured a diving eagle superimposed on a diagonal red, white, and blue stripe.

By late summer of 1957, modifications to the Skyray had been completed and training had progressed to the point where the squadron deployed to MCAAS Mojave on August 16 to undergo their Phase I combat readiness and instrument training. In over 450 sorties flown during their three weeks at Mojave, VMF(AW)-115 pilots accumulated a total of 1028 flight hours, including several hundred simulated ground approach, flame out approach, and instrument approach landings.

During this Mojave deployment and after their return to El Toro, VMF(AW)-115 continued to suffer additional crashes. As a result of these, and others that were occurring in early F4D-1 squadrons, the Skyray were once again grounded in December 1957 for further modifications to the pylons, fuel cells, and afterburners.

Once the unit's Skyrays had been cleared for flight operations, VMF(AW)-115 pilots continued their Phase II training. From October 1957 to January 1958, a portion of the squadron was sent to NAAS El Centro for air-to-air rocketry, gunnery, and missile practice.

VMF-115

On February 11, 1958 the squadron capped a year of training at El Toro and left for San Diego where personnel and aircraft were loaded aboard the USS Windham Bay, bound for Japan. The unit arrived there in March and VMF(AW)-115 was assigned to Marine Air Group 11, 1st Marine Air Wing, and stationed at NAS Atsugi.

The Quemoy Crisis over the Formosa Straits resulted in the squadron's deployment to North Pngtung, Taiwan, on Sept. 8, 1958. From September until March 1959, VMF(AW)-115 Skyrays flew round-the-clock Combat Air Patrol missions in support of Nationalist transport aircraft supplying the island of Quemoy. During this period several VMF(AW)-115 pilots managed to get Sidewinder "lock-ons" to ChiCom MiG-17s, but the Communist aircraft never challenged the Skyrays, much preferring to dodge into the mainland when detected.

The Chinese Communists declared a cease fire approximately six weeks after the squadron had arrived, and VMF(AW)-115 pilots devoted their remaining time on Formosa to training missions. VMF(AW)-115 returned to Atsugi in March 1959, where they remained for the next two months.

The Eagles of VMF(AW)-115 ended their 14-month tour in the Far East in May 1959, when the squadron was "cadred." Nearly all of their personnel were reassigned to other units, and a small nucleus of officers and men took the squadron records to MCAS Cherry Point, North Carolina to form a new squadron. Their Skyrays remained at Atsugi and were taken over by the replacement group, VMF(AW)-115.

Once at Cherry Point, this small cadre of VMF(AW)-115 personnel "reactivated" the squadron, forming it around a sub-unit of VMF(AW)-114. The new squadron became a part of MAG24, 2nd MAW. In a move apparently not uncommon for this sort of transfer, a few of VMF(AW)-114s brightly colored Skyrays were taken over by VMF(AW)-115 with no change in markings.

VMF(AW)-115s Skyrays now sported an orange da-glo spine that continued rearward, tapering up the tail and downward on the fuselage. The drop tanks also featured da-glo designs along with the unit designation, tail code, and nose number painted in black on each side.

It is doubtful whether VMF(AW)-115 carried these da-glo markings on their Skyrays for much more than a year. The squadron was reassigned to MAG 11, 1st MAW at Atsugi in June 1960, where they reverted back to their former markings. In July 1961 the unit was reassigned once again to MCAS Cherry Point.

From April 19 until August 27, 1962. VMF(AW)-115 replaced a Navy fighter unit aboard the USS Independence (CVA-62) as part of a Carrier Air Group 7 Mediterranean cruise. For this tour the squadron's Skyrays were painted in their most flamboyant markings; their traditional red, white, and blue bands on the tail and drop tanks were supplemented by the first appearance of the squadron insignia, which was carried on the rear canopy with a red wing trailing behind it. A red "arrow" outlined in black adorned the white rudder, while the Air Group's "AG" tail code was carried along with "USS Independence" on the rear fuselage.

As far as can be determined, these colorful markings were carried only for this cruise. Photos of VMF(AW)-115 Skyrays taken subsequent to this deployment show a mixed bag of aircraft markings: some with the red, white, and blue stripes of the earlier periods, and other Fords with virtually no special markings other than a very large "VE"tail code.

VMF(AW)-115 had returned to Cherry Point by late summer 1962, but was again off to a new crisis area within a few months. From approximately October 1962 to January 1963 VMF(AW)-115s Skyrays where deployed to NAS Guantanamo Bay, Cuba in support of President Kennedy's naval blockade of the island.

After their return, VMF(AW)-115 continued to operate the Skyray at Cherry Point throughout 1963, while other Navy and Marine F4D-1 units were exchanging their weary mounts for F-4B Phantom IIs as fast as they could get them. By the end of 1963, VMF(AW)-115 began receiving its Phantoms, and the squadron was re-designated VMF(AW)-115 on January 1, 1964 to reflect this. The last F4D-1 Skyray (now F-6A) in an operational fleet squadron was retired on February 29, 1964, marking nearly eight continuous years that the airplane had been flown by the Silver Eagles of VMF(AW)-115

TOP - VMF-115's first F4D-1, 134758, in May 1956 in the early spartan markings which were a black "AE" tail code and nose number. (Clay Jansson) BOTTOM - Flight line at MCAAS Mojave on 11-15-56 with 134822 in the foreground. Note that three Fords have only the "AE" tailcode and two have the red-white-blue tail stripe. (Barry Miller)

TOP - 134807 touches down at El Toro, Ca., in 1957. Stripes on tail and drop tanks are red-white-blue. (NASM) MIDDLE - 134814 in 1957; note red-white-blue wing tip stripes. (Clay Jansson) BOTTOM - 134804 motors over Ca. on 3-17-57. (Douglas)

ABOVE - Four VMF(AW)-115 Fords on 4-8-57, note that the bottom F4D-1 has the "VE" tail code which was adopted in April 1957. (USMC) BELOW - 1957 photo of 134826 showing the addition of the "AW" to VMF(AW)-115 on the spine. (Clay Jansson)

TOP - After reforming around a sub-unit of VMF(AW)-114 in the spring of 1959. VMF(AW)-115 apparently "borrowed" 114's aircraft and markings for a number of months. Colors of tail and drop tank markings is flourescent yellow-orange. (Robert O'Dell). MIDDLE - Double nuts 139145 sans colors and with a large black "VE" on the tail in 1962. (via Burger) BOTTOM - 139079 during carrier landing practice at MCAS Cherry Point in Aug. 1962; fin tip is black. (USMC via Peterson)

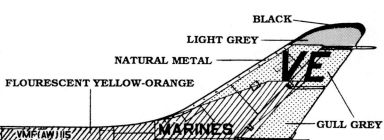

VMF(AW)-115 EAGLES

ABOVE - Four VMF(AW)-115 Fords on 3-23-63 with Carrier Air Wing Seven's "AG" tail code over the Med while attached to the USS Independence (CVA-62). (USN) AT RIGHT - 139093 in storage with "VE" tail code and CVA-62's name on the fuselage. Fin tip is black and stripes are dark blue-white-red, while rudder marking and canopy flash are red. (Swisher) BOTTOM - 139056 in the final VMF(AW)-115 scheme on 3-23-64. (Swisher)

VMF(AW)-314

In December 1957, eleven months after having been redesignated an all weather squadron, El Toro's VMF(AW)-314 began converting from F9F Panthers to F4D-1 Skyrays.

In the first months of 1958, the "Black Knights" began applying distinctive markings to the Skyrays to conform to their nickname. A red-orange scarf-like design, outlined in black, was painted on each tail, with the unit's Modex "VW" slanted rearward inside. The drop tanks carried a black lance along their length, while each wing tip was painted red-orange bordered in black.

On July 1, 1958, after six months of intensive training, VMF(AW)-314 departed San Diego aboard the Utility Carrier USS Cape Esperance (T-CVU-88) and arrive as NAS Atsugi, Japan on July 22, where the squadron became part of MAG 11, 1st MAW.

On September 30, 1958, the squadron, still carrying their colorful paint scheme, was ordered to North Pingtung, Taiwan during the Quemoy Crisis. From September until March 18, 1959, VMF(AW)-314 pilots flew 152 scrambles in support of the Nationalist Chinese Forces. In gratitude, the Nationalist Government presented the squadron with a Chinese ceremonial sword, which was used by the Marine unit to dub each pilot qualifying in the F4D-1, making him a "Black Knight."

VMF(AW)-314 returned to Atsugi on March 23, 1959 and remained there until September 8, when the squadron apparently was "cadred" and reformed on the same day at MCAS El Toro as part of Marine Air Group 15, 3rd Marine Air Wing, AirFMFPac. The squadron's Skyrays remained at Atsugi and were taken over by the replacement unit, VMF(AW)-542.

The "new" squadron received another complement of F4D-1s and within a week of reforming left El Toro for a two-week training deployment of MCAAS Yuma, Arizona. During this period only the squadron's tail code "VW" was painted on their Skyrays, while the wing and tail tips and noses of the drop tanks were painted black. The squadron's earlier colorful paint scheme was never again used on their Skyrays.

Throughout the next year, VMF(AW)-314 made many training deployments to Yuma and Fallon, Nevada for ordinance, radar, navigation, instrument, and field carrier practice. From March 6-18, 1960 the squadron trained jointly with a detachment from Marine Air Control Squadron 3 at Yuma. The Black Knights passed their Phase II training at this time by conducting night air-to-air intercepts under the direction of MACS-3 personnel.

From July 11-14, 1960, the Black Knights flew 68 sorties during the Operational Readiness Inspection at Yuma. At this time, the Wing Inspector stated, "VMF(AW)-314 is the most qualified F4D squadron to depart the west coast since unit rotation began."

On Oct. 14, 1960, VMF(AW)-314 personnel left their Skyrays at El Toro and boarded R5Ds of VMR-352 for a flight to San Francisco. From there the squadron was flown to NAS Atsugi, Japan aboard MATS transport. Once at Atsugi, VMF(AW)-314 replaced VMF(AW)-542 and again acquired the unit's fleet of F4D-1s as part of MAG-11, 1st MAW. With the same black wing and tail tips and drop tank markings applied previously, VMF(AW)-314 pilots spent the nest year in intensive training: carrier qualifications and requalifications, air defense exercises, and numerous deployments.

It should be mentioned here that although the unit's Skyrays often carried an individual pilot's name below the cockpit, this does not necessarily mean the aircraft was flown exclusively by one man. During a tour it was quite possible for a pilot of VMF(AW)-314 to have flow nearly every Skyray in the squadron.

VMF(AW)-314 rounded out its last tour in Japan by undergoing carrier qualifications aboard the USS Hancock (CVA-19) on Dec. 19-20, 1960, Jan. 9-10, 1961, and again on Feb. 22, 1961. On June 14, 1961 the USS Ticonderoga (CVA-14) also hosted the unit's Skyrays for qualifications, as did the USS Midway (CVA-41) on August 11, 1961. At least nine deployments were made during the year to Itazuke AFB, NAF Naha, and MCAF Iwakuni.

The squadron departed Japan in November 1961 and returned to El Toro. They remained there with a new set of Skyrays until the fall of 1962, when these were traded in for McDonnell Phantom IIs.

VMF(AW)-314 F4D-1 134815 at MCAS El Toro, Ca., in 1958. Tail and wing tip designs are red-orange bordered by black. (USMC)

TOP - F4D-1 139077 and 134970 in VMF(AW)-314's early colorful scheme with red-orange tail and wing tip designs bordered by black, and black lance painted on drop tanks; over Ca. on 5-12-58. (USMC) MIDDLE Another view of 134970 showing the wing codes and lance. (Clay Jansson) BOTTOM - Second color scheme on 139124 in 1960 consisting of black fin tip, wing tips and drop tank designs, note white rudder. (Englehardt)

TOP - F4D-1 139125 at MCAS Yuma on 3-19-60. Note grey and white drop tank with black nose. (Swisher) ABOVE - 139127 at MCAS El Toro on 3-10-62 with smaller black drop tank noses. (Swisher) AT LEFT - 139178 at the Seabee base, Port Hueneme, Ca., as seen in the 1970s. (Williams) BOTTOM - VMF(AW)-314 F4D-1 after having a fire extinguished (Clay Jansson)

VMF(AW)-513

On July 26, 1958, the Flying Nightmares of VMF-513 returned to MCAS El Toro, California, from a three-year deployment to NAS Atsugi, Japan. The squadron traded in its F3D-2s for the F4D-1, becoming an all-weather squadron of the 3rd Marine Aircraft Wing, Marine Air Group 15.

VMF(AW)-513 operated the Skyray at El Toro throughout 1959-1961, making many short deployments to training fields in the southwest. During March 1960, for example, the squadron deployed to MCAAS Yuma, Arizona, for parctice in air-to-air gunnery, lead collision rocket firings with the 2.75-inch Mighty Mouse at 30,000 and 50,000-foot altitudes, and Sidewinder missile runs, in addition to cross-country and close air support flights. In December 1960, VMF(AW)-513 competed in the annual Operation Top Gun competition held at Yuma.

Markings then carried by these Flying Nightmare Skyrays were spartan: the squadron tail code "WF" painted in large block letters on the tail, "VMF(AW)-513" on the aircraft's spines, and nose numbers reaching into the low 20s. Quite often, these Skyrays were seen with red or black tail and wingtips, but it is uncertain whether these were true squadron colors, or markings retained from a pervious Marine squadron's use of the aircraft. As far as is known, the squadron insignia of a flying owl was never carried on its F4D-1s.

On October 16, 1961, after returning from a Yuma training deployment, squadron personnel of VMF(AW)-513 boarded the USS Noble (APA-218) for duty in Japan. The squadron arrived at NAS Atsugi on November 4, and was attached to the 1st MAW, MAG 11, Fleet Marine Force, Pacific. Over the next year, VMF(AW)-513 pilots and Skyrays stood hot pad alerts at NAS Atsugi, and on deployment to other Western Pacific airfields. While at NAS Atsugi, the squadron apparently employed a colorful mark-

VMF(AW)-513 F4D01 139139 in flight. (Clay Jansson) ABOVE - 139144 at MCAAS Yuma on 12-3-59, with red fin tip and wing tips and white drop tanks with red tips.(Swisher)

ing scheme for their Skyrays: black or dark blue tail and elevon tips with three gold or silver stars, with similar markings on each drop tank. These color remain to be confirmed, however.

VMF(AW)-513's only long-term deployment with the F4D-1 ended on November 1, 1962, when the unit left NAS Atsugi for the States. The squadron was reestablished once again at MCAS El Toro to began a new training cycle with the F-4B Phantom II.

FLYING NIGHTMARES

TOP - 139054 on 6-12-62 at NAS Atsugi, Japan. Fin tip, wing tips and drop tank trim is either dark blue or black with gold stars and gold borders on drop tank. (T. Matsuzaki via T. Toda) AT LEFT - 139173 in the same scheme, note white rudder (Stride via Williams) BELOW - F-6A 139134 at MCAS El Toro on 12-8-62. Note absence of red wing and fin tips and white rudder. (Swisher) BOTTOM - F-6A 139129 at El Toro in April 1963 with sidewinders in board of the white drop tanks. (Clay Jansson)

TOP - 134833 at El Toro with red wing and fin tips. (USMC) MIDDLE - F4D-1 139193, note wing codes (E.J. Bulban) BOTTOM - F-6A 139177 at Litchfield Park on 3-22-65. This Ford appears to have been reactivated from storage as evidenced by the discolored areas on nose, belly and around cockpit. (Clay Jansson)

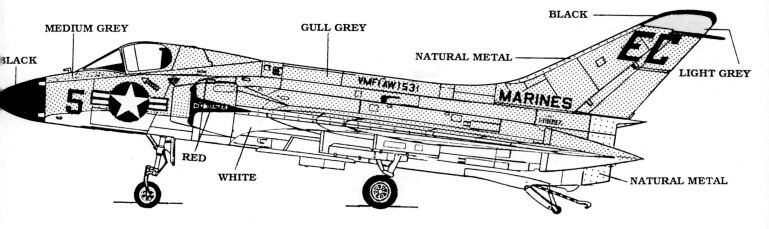

1958 VMF(AW)-531 scheme was grey and white with black lettering which included a slanted "EC" tail code as seen above on 139070. Intake flashes and ejection triangle are red, rescue arrow is yellow and anti-glare panel is medium grey.

GRAY GHOSTS

VMF(AW)-531

Commissioned on November 16, 1942, as the Marine Corps' first night fighter squadron, VMF(N)-531 adopted the nickname The Gray Ghosts. The unit operated the PV-1, F7F, and the F3D-1 before receiving its first F4D-1 at MCAS Cherry Point, North Carolina, on February 22, 1958.

VMF(AW)-531 spent the next year in training at Cherry Point, in preparation for its first Far East Deployment with the Skyray. By March 1959, operations had ceased, orders were cut, and families and personal effects began the relocation to NAS Atsugi, Japan. In April, the squadron took over the Skyrays left previously by the departing VMF(AW)-115, and joined MAG 11, 1ST MAW at Atsugi. In September 1959, the squadron underwent carrier qualifications aboard the USS Lexington (CVA-16), and again in December on the USS Midway (CVA-41). For these deployments, VMF(AW)-531 Skyrays carried only their "EC" tail code, squadron nose number, and the usual unit designation on the spine.

From January to May 1960, the squadron deployed to NAS Cubi Point, Philippines, and in late March made a short deployment to Ping Tung North, Taiwan, to participate in Operation Blue Star. During this exercise, VMF(AW)-531 Skyrays operated off of the Short Expeditionary Landing Field, making Morest landings and steep afterburner takeoffs from the field, which had been constructed of pierced steel matting in less than two days.

VMF(AW)-531 left NAS Cubi Point late in May 1960, returning to NAS Atsugi briefly before being "cadred" late in June and reformed at MCAS Cherry Point. At Cherry Point the squadron was reassigned to MAG 24, 2nd MAW, and the slow process of training virtually a new squadron was begun. The squadron painted its newly acquired Skyrays as before, although slanting their smaller "EC" tail code. While aboard the USS Intrepid (CVA-11) for a short summer carrier qualification cruise, VMF(AW)-531 Skyray displayed their squadron insignia on the aft portion of the canopy.

As a matter of pure conjecture, one photo has been published showing a VMF(AW)-531 Skyray with identical markings to those carried by both VMF(AW)-114 and

VMF(AW)-115: an orange da-glo design painted on the airplane's spine and tail surfaces. Although the date and circumstances of this photo are unknown, it must be assumed that the scheme represents a short-lived period after reassignment when VMF(AW)-531 had taken over the departing squadron's aircraft, most probably at MCAS Cherry Point.

In July 1961, VMF(AW)-531 once again deployed to NAS Atsugi, replacing VMF(AW)-115 and taking over its Skyrays. Its F4D-1s now were painted only with an orange da-glo nose on each drop tank, with the "EC" tail code reverting to the earlier, larger upright block letters. There is no evidence that VMF(AW)-531 Skyrays were painted more extensively, or that they again carried the unit's insignia of a shroud-covered skeleton. The Gray Ghosts of VMF(AW)-531 ended this second Japan deployment with the F4D-1 in July 1962, reforming at MCAS Cherry Point around their new mount, the McDonnell F-4B Phantom II.

VMF(AW)-531

TOP - These orange day-glo markings on the spine and tail are identical to those carried on VMF(AW)-114 and VMF(AW)-115 Skyrays and were in use in late 1958 as seen aboard CVA-42 (see color section). (USN) AT LEFT - VMF(AW)-531 took its Skyrays aboard the carrier Lexington and Midway in the fall of 1959, the aircraft carrying only the unit's "EC" tail code for these carquals. (USN via Col. Bruce Martin, USMC and Harry Gann) BELOW - VMF(AW)-531 F4D-1 comes to a halt as it traps a Morest cable at Taiwan on 3-27-60. (USN)

TOP - VMF(AW)-531 on take-off from a short expeditionary landing field on Taiwan on 3-27-60 during operation "Blue Star". (USMC) MIDDLE - VMF(AW)-531 Skyrays aboard the USS Intrepid (CVA-11) while the squadron was stationed at MCAS Cherry Point in 1960. Note smaller slanted "EC" tail code and squadron insignia on the canopy of #5. (Joe Turner) BOTTOM-139084 in 1961 sporting small slanted "EC" code and black fin and wing tips. (F. Dickey)

TOP - Four VMF(AW)-531 Fords over Japan in April 1962. Note medium grey wing-walks. (USN) ABOVE - 139199 landing at NAS atsugi on 9-29-61 with sidewinder. (T. Matsuzaki via T. Toda) AT LEFT - 134199 which was used as a refueling pit training aid at NAS Miramar. (Williams) BELOW

BELOW - VMF(AW)-531 F4D-1 139187 on the "Hot Pad" at NAS Atsugi. Note combat load of sidewinders and rocket pods and loss of paint on the nose section. (Sherwin)

TOP - LT Sherwin and his VMF(AW)-531 Ford 139158 prior to a mission out of NAS Naha in 1962. Pilots helmet and fuel tank noses are da-glo orange. MIDDLE - LT Sherwin lowering wings prior to launch. BOTTOM - VMF(AW)-531 line at NAS Naha. (Sherwin)

VMF(AW)-542

Originally organized in March 1944 as a night fighter squadron at MCAS Cherry Point, North Carolina, VMF(N)-542 moved to MCAS El Toro in July 1947 and was redesignated as an all-weather outfit in October 1948, flying F7F-3Ns. VMF(AW)-542 joined MAG 33, 3RD MAW, on August 1, 1957, with the F3D-2. The squadron received its first F4D-1 on May 12, 1958, and joined Marine Aircraft Group 15 on July 1.

VMF(AW)-542 remained at El Toro over the the next year while training with the F4D-1, boarding the USS Bon Homme Richard (CVA-31) in late July 1959 for carrier qualifications. At this time, the squadron painted its "WH" tail code on the Skyrays in small connected letters on the rudders. At least one F4D-1 was given special treatment with the addition of a red "arrow" on the tail containing three white stars, signifying the 3rd MAW, with each elevon tip painted red with a single white star on both upper and lower surfaces.

On August 20, 1959, VMF(AW)-542 sailed westward for duty in Japan. The squadron replaced VMF(AW)-314, being assigned to MAG 11, 1st MAW at NAS Atsugi on August 28. The unit deployed to NAS Cubi Point, Philippines, from January to May 1960. While based at Cubi Point, VMF(AW)-542 Skyrays made a two-week deployment to Taiwan to participate in Operation Blue Star, a joint American-Nationalist Chinese amphibious exercise.

After being replaced by VMF(AW)-314 at Atsugi, VMF(AW)-542 returned to El Toro on November 2, 1960, where it rejoined MAG 15, 3rd MAW. Over the next two years, the squadron embarked on a new training program with the Skyray, making several temporary deployments to Yuma, Arizona, and Pt. Mugu and El Centro, California. At this time, the unit's Skyrays carried a larger "WH" tail code, while the front portion of each drop tank and the tail and wingtips were painted a very dark blue. By late 1962, these markings were modified by the addition of many small white stars painted on each drop tank nose in a spiral pattern. Each aircraft's nose number was painted on the lower tip of each pitch trimmer, and the wingtip color was deleted.

VMF(AW)-542 F4D-1 134795 in the squadron's first scheme. This was a very unique and unusual placement of the "WH" tail code on the rudder. (Clay Jansson)

On October 30, 1962, squadron personnel boarded government aircraft for their second Far East deployment with the F4D-1 (now redesignated F-6A), arriving at NAS Atsugi on November first. VMF(AW)-542 Skyrays now apparently reverted back to the "plain" dark-blue drop tanks markings, although their pitch trimmer numbers were retained. During the following year, VMF(AW)-542 made short deployments to Okinawa and Taiwan. The squadron returned to MCAS El Toro in the fall of 1963, and was redesignated VMFA-542 on November 2 in preparation for its new role with the F-4B.

El Toro based VMF(AW)-542 aircraft off the southern California coast. 134851 #7, 134804 #9, 139149 #16 and 134795 #13. (Clay Jansson) BOTTOM - 134795 banking away with a sidewinder. (Clay Jansson)

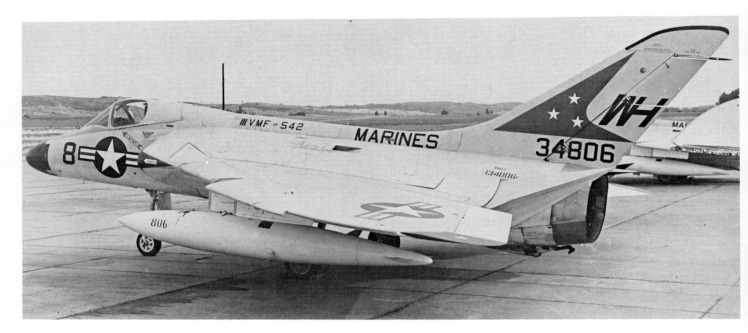

TOP - 134806 in what is thought to be a one off scheme. The tail arrow and wing tips are red with white stars. The three white stars signify the 3rd MAW. (Tailhook photo service)- ABOVE - Head on view of 134806 showing the wing tips and wing code. (Clay Jansson) BELOW - 139047 in the squadron's second scheme which featured standard block letters on tail in Jan. 1961. (Clay Jansson)

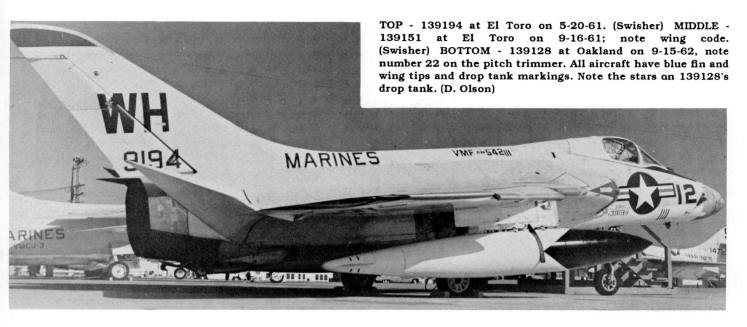

TOP - 139194 at El Toro on 5-20-61. (Swisher) MIDDLE - 139151 at El Toro on 9-16-61; note wing code. (Swisher) BOTTOM - 139128 at Oakland on 9-15-62, note number 22 on the pitch trimmer. All aircraft have blue fin and wing tips and drop tank markings. Note the stars on 139128's drop tank. (D. Olson)

FLYING QUALITIES OF THE FORD AND VMF(AW)-542

AS RECALLED BY COL. JACQUES NAVIAUX USMC RET.

After graduating from the Naval Academy and completing flight training Jacques Naviaux flew Fords. He then became a T-39 NFO instructor and received a masters degree from Monterey. He flew F-4B Phantoms with VMFA-122 in Vietnam and served as of VMO-8 and CO of VMA-134 as well as CO of the 3rd. Air Naval Gunfire Liaison Co. at Long Beach. He retired in 1986 and is a executive with General Electric.

"The flying qualities of the aircraft bordered on the bizarre. The high (for its time) thrust-to-weight ratio resulted in rapid acceleration and short take-off rolls. At the same time, the aircraft had neutral-to-negative roll stability and high coupling between roll and yaw. Many pilots were very surprised on their first take off when the normally slightly asymmetric landing gear retraction resulted in a spectacular yaw. Since most jets require very little rudder, the maneuver was unexpected. Rumor had it that nose gear doors had been ripped off by the yawing moment, but I

TOP - First Lt. Jacques Naviaux. MIDDLE - VMF(AW)-542 Skyray launching from the USS Ranger (CVA-61). (Naviaux) BOTTOM - "542" Ford about to trap. Note the drunken attitude common to the Skyray's landing. (Naviaux)

never saw any. The first takeoffs were considered to be worthy of note — the ready room vultures went out to watch.

The aircraft was simple enough - no flaps and aerodynamic slats. Later on we would have difficulty with asymmetric slat extension in the A-4 in extreme maneuvers. I am not aware of any similar problems with the Ford, probably because we did not focus on air combat maneuvering and, hence, did not fly the aircraft as close to the limits as we did with the A-4. In the transonic speed ranges, the Ford had an extreme nose tuck - 25 to 35 lbs. of stick pressure. Production aircraft were equipped with the J-57, one of the more successful engines of all time. In the Ford, the inlet design led to duct blockage at high angles of attack. Going into afterburner with anything over 3g on the aircraft resulted in a compressor stall, which was usually spectacular. Flames would shoot out the intakes. In most flight lines, half of the aircraft would exhibit evidence of burned paint in the intakes. Having one of these compressor stalls at night was generally a truly memorable experience. Fortunately, the engine was very tolerant of this type of abuse and never suffered from the stalls. It was also very forgiving of foreign object damage. It did have one very undesirable characteristic - the bleed air valve tended to ice over. During the winter months in Japan when days seemed to have clouds from 500 to 50,000 feet. If the bleed air valve iced over, you couldn't use the afterburner above 35,000 feet which meant that you couldn't climb above 35,000 feet and, therefore, couldn't get VFR on top, couldn't fly a mission and went to the holding pattern until your block time for penetration came up. We operated on block times for instrument approaches, and one had to plan well on an IFR day with the Ford, which combined a very high fuel consumption rate with a very limited supply of fuel. The Navy had a very cavalier attitude about block times and often launched carrier air wings for NAS Atsugi where we were stationed. It was not at all uncommon to return to the initial approach fix to find out that the Navy usurped all of the block times for the next two hours. We had to divert, of course, and some of the diversions were a bit uncomfortable. I had to land on a taxiway at an Air Force base once.

The transonic nose tuck was a problem we learned to live with. Douglas had developed a device called the Transonic Trim Compensator or "TTC" to deal with the problem. Without the TTC, as the aerodynamic center shifted from the quarter to the half chord in the Mach .87 to .89 range, it would take 25 to 35 lbs to stick pressure to keep the nose from tucking. On the other end, when decelerating from supersonic to subsonic speeds, the nose would pitch up. In high g turns that were usually marked by rapid deceleration, the unwary pilot could be caught by a nose pitch up that could produce an eye watering maneuver that would overstress the aircraft.

Before fly-by-wire systems in which control inputs are vectored through a computer, the aircraft designer was faced with the problem of introducing control feel in to the system, since the actual control surface deflection was accomplished by an irreversible hydraulic system. Control effectiveness is a function of the square of the calibrated airspeed. In light aircraft with mechanical controls, aerodynamic loads are transmitted back to the pilot through the control stick. This is not the case with a hydraulic system. The designer is thus faced with the problem of producing an artificial feel into the system so that the pilot will have adequate response at low airspeeds and yet not overstress the aircraft at high speeds. This was a non-trivial design problem in the pre-fly-by-wire era. The control systems involved a Rube Golberg lash up of counterweights, springs, etc. Designing a control system that could be flown by the average pilot turned out to be a lot harder than one that could not.

Many of the control system artificial feel designs of that era were not flyable under certain conditions by the average pilot, and the consequences were tragic. The downsprings initially designed into the Phantom II are a case in point.

In the Ford, the ratio of stick throw to control surface deflection was changed as a function of airspeed by a device called a mechanical advantage changer. This is one of those things that one checks in the post start sequence and never thinks about again until it fails. I had one failure in the Ford.

We were conducting carrier qualification landings on the USS Ranger, and after my second pass, the MAC went to the high speed position which meant that it now required three times the stick deflection to produce the same results. The Ford control surfaces consisted of elevons controlled by the stick and pitch trimmers actuated electrically by the trim system.

My first two cat shots and traps had been something less than a superlative demonstration of airmanship, and since I had aced the Field Mirror Landing Practice flights, I was determined to do so on the ship. Instead, since I did not analyze the failure immediately, I was all over the cockpit with the stick. My initial reaction was to ascribe the difficulty to pilot technique and I tried harder with the result that things got worse. I did manage to trap on the next pass but not without some scathing comments from the LSO. The failure became obvious on the deck and I was relieved to think that perhaps I wasn't as bad as I thought I was.

The Ford had very little margin between maximum landing weight and bingo fuel, or fuel required to reach a land base at normal carrier landing practice distances. On the Ranger, we usually had fuel for three passes. This is one of the attributes that limited carrier operations. We had no inflight refueling capability (although some aircraft had a refueling probe on one drop tank). This made the prospect of operating out of range of a bingo field a rather unpleasant one. We never did that, although we came close once.

Operating in the rain was a challenge. In addition to the flat front windscreen with no rain removal system which meant that you couldn't see out of the front when landing in the rain, the small high pressure tires were subject to hydroplaning. We either landed into the arresting gear on a wet runway or shut the engine down on touchdown if arresting gear was not available. One could shut the engine down at touchdown and relight at 12% to 15% RPM thus eliminating the effect of the fairly high residual thrust at idle. For an all-weather fighter, the Ford's characteristics on a wet runway left a lot to be desired.

The aircraft was also known as the "Lead Sled". With the gear down and speedbrakes out, the L/D ratio was about 6/1. A similar airframe, the F5D, equipped with extra large speed brakes, was used as a chase plane for the early lifting body flight tests that led to the Space Shuttle - an L/D of 3/1. Descending was never a problem."

The Ford was one of the two true all-weather fighters in the Naval inventory, in 1961, the other being the Demon. With a properly working radar which was somewhat of a rarity, we could detect and initiate a track against a fighter at about 20 nautical miles. Our mission was to intercept and shoot the enemy down with our primary weapon, 2.75" rockets. We also carried Sidewinders and the aircraft had 20 mm guns. We flew with the guns installed but without ammunition. The guns were serviced through panels in the wing. When the ammo cans were out, one could carry a limited amount of baggage in the gun bays. I came back from a deployment once on the wing of one of our senior captains who had neglected to tighten the fasteners on the gun bay where his clothing was stored. Enroute I noticed that he had something flapping in the breeze. It turned out to his only uniform shirt which had one arm chewed off. He stormed into the ready room for the flight debriefing in his uniform shirt with one arm frayed off to the shoulder. He didn't think that it was nearly as funny as we did.

The Ford was typical of every airplane I flew — it had a good many things in the cockpit that never worked and indeed could not be maintained. The auto-pilot was one of these. The auto-pilot was supposed to ease pilot workload when flying intercepts, but never worked. This was typical of the analog era. Now when you step into an F-18, everything works nearly all the time.

Our wartime ordnance load would have been four 19 shot 2.75" rockets pods, two Sidewinders and guns. Our all-weather tactic was to fire all 76 rockets on a 100 degree lead collision run at a range of 500 yards, a true shotgun. It sounds awesome, but in reality, we would have been lucky to hit anything. I was fortunate enough to knock down a drone in a live firing exercise at Pt. Mugu and as far as I know, that was the only time that anything was shot down with the Ford system (a Skyraider pilot bagged a MIG in Vietnam with a visual 2.75" rocket firing).

Our live fireings were conducted against a device known as the Delmar Scorer. The Delmar, which looked like a large bomb, was made of styrofoam and streamed behind the tractor aircraft on 7,000 feet of piano wire for rockets or 25,000 feet for Sidewinders. It had flares which were used as a heat source for Sidewinders. The pilot had two controls in the cockpit to reel the Delmar in and out. It was fairly easy to snap the Delmar off the wire, so towing had to be done within fairly severe airspeed and g limits. If you did snap it off, the reel would back-lash and it took the long suffering ordnance crew the better part of a day and a wholly unique vocabulary of invectives to rewind the reel.

The thing would snap off when you didn't want it to, but as is typical of the perverse nature of things, when you wanted to get rid of it you couldn't. We had one tow pilot who was reeling the Delmar in for landing when the reel jammed. He attempted to get rid of it, but it wouldn't come off. Being low on fuel, he landed at MCAS Yuma, dragging the Delmar behind which separated a power line and darkened part of the city of Yuma for several hours.

The fireing aircraft carried a pod which contained a high speed 35mm camera and a small radar. When you fired at the Delmar Scorer, the camera would be triggered and you would photograph the rockets in flight and get a range from the radar so you could score your firing.

We flew a lot of the fireing missions under a hood with a chase plane, including low altitude hops. At least two pilots flew through the tow wire, fortunately with little damage.

When you were flying the tow (a good job for Lieutenants) you had to ensure that the firing aircraft was locked on to the Delmar and not you. On a lead collision run, the firing aircraft appeared to be heading straight for you. The bearing drift at the last minute was the clue. If the firing aircraft was on more than a 110 degree run, this could be difficult to call. As far as I know, we never fired at the tow.

Air-to-air gunnery was flown against a nylon banner in a squirrel cage pattern with a flight of four using paint dipped bullets so that the hits could be attributed to the individual. I had the ill luck one day to lose the banner while flying tractor for a flight led by the Skipper. To make things worse, it was one of those days in which he thought that he was really hammering the banner. I had the definite impression that it was in both my short term and long term career interests to retrive that banner.

I went over to one of the helicopter squadrons and explained my dire circumstances. They really didn't care much for fighter pilots, but I must have looked as though I was in a desperate situation, so we went banner hunting into the Arizona desert. I found the banner, but immediately became involved in an ownership dispute. One of the local ranchers had also found the banner and felt that it had potential as a sunshade for cattle. He furthermore held the opinion that anything that fell from the sky onto his property was his and was also of the opinion that the noisy helicopter that was creating big clouds of dust was guilty of trespassing too. I wound up with the banner but only by the narrowest margin. My return to base was ignominious as well — the banner failed to exhibit the number of holes that the Skipper felt that he had made so he was of the opinion that I had compounded my previous errors by bringing home the wrong banner. Short hop-long day. I've had a lot of those.

I reported into MAG-15 at MCAS El Toro in the summer of 1961 with a fresh set of gold wings and a burning desire to fly the F-8U crusader. My desire was to go unfulfilled. I was the first regular officer they had seen in months, and VMF(AW)-542 was in need of Ford pilots to complement the planned unit rotation to Japan the following year. A Lt.Col. at Group Headquarters said, "Son, you'll love the Ford - it has a big afterburner." Off I went to Fords.

I remember that tour as being a very good time in my life. Who could be happier than a lieutenant in a fighter squadron (even if the Ford wouldn't go Mach 2.0 qualifying me for a 1,000 mile per hour club patch)?

We trained in the states for the next year deploying to MCAS Yuma every other month for weapons training. In September 1962, we rotated to NAS Atsugi for thirteen months. We flew all over the Far East, Japan, Okinawa, PI, Taiwan, day and night carrier qualified and never scratched an airplane, outside of a couple of radomes. We had a competent squadron at all levels, flew in all types of weather and loved it. At the end of the tour, we delivered the Fords to Kisurazu and they went to wherever old airplanes go. That was the last Ford squadron to deploy to WestPac.

Other units were not so fortunate. I remember one week at Yuma when we lost a Crusader per day Monday through Thursday in the gunnery pattern due to outter wing panel failures. On Friday, a Crusader shot down the FJ4 towplane. On Saturday, a helicopter that was attempting to retrieve the wreckage of one of the Crusaders that had fallen in Mexico lost power and settled on top of the wreckage. The base commander had enough by then too, and declared that Sunday would indeed be a day of rest - there would be no more accidents for the week because

ABOVE - VMF(AW)-542 Skyrays in flight. BELOW - F4D-1s 139179, 139127, 139058 and 139095 at Ping Tung North, Taiwan in 1963. (Naviaux)

there would be no flying.

In those days, the tactical focus was on missile intercepts and the analysts had convinced people that the probability of kill approached 100%. Dog fighting, or visual tactics, or air combat maneuvering was thought to be a thing of the past now that we had radars and computer-based fire control systems. Things didn't work out that way at all when we went to war in Vietnam. The combat stituation, rules of engagement, missile envelopes and delicate systems did not match the combat situation, and we did very poorly initially. It took a dedicated effort by Navy fighter pilots like Sam Leeds, who initiated what became Top Gun to turn things around. Now we fly fighters and fly them very well. Today's lieutenants are vastly better trained than we were.

Our training consisted of a couple of lieutenants going out to mix it up and trying to figure out what to do. There were very few rules and restrictions. We used to do a lot dog fighting in the Mount Palomar area which was called Tom and Jerry. If you wanted a fight you hung around there. I can remember once winding up in a dog fight over Oceanside and being pointed straight down at 25,000 feet and Mach 1.3. It must have been a dandy sonic boom. I turned off the transponder so that I couldn't be tracked on radar and short of slithered home. I scanned the sonic boom reports for several days afterwards. Nothing was said - people were more tolerant in those days. I remember a television interview with a very attractive and obvisouly Southern belle. When asked what she thought about the nuisance of sonic booms, she replied that she loved them because every time she heard one she thought that there must be some cute little ensign up there in his fighter.

In the winter months at El Toro and in Japan we had to fly in exposure suits. The early model of these suits was a dry suit like a divers suit. Getting into this thing was no small undertaking. You crawled in through a zippered hole in the chest and then two parachute riggers pushed your head down into it and pulled it up through the neck ring which was like a rubber turtleneck. Once you were in it you were there for good until help came. I don't think there was any conceivable way an average person could get out of the suit by himself. I remember one time I bingoed off the carrier and went into NAS Alameda, where I desperately needed to make a nature call. There wasn't any way to do that in that suit, so I went to the head attempted to get out of the suit myself. While in the process of extricating myself from the suit I got my head stuck underneath my armpit. I went staggering out of the mens room, blind, head stuck in this black rubber suit looking like the man from Mars to a group of dependents waiting in operations for their loved ones to come home. I finally got someone to help me, but had a hard time trying to convince him that what he had to do was push hard down my head so I could get it to pop out through the chest cavity.

Later on we replaced those suits with a MK 5 suit which proved to be more comfortable. The new suit had a blower and you wore a set of ventilated underwear. The blower would blow cold air through it and out through the neck and that would at least keep you at a reasonable temperature.

In the winter months at NAS Atsugi we would stand five minute strip alerts as part of the Air Defense Command. This would be a 12-hour watch and you would be in the suit the whole time. We used to stay in a little shack at the end of the runway and the pilots would, of course, turn the heat down and the poor groundcrew would turn it up. The only way to recover from a watch was to go for a hot bath and massage in the BOQ for the princely sum of $1.25.

Since we were first to get the new suits, the flight surgeon decided it was time to see how effective they were, so he picked several hapless lieutenants, one of them being myself and put us in the sump tank. These tanks were open water cysterns that were used for fire fighting, and dated back to WWII when Atsugi was a Zero and Kamakazi field. The surgeon kept us in the sumps until our body temperature dropped 2 degrees. That was the coldest I have ever been. Today we call that hypthermia.

We adhered very closely to a wingman concept and always launched at least two aircraft. The whole time that we stood strip alert in Japan we only had two launches and I happened to be on one of them. We launched into the blackest night I can remember. It was about three o'clock in the morning and I was already at 35,000 feet before I really woke up. I never did find the target I was chasing. It was probably a radar whisp around the Japanese Alps.

One of our flights did go out one day to pick up an airliner and escort it to Japan. The airliner had experienced an extensive electrical failure and had lost all its radios.

The hangar that we had inherited at Atsugi was an unusual place. It had been a U-2 hangar and had all kinds of inner and outer walls with double partitions. The whole thing was also painted black. Since the U-2 was still under tight wraps, we were never sure as to the theory behind the construction.

While we were in Japan a typhoon was supposed to hit and it was decided that we would have to evacuate the airplanes. The only problem was nobody knew where to send us. We manned the aircraft anyway and prepared to launch. The though was that we would go to MCAS Iwakuni. I was not particularly enthusiastic about that because it was the worst weather that I have seen outside of Vietnam or some of the big thunderstorms in Texas. About thirty minutes after having started our engines and taxiing out to sit on the end of the runway, the recall came and we taxied back and tied down the airplanes. We then went to the "O" club and drank whiskey until the typhoon passed two days later. Fortunately, there was no damage just lots of wind and rain.

Unlike the airplanes of today, radio failures were all too common and normally accompanied by a TACAN failure and two or three other evil things. I remember launching out of Iwakuni once in terrible weather. I proceeded to have TACAN failure so I went into the holding pattern where my wingman would lead me in. We held for what seemed like forever, but was actually about 45 minutes and by that time I had a wild case of vertigo. We broke out at 500 feet in a driving rainstorm, and my wingman was a little bit fast. In fact, I was really too fast to land, but not interested in another approach. I plunked that thing down on the runway and hadn't slowed very much by the time I passed the midpoint, so I put the hook down. The hook skipped over the arresting cables whereupon I tapped the brakes and blew both tires. I then continued into the chain gear off the end of the runway and sat there ignominiously. It was raining so hard that the tower didn't know I was off the end of the runway until I turned on the battery and told them. Of course, the safety officer was out to discuss my landing techniques in short order.

TOP - VMF(AW)-542 Skyray traps. MIDDLE - Squadron photo in front of 139044 and another Skyray. (Naviaux) BOTTOM - VMF(AW)-542 Skyray launches from the USS Lexington (CVA-16) while three "542" Fords watch. (Naviaux)

During our tour to the Far East, we spent about two months off and on at Pingtung North, an airfield on the island of Formosa. Living at Pingtung North was a lesson in living in abject squalor. For about three weeks I lived in a pup tent under the wing of my plane while it was parked in a revetment. After that they modernized the facilities and got us some tents to live in.

While we operated out of Pingtung North, I did one of those unforgivable, unforgetable things, I managed to make a wheels up pass. I had been out flying with the skipper, Lt. Col. Parnell, and we came back from the last flight and made several low passes over the revetments where the troops were. On the last pass I had a runaway nose up trim. The pitch trimmers went full nose up and I did an Immelmann over the field, but not intentionally. I then came back around and made what I though was a magnificent approach, but I had forgotten to put the rollers down. My best friend at the time was the runway duty officer and, of course, he fired a flare at me which was the signal to an incoming aircraft that his wheels were up. I thought he was just being funny until at the last minute I glanced down at the gear indicators and saw three flags "up, up, up". Fortunately, the airplane had good power response and I was able to save myself from a wheels up landing. I did see one wheels up landing in the airplane and the only damage was to the drop tanks.

While at Pingtung, I saw one of the funniest things I have ever seen. We were doing a big airshow for the Chinese officials and had a whole grandstand full of generals. We had been briefed and were flying in an operation called Silver Wing. Our mission was to show how the great yankee birds went off to get the bad guy. The script called for the aircraft to launch from a strip alert position, taxi past the grandstand and takeoff into the wild blue yonder. At the time, about half of the squadron was inflicted with the Chinese two step. As one of the planes right in front of the grandstand the pilot realized that he had to go and there was no stopping it. He shut down the engine, braked to a stop and ran for the bushes ripping off his clothes as he went. The Chinese never commented on this part to the show.

We also did some air-to-ground work with the 2.75 rockets while we were in Taiwan. I went out to this range as the range safety officer with a first lieutenant in the Chinese Air Force as my counterpart. He spoke very little English and I didn't speak any Chinese. When the first flight got on station, there still were alot of civilians down in the target area, so I asked my Chinese friend how do we get the people out of there? He told me to have the Fords make a low pass. So I did and all the people who were scavaging hit the dirt. We then started firing into the target area which was hard pan surface. Sometimes the rockets with plaster warheads would ricochet and skitter along the ground. I saw one guy pick one up while on the run. I could just see the headlines, "Marine officer responsible for death of a Chinese civilian, because he did not clear the range properly." If there were any casualties among the scavengers, we never heard about them. They continued to work in the target area under fire.

It was very uncomfortable to be flying over the Formosa Straits in those days because we were not allowed to be armed and the Chinese were not all that far from a shooting war. The Chinese at that time would regularly fly north and south fighter sweeps over the mainland of China. Qumoy and Matsu were shelled with regularity and the situation was tense.

One time in an exercise with the Chinese we acted as the aggressor. Our mission was to go out to a predetermined point turn around and come back in. I plotted the point I was given, plotted it again, got someone else to plot it, got a third person to plot it and still came up with the same position. The turn-around point they had given me was about 25 miles inside mainland China. I asked the Chinese liaison officer about it, and he said there was no mistake, that is the way we do it. Well they may have done it that way, but we didn't. I was not about to fly over mainland China in an unarmed Skyray.

When we came back to Japan from group deployment at Pingtung North in the spring of 1963, a crisis was brewing and it was decided that our services were needed. They were going to send us to Thailand to what was described as a very bare base called Udorn. We didn't have the range to fly to Thailand so the concept was to launch out of Cubi Point, land on an aircraft carrier 600 miles out, refuel and launch into Thiland. We didn't think this was vary smart plan because we were going to launch out to the ship at the limit of our range and land aboard the carrier with no bingo field. We hadn't been aboard ship for a year and our carrier landing proficiency left alot to be desired. They gave us three practice periods and we were ready.

We then had the strangest briefing I have ever had. A civilian from an unidentified agency gave the brief. He provided us with a list of things to carry in the event we went down. One of the items on the list was a labor union card if we had one. Of course, labor union cards were a common commodity in a Marine fighter squadron. That gaggle was cancelled without comment."

F4D-1 139112 at Oakland, Calif., on 9-15-62. **Front of wing tanks are blue with white stars and fin tip is blue. Radome, anti-glare panel and front of NavPac is black. Natural metal leading edges on intakes, wings and fin. (Olson via Williams)**

U.S. NAVAL TEST PILOT SCHOOL

The U.S. Naval Test Pilot School, located at NAS Patuxent River, had its beginnings early in 1945 as an informal Flight Test Pilot's Training Program attached to the Flight Test Division of Pax River's Naval Air Test Center. The program had evolved by 1948 into the Test Pilot Training division when a formal six-month course of instruction was begun. In 1958, this course was lengthened to eight months and the school was officially renamed the U.S. Naval Test Pilot School.(TPS).

The mission of the TPS is to train experienced aviators, Naval Flight Officers, and engineers to become qualified engineering test pilots, test flight officers, and test project engineers for duty at the nearby Naval Air Test Center and other Navy research and development facilities, as well as at the testing centers of the other U.S. military services and those of foreign allies. During the 1960s, this eight-month TPS course of instruction (with a new class starting every four months) was divided into two phases: academic and flight. Each student averaged approximately one flight and 3½ hours of classwork daily. The course's academic topics included aerodynamics, themodynamics, dynamic and static stability, jet engine theory, and weapons systems. For the flight phase, each student was required to plan, fly and write test reports on various flight test assignments in two basic disciplines: performance testing and stability and control testing.

To accomplish these tasks the TPS of the 1960s era maintained, as it does today, a large stable of fascinating aircraft. The majority of student flight hours was spent in the F-8 Crusader and A-4 Skyhawk but test hops might also be required in the TPS T-1A, T-28, OV-1, C-54, S-2, de Havilland Beaver or Otter, Schweitzer 2-32, or one of several F-6A Skyrays. While the exact date of the Skyray's first use at the TPS has been difficult to determine, it is believed that F4D-1 134764 was initially assigned there in November 1961. By the mid-1960s, 764 was joined by F-6As 134806 and 139177. At this time 764 was given a fluorescent red-orange (da-glo) fin and rudder, outer wing panels excluding elevons and nose band. The wing leading edges and intake lips were painted silver. A blue TPS book was painted on the airplane's tail, and "U.S. Naval Test PIlot School" was painted in block letters on the airplane's dorsal spine. The last three digits of the airplane's serial

F-6A 139177 in Aug. 1966, with red da-glo tail, nose and outer wings. Book on fin is blue with white pages and TPS. Leading edges of wings, intakes, pylons and drop tank noses are gold. (Oestricher)

Test Pilot School insignia

number were painted on the top and bottom outer elevon tips so that these numbers could be read with the airplane's wings were folded. Skyray 134806 was painted similarly, but "TPS" in large block letters stepped upward on the fin replaced the TPS book. F-6A 139177 was also painted identically to 764, but in 1966 the airplane's intake lips, wing leading edges, and drop tank noses were painted gold for the annual Patuxent River Show. Also in 1966 the Test Pilot School Skyrays were honored when a stylized Skyray planform was incorporated into the TPS insignia. This Skyray silhouette was painted on the tails of all TPS aircraft with the exception of F-6A 134764, which apparently was retired prior to the change but kept in storage at Patuxent River.

The reasons for retaining these Skyrays at the TPS, so long after the type had left active service with the fleet, have been described as providing the student test pilot with everything from experience in a "delta-winged" fighter to that of furnishing an airplane with "poor low speed handling qualitites." For example, Phil Oestricher, a TPS

F-6A 139177 in its final scheme as seen today on display at Quantico, Va. The TPS book has been traded for a black stylized Skyray on the tail. (via Williams)

student pilot in 1966 now test flying the F-16 for General Dynamics, conducted a typical exercise on F-6A 139177 in August of that year when he investigated the maneuvering stability of the type during an hour and 45-minute flight. Using a hand-held force gauge and cloth measuring tape, Oestricher measured the airplane's stick forces during steady turns, sudden pull-ups, and steady pull-ups while flying at 300 KIAS at 30,000 feet in order to "determine the service suitability and specification conformance of the maneuvering stabillity of the F-6A airplane."

On September 12, Oestricher flew 1139177 once again in an "investigation of the transonic flying qualities of the F-6A airplane," concluding that the Skyray was unsatisfactory and not suitable for service use: "The observed changes of longitudinal stick force during accelerations through the transonic region were excessive and very distracting to the pilot. The tactical value of the F-6A airplane in the transonic region is seriously compromised because the pilot is required to devote a major portion of his attention to basic airwork at the expense of other duties such as fire control system operation."

Addressing the question of why the TPS Skyrays were retained for so long, Oestricher makes some unusual observations: "My opinion was that it was kept as an interesting and not particularly dangerous 'horrible example' or a 'Don't ever buy another one like this airplane. Structurally, the 'Skyray' was something of a paradox: a very strong landing gear attached to a thin-skinned, fatigue-prone, and (might as well say it) flimsy airframe. In VMF(AW)-114, we were forever stop-drilling skin cracks, putting on doublers, etc. Somewhere I saw a 'Skyray' picture—supposedly at high speed—which showed virtually every skin panel bulged out (or in) from airloads, a far cry from the F9F series!

"It was very poor handling airplane in the transonic regime but, to me at least, handled reasonably well in the landing pattern so long as one was willing to learn how to fly it properly. Despite the turn coordination feature of the upper (or servo) rudder, the 'Skyray's' highs adverse yaw, high dihedral effect, and low directional stability combined to keep it out of the typical 'feet on the floor' jet fighter category. Only the Aeronca 'Defender' and 'Champion' (in my experience) required more pilot rudder input to turn properly at pattern speeds! A turn to the downwind immediately after takeoff (as in a field carrier landing practice operation) was best initiated with a small amount of rudder which was followed with lateral stick.This kept the ball reasonably centered throughout the turn. I never flew a 'Cutlass' so I don't know how that tailless fighter handled, but all this rudder pushing was not necessary in F9F, FJ,F3D, TV, F8U or, for that matter, AD-5 airplanes. The 'Skyray' handled very well on the final portion (on the mirror) of a carrier or runway landing. Sink rate control was very precise and easy and the airplane held the trimmed angle of attack (and hense, airspeed) very well. When I cruised with the airplane in 1959, we did not have angle of attack indications in the cockpit. These were incorporated by the time I flew the airplane at TPS. Even when discounting my additional pilot experience by that time, it was obvious that believing the AOA indicator and ignoring the buffet made the approach turn much more confortable and enhanced the precision of control down the glideslope to touchdown."

By 1969 the Test Pilot School F-6As had outlived their usefulness, due mainly to their poor serviceability, and were replaced by Northrop T-38s. On November 25, 1969, the last flyable Skyray was ferried from NATC Patuxent River to NAS Pensacola, Flordia. Piloting F-6A 134806 on the 2.3-hour flight was Captain George Watkins, who presented the airplane to representatives of the Naval Aviation Museum. On February 4, 1970, Captain Watkins "carried" F-6A 139177 beneath a CH-53D from Pax River to the Marine Corps Air Museum at MCAS Quantico, Virginia. In the meantime, the last TPS Skyray, F-6A 134764, had been painted a glossy dark blue overall and put on display in 1969 at the entrance to the Test Pilot School. When the school relocated to another hangar in 1975, the F-6A was stored in one of Pax River's Strike hangars. By 1976, the airplane had been repainted in standard gray and white with the full TPS insignia displayed on its tail. The Skyray had again been repainted by April 1978 in gloss white overall with a gloss red radome, wings and tail. In these gaudy colors the Test Pilot School's only remaining Douglas Skyray was placed on display in July 1978 at the new Naval Air Test and Evaluation Museum at NAS Patuxent River.

TOP - F-6A 134764 in July 1966; colors are the same as 139177. (via Besecker) ABOVE - 134764 on display at Pax River on 4-22-74 with TPS insignia on the tail. (Besecker) AT LEFT - 764 in 1970 painted blue with red cockpit, spine and tail. Black TPS on spine and 764 on fin cap. (Besecker) AT LEFT - April 1978 photo of 764 in a white and red scheme. Red tail, wings, nose and intakes (R.F. Dorr) BELOW - 134806 in Dec. 1966 in the same scheme as 139177. TPS on tail is in blue. (Oestricher)

Miscellaneous

Finally, while 134769 also was briefly in the custody of the Bureau of Aeronautics Representative, Research and Development (BAR R&D), Dallas, Texas, from May to August 1956, 134751 spent its entire service life in the custody of the BAR R&D Baltimore, Maryland, beginning in January 1956. The aircraft was stricken in April of that year after having accumulated only 32 hours of flight time.

PERFORMANCE SUMMARY

TAKE-OFF LOADING CONDITION		① G.P. FIGHTER 4-SIDEWINDERS 2-300 GAL. TANKS	③ G.P. FIGHTER 4-19 SHOT RKT. PKGS. 2-300 GAL. TANKS	⑤ G.P. FIGHTER 2-SIDEWINDERS 2-19 SHOT RKT PKGS. 2-300 GAL. TANKS	⑦ G.P. FIGHTER 4-SIDEWINDERS 2-150 GAL. TANKS	⑨ FERRY 4-ROCKET RACKS 1-NAVPAC 2-300 GAL. TANKS
TAKE-OFF WEIGHT	lb.	27,116	27,937	27,517	24,910	26,529
Fuel Internal/External (JP-5)	lb./lb.	4352/4080	4352/4080	4352/4080	4352/2040	4352/4080
Payload	lb.	830	1558	1194	830	----
Wing loading	lb./sq. ft.	48.7	50.2	49.4	44.7	47.6
Stall speed - power-off	kn.	120	122	121	115	119
Take-off run at S.L. - calm	ft.	3295	3515	3400	2740	3140
Take-off run at S.L. 25 kn. wind	ft.	2300	2460	2380	1870	2180
Take-off to clear 50 ft. - calm	ft.	5055	5360	5210	4280	4850
Max. speed/altitude (A)	kn./ft.	529/15,000	505/15,000	514/15,000	540/15,000	532/20,000
Rate of climb at S.L. (A)	fpm	5400	5000	5230	6250	5600
Time: S.L. to 20,000 ft. (A)	min.	5.1	5.7	5.4	4.4	4.9
Time: S.L. to 30,000 ft. (A)	min.	10.5	12.0	11.2	8.4	10.0
Service ceiling (100 fpm) (A)	ft.	37,600	36,400	37,000	39,600	38,000
Combat range	n.mi.	973	879	923	702	1000
Average cruising speed	kn.	447	437	441	452	448
Cruising altitude(s)	ft.	34,900-41,800	31,800-40,100	33,200-40,900	37,600-41,900	35,900-42,400
Combat radius	n.mi./hr.	306/1.7	290/1.7	297/1.7	151/1.0	
Average cruising speed	kn.	452	447	450	457	
CAP Loiter time/mission time	hr./hr.	0.7/1.7	0.6/1.7	0.6/1.7	0/1.0	
CAP loiter altitude	ft.	28,000	37,200	27,600	29,400	
COMBAT LOADING CONDITION		② TANKS OFF MISSILES ON	④ TANKS OFF ROCKETS ON	⑥ TANKS OFF, ROCKETS ON, MISSILES ON	⑧ TANKS OFF MISSILES OFF	
COMBAT WEIGHT	lb.	22,648	23,469	23,049	22,008	
Engine power		MAXIMUM	MAXIMUM	MILITARY	MAXIMUM	
Fuel		FULL INTERNAL	FULL INTERNAL	FULL INTERNAL	FULL INTERNAL	
Combat speed/combat altitude	kn./M/ft.	565/.98/35,000	557/.97/35,000	531/.92/35,000	566/.98/35,000	
Rate of climb/combat altitude	fpm/ft.	8400/35,000	7300/35,000	1540/35,000	9300/35,000	
Combat ceiling (500 fpm)	ft.	51,000	49,400	39,600	52,100	
Rate of climb at S.L.	fpm	17,300	15,900	6,900	18,300	
Max. speed at S.L.	kn./M	625/.94	612/.92	512/.77	627/.95	
Max. speed/altitude	kn./M/ft.	623/.94/S.L.	612/.92/S.L.	544/.89/20,000	627/.95/S.L.	
LANDING WEIGHT	lb.	18,982	18,894	18,930	18,877	19,446
Fuel	lb.	1326	1337	1333	1221	1349
Stall speed-power-off/appr. pwr.	kn./kn.	100/100	100/100	100/100	100/100	102/101
Distance-gr. run/over 50 ft. obst.	ft./ft.	5430/6145	5410/6125	5420/6135	5400/6115	5565/6285

NOTES

(A) Military thrust
(B) For effect of JP-4 fuel on combat radius and mission time see Notes page.
(C) All loadings include 4-20mm guns and ammunition.
(D) Mission Time: Any time where fuel is used and distance gained, including CAP loiter and combat time.
(E) Performance Basis: Contractor and NATESCEN flight test data. Combat range and radius are based on fuel consumption of Pratt and Whitney J57-P-8B engine derived from contractor and NATESCEN flight tests.
(F) Tanks dropped when empty
(G) Operational Spotting: A total of 84 airplanes (wings folded) can be accommodated in a landing spot on the flight and hangar deck of a CVA-19 class angled-deck carrier.

F4D-1 SKYRAY DEPLOYMENTS

YEAR	CODES	SQUAD.	SHIP	AREA	AIR GROUP
1957	200/NF 200/S	VF-141	CVA-31	W.P.	CVG-5
1957/58	200/AL	VF-74	CVA-42	MED	CVF-17
1958	200/NL	VF-23	CVA-19	W.P.	CVG-15
1958	300/NP	VF-213	CVA-16	W.P.	CVG-21
1958/59	100/AK	VF-102	CVA-59	MED	CVG-10
1959	100/AF	VF-74	CVA-11	MED	CVG-6
1959	200/NK	VF-141	CVA-61	W.P.	CVG-14
1959	300/NP	VF-213	CVA-16	W.P.	CVG-21
1959	200/AB	VMF(AW)-114	CVA-42	MED	CVG-1
1959/60	100/AK	VF-13	CVA-9	MED	CVG-10
1960	100/AJ	VF-102	CVA-59	MED	CVG-8
1960	100/NF	VF-51	CVA-14	W.P.	CVG-5
1960/61	100/AF	VF-74	CVA-11	MED	CVG-6
1961	100/AJ	VF-102	CVA-59	MED	CVG-8
1961	100/AK	VF-13	CVA-38	MED	CVG-10
1961/62	100/AF	VF-162	CVA-11	MED	CVG-6
1962	100/AG	VMF(AW)-115	CVA-62	MED	CVG-7
1962	100/AK	VF-13	CVA-38	MED	CVG-10

BACK COVER - Third Annual Naval Air Weapons Meet at El Centro on April 14-18 1958. TOP - Winner of the air-to-air event, the VF-213 line. (Harry Gann) BOTTOM - Front to back, two FAGU Fords, followed by the believed-to-be one-off FAWTUPAC red trimmed F4D, followed by a VF-101 Ford, followed by a FAWTUPAC Ford, followed by a line of FJ-3/-3M Furys. (Harry Gann)